Mainstreaming Torture

Mainstreaming Torture

*Ethical Approaches in the Post-9/11
United States*

REBECCA GORDON

OXFORD
UNIVERSITY PRESS

OXFORD

UNIVERSITY PRESS

Oxford University Press is a department of the University of Oxford.
It furthers the University's objective of excellence in research, scholarship,
and education by publishing worldwide.

Oxford   New York

Auckland   Cape Town   Dar es Salaam   Hong Kong   Karachi
Kuala Lumpur   Madrid   Melbourne   Mexico City   Nairobi
New Delhi   Shanghai   Taipei   Toronto

With offices in

Argentina   Austria   Brazil   Chile   Czech Republic   France   Greece
Guatemala   Hungary   Italy   Japan   Poland   Portugal   Singapore
South Korea   Switzerland   Thailand   Turkey   Ukraine   Vietnam

Oxford is a registered trade mark of Oxford University Press
in the UK and certain other countries.

Published in the United States of America by
Oxford University Press
198 Madison Avenue, New York, NY 10016

© Oxford University Press 2014

Library of Congress Cataloging-in-Publication Data
Gordon, Rebecca.
Mainstreaming torture : ethical approaches in the post-9/11 United States / Rebecca Gordon.
p.   cm.
ISBN 978-0-19-933643-2 (hardback) — ISBN 978-0-19-933644-9 (ebook)
1. Torture—Moral and ethical aspects—United States. 2. Terrorism—United States—Prevention.
3. War on Terrorism, 2001–2009—Moral and ethical aspects. I. Title.
HV8599.U6G67 2014
364.6′7—dc23

2013037640

1   3   5   7   9   8   6   4   2

Printed in the United States of America on acid-free paper

Para ti, compañera de mis días, y del porvenir.

CONTENTS

ACKNOWLEDGMENTS

It takes a village (or more than one) to raise a book. This is a better book because of the variety of village communities in which it grew up. They include the department of Ethics and Social Theory at the Graduate Theological Union in Berkeley, California; my *compañeros/as* at War Times/Tiempo de Guerras (www.wartimes.org); the colleagues in my philosophy department at the University of San Francisco; a certain Closed Group with No Name; the Ivory Tower Fiber Freaks and Friends of Abby's Yarns on ravelry.com; the Guerrero Street Writers and our meeting place, Que Tal coffee shop; the Episcopal Church of St. John the Evangelist and especially Liz Specht; and, finally, the other residents of the Bartlett Street compound, including Trish, Catherine, Jojo, Molly, the inimitable Morty, and of course Jan. Each one of these communities left its own indelible stamp on the work, holding the writer accountable to a variety of audiences.

Mainstreaming Torture began life as a doctoral dissertation. My committee, including advisor Martha Ellen Stortz, Lisa Fullam, and William M. Sullivan, shepherded it—and me—through the process of turning an idea into an argument and, ultimately, a book. It was Marty who first got me thinking about virtue ethics as an approach to the moral life. Lisa kept me honest about what St. Thomas *really* meant by the irascible and concupiscible powers (no mean feat). And Bill has been a mentor and sounding board throughout the whole process.

Among my University of San Francisco colleagues, two have been particularly generous with their support. Ron Sundstrom talked through early versions with me and encouraged me to keep on. Kim Connor had enough faith in the project to push me to seek publication and to put me in contact with Oxford University Press.

Cynthia Read, my editor at OUP, led me through the review process, encouraged me to believe that the book might one day be published, and helped me to interpret and make use of the reviewers' comments. Charlotte Steinhardt helped

ix

me through manuscript preparation and production. I am particularly indebted to one anonymous reviewer for the suggestion to include reference to the three Christian "graces"—faith, hope, and love—in addition to the classical virtues and for a reminder about the (anti-) liturgical nature of interrogation under torture. A second reader provided *many* valuable pages of questions and comments. Every writer should be so fortunate as to have her work treated with this quality of attention. To the extent that I have succeeded in resolving the issues raised by this reader, *Mainstreaming Torture* is a much better book. It was also this reader who suggested that I give the work a title with a bit more impact than the original, which I hope she or he will think that I have done.

Several friends, both academics and laypeople, have given the manuscript very close readings, for which I am profoundly grateful. Elizabeth Freeman's suggestions led to a reorganization that I believe substantially strengthens the arc of argument across the book. I don't know which I appreciate more, her faithful friendship or her sharp critical eye. Max Elbaum gave the manuscript an intelligent, well-informed layperson's reading. This was particularly helpful for the technical philosophical sections, where a layperson might reasonably be expected to lose interest. Catherine Cusic read every word and provided line edits throughout, which have sharpened both the argument and the prose.

Other friends, new and old, have given help and support along the way. Fellow writer Ellinor Mitchell understands like no other the power of productive procrastination. Sharon Martinas's faithful anti-racist organizing remains an inspiration always. Rima Vessely-Flad's work on race and incarceration helped shape the section on U.S. prisons. Patrisia Macias provided a model of courage and commitment.

Finally, I do not know how many times Jan Adams has slogged through this manuscript, from its first beginnings a decade ago to its present form. It's a rare thing when a life partner also serves as one's most honest editor and does it with such grace that the writer feels only gratitude for the most devastating critique. Without Jan, who remains my first, best audience, there would be no book.

Everyone named here has contributed to this project. It remains only to say that responsibility for all errors, omissions, or lapses in judgment is mine alone.

Mainstreaming Torture

Introduction

Are we so scared that we are willing to knowingly let others per-
petrate, in the dark and in our name, acts of terror which will eter-
nally corrode and corrupt us?[1]
                                    —Ariel Dorfman, *Chilean novelist*

This is a book about institutionalized state torture carried out by the United
States of America. It describes how this country's relationship to torture
changed after the terrorist attacks of September 11, 2001, and how that relationship continues previous practice. This is also a book about the ethics of
torture. In it I argue that we must stop thinking of torture as a series of *isolated
actions* taken by heroic individuals in moments of extremity and begin instead
to understand it as a socially embedded *practice*. Institutionalized state torture
has its own histories, its own traditions, its own rituals of initiation. It encourages, both in its individual practitioners and in the society that harbors it, a
particular set of moral habits, call them virtues or vices as you prefer.

I have written with two audiences in mind: academics interested in philosophical ethics and the general public, in particular people living in the United
States. My hope is that both audiences will find enough of value here to sustain the effort of working thorough a somewhat complex argument about a
difficult, distressing, and important subject. General readers are encouraged
to explore some of the ways that philosophers think about ethical questions;
philosophers, to remember Aristotle's dictum about the purpose of doing
ethics, that "we are inquiring not in order to know what virtue is, but in order
to become good, since otherwise our inquiry would have been of no use."[2]

How did the U.S. relationship to torture change after September 11? In some
ways it was a continuation of past involvement, on the levels both of theory and
of practice. For many years, the United States had secretly funded research
on torture at U.S. and Canadian universities.[3] One product of this research
was the Central Intelligence Agency's (CIA) *KUBARK Counterintelligence
Interrogation* manual with its sections covering "non-coercive" and "coercive"

techniques, first printed in 1963. In it can be found many of the methods, such as noise bombardment, sleep and sensory deprivation, and "stress positions," that would later become the hallmarks of U.S. torture in the "war on terror."[4]

The United States had also provided covert training and support to torture regimes in other countries around the world—from Greece to Uruguay, Chile to El Salvador, Indonesia to Vietnam. The Phoenix Program, implemented during the Vietnam War by U.S. armed forces and the CIA, involved the torture and deaths of tens of thousands of Vietnamese, as part of the U.S. counterinsurgency project designed to break the will of the Viet Cong. In testimony before Congress, military intelligence officer K. Milton Osborne provided some details of the methods used:

> The use of the insertion of the 6-inch dowel into the 6-inch canal of one of my detainees' ears and the tapping through the brain until he dies. The starving to death of a Vietnamese woman who was suspected of being part of the local political education cadre in one the local villages. They simply starved her to death in one of the hooches at that very counterintelligence headquarters. There were other methods of operation which they used for interrogation, such as the use of electronic gear such as sealed telephone attached to the genitals of both the men and women's vagina and the man's testicles, and wind the mechanism and create an electrical charge and shock them into submission.[5]

The Phoenix Program was kept "under wraps," in part to avoid the problem of "collecting information that could stand scrutiny in open court," that is, that would allow prosecution of people based on testimony produced under torture. Instead, Phoenix replaced "the formalities of prosecution with pump and dump—pumping suspects for information by torture, and then dumping the bodies, more than twenty thousand of them between 1968 and 1971."[6]

The "wraps" didn't hold, however, and in the 1970s, Phoenix became the subject of more than one congressional inquiry. This activity culminated in the 1975 Church Committee, chaired by Idaho Senator Frank Church. The committee held nine months of hearings into CIA activities including assassinations and torture on several continents. In response to the final report, then-President Gerald Ford issued an executive decree, which, among other measures, prohibited the assassination of foreign leaders, and the Senate established the Select Committee on Intelligence, which remains in existence today. Citing, among other concerns, "revulsion at the Phoenix program," the Committee recommended "a new statutory framework for American intelligence activities,"[7] under which the CIA's operations, like its involvement in the 1973 coup against Chilean President Salvador Allende and its spying on U.S. citizens at home, would be reined in. Clark Clifford, who had served many Democratic administrations since the end of World War II, summarized his confidence in the Church Committee. "Our national spirit," Clifford testified, "seems to have been replaced by a national malaise." Concerned about the public's cynicism about national institutions, he commended the committee's efforts to "assist us in regaining confidence in our national integrity, and in helping to restore to our nation its reputation in the world for decency, fair dealing, and moral leadership."[8] After the Church Committee's well-publicized deliberations, a national consensus about torture reigned; U.S. torture was incompatible with U.S. "decency, fair dealing, and moral leadership."

This is not to say that the United States ceased all involvement in torture after the mid-1970s. Rather, torture once again went underground. The U.S. military and the CIA continued covertly training military and police forces in many countries. The CIA's 1963 KUBARK interrogation manual, now renamed the *Human Resource Exploitation Training Manual*, was reissued in 1983 and used to orchestrate the operations of, among others, the Salvadoran military and the Nicaraguan anti-Sandinista *contra* forces.[9] Those who were interested could glean information about these activities from mainstream news sources. However, apart from the efforts of activist groups such as the School of the Americas Watch, the Committee in Solidarity with the People of El Salvador, and the Nicaragua Network, there was little public interest in the issue of torture. Similarly, in the scholarly arena, the wrongness of torture was taken to be a more or less settled matter. The world seemed to be moving toward a public international consensus, and in 1994, the United States, albeit with reservations, ratified the 1986 United Nations Convention against Torture and Other Cruel, Inhuman, and Degrading Treatment or punishment.

All this changed after September 11, 2001. In the aftermath of the attacks, the United States recommended direct use of torture by U.S. personnel against perceived U.S. enemies for the first time since the 1970s, and a new discussion about the ethics of torture began to appear both in the popular press and in scholarly journals. In an early November 2001 issue of *Newsweek* magazine, journalist and historian Jonathan Alter observed, "In this autumn of anger, even a liberal can find his thoughts turning to . . . torture." He wondered whether it might be a good plan to deport the Muslims living in the United States whom the FBI had rounded up to "Saudi Arabia, land of beheadings." Americans who weren't thinking about new methods to "jump-start the stalled investigation of the greatest crime in American history" had failed to recognize that they lived in a transformed world. "Some people still argue," wrote Alter, "that we needn't rethink any of our old assumptions about law enforcement, but they're hopelessly 'Sept. 10'—living in a country that no longer exists."[10]

Like the Phoenix Program in Vietnam, the post-9/11 torture programs have instituted their own version of pump-and-dump. They also have sought to side-step the "formalities" of prosecution of their targets, on occasion attempting to try them through military "commissions" held outside the United States. The post-9/11 torture programs have new dumping grounds; prisoners are no longer shoved to their deaths from helicopters over the South China Sea but instead face indefinite detention in a variety of institutions. These include the prison at Guantánamo Bay, Cuba; the detention centers now handed over by the U.S. military to Iraqis and Afghans; "supermax" prison facilities in the United States; and the countries that receive our prisoners in the procedure known as "extraordinary rendition," all described more thoroughly in Chapters 1 and 2.

One post-9/11 change is that U.S. involvement in torture is no longer entirely covert. The administration of George W. Bush and Dick Cheney may not have intentionally exposed torture at Abu Ghraib, in Afghanistan, in CIA "black sites," or at Guantánamo. Still, as early as September 2001, they were quite content to hint at what would be happening, beginning with Dick Cheney's warning less than a week after 9/11 that the United States would now need to work the "dark side."[11] In 2002, Cofer Black, the administration's Ambassador at Large and Coordinator for Counter-Terrorism, made his famous statement to Congress that "there was 'before' 9/11 and 'after' 9/11. After 9/11 the gloves come off."[12]

Theologian William Cavanaugh has called this now-you-see-it-now-you-don't approach to torture a "striptease of power."[13] Like any striptease, its aim is to fascinate the audience, to fire up the imagination. What lies behind the veil? What lurks beneath the glitter? In this case, people living in the United States have been asked to imagine just how terrible the danger must be that requires *our* government, the *American* government, to do such terrible things. At the same time, we are invited to be soothed by the knowledge that, terrible though it may be, torture keeps us safe, and safety has become a primary national concern.

There is a word for people whose first concern is always for their own safety, a name for people who will permit anything to be done that they believe is necessary, as long as it keeps them safe. Such people are sometimes called cowards. Has the United States has become a nation of cowards? The suggestion is more than a little hyperbolic. A "nation," even in the original meaning of a political entity whose people share a single culture and language, is a complex creature. The United States, in all its multicultural, polyglot glory, is complex on another order of magnitude—enough so as to render any blanket statement about its people absurd.

Nevertheless, there are signs that many people in this country have become more or less habituated to the idea that preventing terrorist attacks sometimes requires torture. In 2012, Amy Zegart, a Stanford researcher, commissioned a poll on U.S. attitudes toward torture, replicating a series of questions that were asked in a January 2005 USA Today/CNN/Gallup poll. Four years into the Barack Obama administration, it appears that people in this country are more comfortable about torture, including specific methods of torture, than they were in 2005. "In 2005," for example, says Zegart, "only 16 percent approved of waterboarding suspected terrorists, while an overwhelming majority (82 percent) thought it was wrong." In 2012, however, "25 percent of Americans believe in waterboarding terrorists," while the number who think it is wrong has shrunk to 55 percent. On "a lark" Zegart also "threw in" a question about using a nuclear bomb, not expecting much response. She was startled to find that "a quarter of all Americans are willing to use nuclear weapons to kill terrorists."[14]

Zegart's research shows that people in this country are much less likely than they once were to disapprove of assassinating "known terrorists," whether through the use of unpiloted aircraft known as drones or by other means. In 2005, 33 percent of respondents were opposed to assassination; by 2012, this number had shrunk to 12 percent.[15] A February 2013 poll conducted by the Pew Research Center for People & the Press phrased the question a bit differently, describing the assassination targets as "extremists," rather than "known terrorists." It is possible that people are less willing to approve the killing of mere "extremists" than of "terrorists." The poll showed that "overall, 56% approve of the U.S. conducting missile strikes from pilotless aircraft to target extremists in countries such as Pakistan, Yemen and Somalia; just 26% say they disapprove." The poll also showed that that people were less willing to approve hypothetical strikes that accidentally killed civilians along with extremist targets. Whether such a hypothetical distinction is possible in real-life drone attacks is a separate question.[16]

Similarly, a majority of people polled in June 2013 were willing accept surveillance by the National Security Agency (NSA) as the price of security. A week after it was revealed that the Obama administration has continued the massive collection of telephone and Internet data begun under the Bush administration, 56 percent of respondents to a *Washington Post*–Pew Research Center poll agreed that the NSA "program tracking the telephone records of millions of Americans is an acceptable way for the government to investigate terrorism." Asked a more general questions, "62% say it is more important for the federal government to investigate possible terrorist threats, even if that intrudes on personal privacy."[17] It would seem that many people in the United States are frightened enough of terrorism that they would, if offered the choice, trade personal privacy (along with allowing torture and assassination) in return for security.

The offer of such a trade is, of course, a false one, another instance of now-you-see-it-now-you-don't. In fact, the NSA has not been able to come through with their end of the bargain; none of this immense effort could prevent two young men from detonating backpack bombs at the finish line of the 2013 Boston Marathon. In fact, no government program can completely eliminate the possibility that some human beings will make violent attacks on other human beings, whether for personal or political motives, any more than it can eliminate human mortality itself. This is not to argue that the U.S. government should make no attempt to forestall terrorist attacks (or for that matter, random assaults on schoolchildren such as the 2012 massacre in Sandy Hook, Connecticut).[18] It is rather to ask what practices people in this country ought to permit as the price of a real or illusory safety.

Constructing an Argument

This book makes several arguments. The first is that the scholarly and popular discussions about torture—both torture in general and as it has been practiced by the U.S. government since September 11, 2001—have consistently mischaracterized the problem. By treating torture as occasional acts, rather than as an ongoing practice, these arguments have lifted the conversation too far into the hypothetical realm. The resulting discussion fails to address the messy anguish of what actually happens in prisons and detention centers; instead we focus on the finely hewed contours of well-constructed "limit cases." Thus, all ethical arguments that treat torture only as episodic behavior are inevitably incomplete approaches to the problem. While they may provide useful exercises in theoretical ethics as Fritz Allhoff has suggested, they cannot provide an adequate moral grasp on institutionalized state torture as it actually is practiced.[19]

A corollary to this argument is that because torture is not a series of discrete actions, it cannot best be understood and judged through ethical methods that focus on actions, such as deontology and the various forms of consequentialism. I have proposed an approach that, rather than evaluating torture as isolated *acts*, treats torture as a *practice*, in the sense intended by Alasdair MacIntyre, a pioneer of contemporary virtue ethics. Several conclusions arise from this effort:

First, when torture is understood as a practice, it becomes possible to examine the "goods internal" to that practice and to identify the intellectual and moral habits necessary to achieving such goods. These "goods" and habits can then themselves be subjected to moral scrutiny.

Second, the effects of the practice of institutionalized state torture will necessarily extend beyond individual victims and torturers, although the precise nature of those effects is a subject for empirical study. A decades-long practice of state torture cannot survive and expand without the knowledge and approval of some portions of the government apparatus. In a democratic nation that practices torture, questions must also be raised about the relationship between the general population and the practice. To what extent, for example, might certain pervasive habits of intellect or character either be formed by or contribute to the furtherance of that practice?

Finally, because torture is not an episodic occurrence but a socially embedded practice, only a systemic approach to ending torture in the United States can have a hope of succeeding. Prosecutions of individuals like Charles Graner and Lynndie England (low-level soldiers convicted in the Abu Ghraib scandal) do nothing by themselves to end the practice of torture.[20] If anything, they reinforce the rhetoric of denial that insists that any report of torture in the "war on terror" reveals an aberrant action, rather than what it really is: a glimpse of a larger, systemic practice.

This book is organized in seven chapters. Chapter 1 offers a definition of the subject of this book—institutionalized state torture. It addresses the legal, phenomenological, and political criteria that qualify this practice, ultimately defining such torture in three parts, as (i) the intentional infliction of severe mental or physical suffering by an official or agent of a political entity (ii) that aims to dismantle the victim's sensory, psychological, and social worlds (iii) with the effect of establishing or maintaining that entity's power.

Chapter 2 asks whether U.S. practice in the post-9/11 period satisfies this definition of institutionalized state torture and concludes that it does. Information from a wide variety of sources demonstrates that prisoners held in the "war on terror" have been subjected to severe mental and physical suffering. Treatment has included harsh beatings, agonizing physical immobilization, suffocations, sensory deprivation, prolonged sleep deprivation, prolonged isolation from all human contact, sexual and other forms of humiliation, anal and vaginal rape, canine attacks, and the experience of drowning induced by "waterboarding."[21] Contemporaneous journalism, recent historical works, and even more recently declassified government documents make it abundantly clear that the use of torture is not an deviation from ordinary practice but the result of specific policies issuing from the offices of the Department of Justice, the Secretary of Defense, the vice president, and the CIA. Those who practiced torture have indeed been acting as officials or, in the case of private contractors, as agents of the U.S. government.[22]

Chapter 2 further demonstrates that many of the methods used on prisoners held by the United States during this period were designed with the express intention of dismantling the victims' sensory, personal, and social worlds. This is precisely the objective laid out, for example in the CIA's KUBARK interrogation manuals, with their emphasis on creation of the experience they label "DDD": debility, dependency, and dread.[23]

Finally, Chapter 2 argues that the power of the U.S. government has indeed been enhanced and maintained by its various "interrogation" programs. In countries where the United States has been involved in direct military action, such as Iraq and Afghanistan, the United States has used torture with the usual goal of frightening potential adversaries. At home, the awareness that the government had undertaken such extreme measures on U.S. citizens' behalf has served to reinforce citizens' belief in an existential threat to themselves and the nation. This belief has also rendered citizens more amenable both to restrictions on civil liberties in this country and, at least for some years, to undertaking wars abroad.

Chapter 3 presents the range of ethical arguments about torture, as found both in the scholarly literature and in the editorials of two major newspapers, the *New York Times* and the *Wall Street Journal*. While scholars and editorialists may employ different vocabularies, their actual arguments turn out to be remarkably similar. The majority of discussions in both arenas take one of two ethical approaches: consequentialism or deontology. The former bases ethical judgments about individual actions on the *outcomes* of those actions. The latter approach is more concerned with questions of duty and the *motives behind* actions. Both approaches, however, tend to treat torture as a series of isolated acts, rather than as an ongoing, socially embedded practice.

The discussion of consequentialist approaches to torture begins with an investigation of an argument that is so common that it has its own name—the "ticking time-bomb" case. I argue, as have other ethicists, that this hypothetical approach to torture is so far removed from actual practice as to render its conclusions irrelevant to any serious discussion of torture. Nevertheless, the "ticking time-bomb" case remains the emblematic presentation of torture as a moral puzzle, both in academic ethics and in the popular press.

More generally, consequentialist arguments *in favor of* torture recommend permitting the suffering of some person or persons to prevent injury to, or the death of, others. These arguments differ primarily as to which "others" ought to be thus protected. Strict utilitarian arguments, which focus on bringing about the greatest good for the greatest number, are primarily addressed to the "ticking time-bomb" problem, justifying the torture of one person to save the lives of thousands. Other consequentialist arguments in favor of torture place less emphasis on the number of people to be saved through torture than on the difference between the guilt of the person to be tortured (who is presumed to be a criminal or terrorist) and the innocence of those to be saved (e.g., schoolchildren).[24] A third consequentialist approach argues that torture is justified if it provides information that might save the lives of a smaller number of specific people—soldiers on the battlefield. Consequentialist arguments *against* torture, on the other hand, focus on two main questions: whether torture "works," that is, whether it really is an effective means of acquiring intelligence, and whether using torture during wartime increases danger to one's own soldiers if they are captured.

Chapter 3 then takes up deontological arguments about torture. Those *in favor* of torture posit a duty—generally constructed as the duty of individual government officials—to protect civilians from terrorist attack, even when by doing so one incurs personal moral guilt. Deontological arguments *against* torture invoke and amplify Immanuel Kant's imperative against the use of human beings as mere instruments to achieve some other end.

While they differ in emphasis, most consequentialist and deontological approaches share a fundamental limitation: they treat torture itself as a series of discrete and unusual *actions*, arising suddenly in situations of great extremity. This view makes it possible to examine hypothetical acts of torture as if they were freestanding moral problems, devoid of any social or historical particularity, rather than parts of a larger whole.[25] However, such hypothetical situations prove inconsistent with the extended definition of torture developed in Chapter 1, which is based in real-world experience, rather than hypothetical argumentation. Chapter 3 concludes with the suggestion that torture may best be treated as a practice, especially as that term is used by virtue ethicist Alasdair MacIntyre.

Chapter 4 outlines MacIntyre's ethical approach, a teleological method that describes the good human life as a profound quest to understand what is good for human beings. In the context of searching for this human *telos*, people participate in *practices*, in the course of which they are formed in the *virtues* required for successful practice. A practice, in MacIntyre's understanding, is a "coherent and complex form of socially established cooperative activity through which goods internal to that form of activity are realized in the course of trying to achieve those standards of excellence which are appropriate to, and partially definitive of, that form of activity."[26] The virtues are those habitual forms of human excellence necessary to, and developed through participation in, practices.

Next, Chapter 4 addresses a critique of MacIntyre's approach, which is that, like virtue ethics in general, it is inescapably relativistic. This criticism argues that in MacIntyre's system a particular set of virtues can only be meaningful within a particular tradition and the community that carries that tradition. This implies that there is no possibility of making legitimate ethical judgment across traditions, that each tradition remains a self-consistent, impermeable whole. In this context I introduce "capabilities" theory, an approach to cross-cultural ethical judgment developed by Amartya Sen and Martha Nussbaum.

Chapter 4 then addresses the question of the unity of the virtues. That is, is it possible for a person to possess some key virtues while lacking others or while simultaneously possessing the opposing vices for some of them? MacIntyre has changed his own position on this question. His more recent work, along with that of his interpreter Christopher Stephen Lutz, argues that human virtues do indeed function as a unified whole within a person's character. In particular, moral virtues such as courage, temperance, and justice cannot be practiced without the presence of the intellectual virtue of practical wisdom, which helps a person know, as Lutz puts it, "What is to count as cowardice? What is to count as rashness? What is the purpose to which my courageous acts are to be directed?"[27]

Finally, Chapter 4 considers the question of whether an intrinsically evil human endeavor, specifically torture, qualifies as a practice at all in MacIntyre's sense. This is a relevant question in part because MacIntyre himself has suggested that it does not.[28] It would seem that the "coherent and complex form of socially established cooperative activity" of institutionalized state torture should generate in its participants *evil* dispositions of character, that is, vices rather than virtues. For this reason, torture does not perfectly satisfy MacIntyre's definition of practice. Nonetheless, it bears enough similarity to what MacIntyre means by a practice, especially in that it possesses its own internal goods and generates in its practitioners stable moral and intellectual qualities, to render MacIntyre's approach a useful tool for making a normative judgment about torture. Chapter 4 concludes by accepting Lutz's proposed appellation, "false practice" to characterize torture.[29]

Chapter 5 demonstrates the ways in which institutionalized state torture as defined in Chapter 1 and, in particular, the use of torture by the United States in the "war on terror" satisfies the structural requirements of a practice as elaborated in Chapter 4. Here it is shown that torture is indeed a "coherent and complex form of socially established cooperative activity." At this point, a possible empirical challenge to this conception of torture as a practice emerges, in the form of the "obedience to authority" experiments of Stanley Milgram and Philip Zimbardo's Stanford Prison project. One implicit argument arising from these studies is that if many people can quickly and easily be induced to torture others, the situations in which people find themselves may have a greater role in determining their behavior than does moral character. However, as philosophers Sabini and Silver argue, the fact that many people are more likely to engage in torture in some situations than in others does not by itself rule out a virtue ethics approach to torture.[30]

Chapter 6 describes the "goods internal" to institutionalized state torture: the production of truth, the production of enemies, and the production and reproduction of torturers themselves. It then addresses ways in which torture deforms in its practitioners each of the four cardinal virtues, which are justice, temperance, courage, and prudence. A brief excursus addresses the implications of torture for another set of human qualities, sometimes called the Christian graces, which are faith, hope, and love.

Having established the view of torture as a practice with particular effects on its practitioners and suggested that those effects may well extend to the larger society in which torture is embedded, Chapter 7 concludes the book by asking what is to be done about U.S. torture. In the short term, I argue, we should focus efforts on genuinely ending the practice of torture, which has so expanded during the "war on terror." This effort begins with closing the prison at Guantánamo, which President Barack Obama has twice sworn (and as of yet failed) to do. It means ending the practice of extraordinary rendition, the "outsourcing" of torture to other countries. Such rendition is prohibited by the UN Convention against Torture, and the United States should comply with its obligation to honor a convention that it has signed. And it means dismantling the torture apparatus maintained by the tangle of intelligence agencies that has grown up over the last sixty years.

We will not be able to achieve this last, however, without a full accounting of what has been done since 9/11 in the name of protecting Americans from terrorism. That is one important project for the medium term. Such an effort will depend on the courage and dedication of a wide variety of people: journalists and historians, officials of all three branches of government, and ordinary residents of this country. In addition to a full accounting of what has been done, we must hold persons accountable for what they have done. This does not mean prosecution of more enlisted members of the armed forces, such as Charles Garner and Lynndie England of Abu Ghraib fame. The call for accountability refers rather to those people who in Latin American parlance are called the "intellectual authors" of torture. I argue in this final chapter that for several reasons, justice requires an end to impunity for high public officials.

In addition to the requirements of justice, this last chapter reexamines the other three classical virtues in relation to how the country might move forward to end torture and regain our courage, temperance, and practical wisdom.

A Personal Note

Although this is an academic book, my own interest in the problem of torture is not academic. I had the privilege of spending parts of the 1980s in the war zones of Central America, including six months of travel in the countryside of Nicaragua during 1984. There I worked with an organization called Witness for Peace. Its purpose was twofold: to provide some meager accompaniment to Nicaraguans caught up in the *contra* war and to gather testimonies of those who had survived *contra* attacks at a time when the Reagan administration was illegally funding those attacks and training the attackers.[31]

The *contra* strategy in the Nicaraguan countryside was classic terrorism: unpredictable violence directed against civilians and civilian infrastructure such as family farms, schools, clinics, roads, and telephone lines. A typical attack involved murder, kidnapping of fighting-age youth, torture, and the display of mutilated bodies as a warning to others not to support the Sandinista government. I met people who had been tortured and a few who may have been torturers. I met teachers who buried their books every morning and dug them up again at night to teach. I met a woman whose son, an elementary school teacher, was tortured to death in front of his students. I met people of extraordinary courage, like the twenty-one-year-old woman communications operator in Occotal, who told me, "If I die, it doesn't matter. Someone will come after me" to continue the work.

When the terrorists struck on September 11, I hoped that the people of my own country would demonstrate the same kind of courage. I still believe we can.

Notes

1. Ariel Dorfman, "Untying an Ethical Question on Torture," *San Francisco Chronicle*, May 9, 2004, http://www.sfgate.com/opinion/article/Untying-an-ethical-question-on-torture-2760599.php#page-1.
2. Aristotle, *Nicomachean Ethics*, trans. David Ross (New York: Oxford University Press, 1998). 1103b26.
3. Alfred W. McCoy, *A Question of Torture: CIA Interrogation, from the Cold War to the War on Terror*, 1st ed. The American Empire Project. (New York: Metropolitan Books/Henry Holt, 2006), Chapter 2.
4. CIA, *KUBARK Counterintelligence Interrogation* (1963).
5. Committee on Government Operations, "U.S. Assistance Programs in Vietnam" (Washington, DC: 1972), 100–01.
6. McCoy, *A Question of Torture*, 64–71, 119.
7. Select Committee to Study Governmental Operations with Respect to Intelligence Activities, "Final Report on Foreign and Military Intelligence," ed. U.S. Senate (Washington, DC: 1976), 27–29.
8. Ibid., 29.
9. CIA, "Human Resource Exploitation Training Manual" (1983).
10. Jonathan Alter, "Time to Think about Torture," *Newsweek*, November 5, 2001.
11. Tim Russert, "NBC News' Meet the Press: Dick Cheney," September 16, 2001, http://www.fromthewilderness.com/timeline/2001/meetthepress091601.html; Select Committee to Study Governmental Operations with Respect to Intelligence Activities, "Final Report on Foreign and Military Intelligence."
12. Cofer Black, "Joint Investigation into September 11th: Fifth Public Hearing," September 26, 2002, http://www.fas.org/irp/congress/2002_hr/092602black.html.
13. William T. Cavanaugh, "Making Enemies: The Imagination of Torture in Chile and the United States," *Theology Today* 63, no. 3 (2006).

14. Amy Zegart, "Torture Creep: Why Are More Americans Accepting Bush-Era Policies than Ever Before?"*Foreign Policy*, September 25, 2012, http://www.foreignpolicy.com/articles/2012/09/25/torture_creep. Zegart believes that exposure to fictional films and television shows about spies is the main factor in the uptick in support for torture revealed by her poll. This book suggests additional possible explanations.

15. Ibid.

16. Pew Center for People & the Press, "Continued Support for U.S. Drone Strikes," February 11, 2013, http://www.people-press.org/2013/02/11/continued-support-for-u-s-drone-strikes/.

17. Pew Center for People & the Press, "Majority Views NSA Phone Tracking as Acceptable Anti-Terror Tactic," June 10, 2013, http://www.people-press.org/2013/06/10/majority-views-nsa-phone-tracking-as-acceptable-anti-terror-tactic/.

18. James Barron, "Children Were All Shot Multiple Times with a Semiautomatic, Officials Say," *New York Times*, December 15, 2012.

19. Fritz Allhoff, "A Defense of Torture: Separation of Cases, Ticking Time-Bombs, and Moral Justification,"*International Journal of Applied Philosophy* 19, no. 2 (2005).

20. Graner and England are among the seven soldiers prosecuted for the torture revealed at Abu Ghraib. The Taguba Report describes Graner as a "ringleader." England is probably best known as the woman photographed holding an Iraqi man on a leash as if he was a dog.

21. Extensive documentation for this claim can be found in Chapters 1 and 4.

22. See, for example: Philippe Sands, *Torture Team: Rumsfeld's Memo and the Betrayal of American Values*, 1st ed. (New York: Palgrave MacMillan, 2008); Jane Mayer, *Dark Side: The Inside Story of How the War on Terror Turned into a War on American Ideals* (New York: Doubleday, 2008); Maj. Gen. Antonio M. Taguba, *Article 15–6 Investigation of the 800th Military Police Brigade* (U.S. Department of Defense, 2004).

23. CIA, "Kubark Counterintelligence Interrogation," 83.

24. See, for example, Jean Bethke Elshtain, "Reflection on the Problem of 'Dirty Hands,'" in *Torture: A Collection*, ed. Sanford Levinson (New York: Oxford University Press, 2004).

25. One important exception is the consequentialist argument of Arrigo and Bufacchi, who cite inevitable long-term damage to social and governmental institutions that arises from the creation of the infrastructure necessary for torture. See Vittorio Bufacchi and Jean Maria Arrigo, "Torture, Terrorism and the State: A Refutation of the Ticking-Bomb Argument," *Journal of Applied Philosophy* 23, no. 3 (2006); Jean Maria Arrigo, "A Consequentialist Argument against Torture Interrogation of Terrorists," paper presented at the Joint Services Conference on Professional Ethics (Springfield, VA: January 2003).

26. Alasdair MacIntyre, *After Virtue*, 2d ed. (Notre Dame, IN: Notre Dame University Press, 1984), 187.

27. Christopher Stephen Lutz, *Tradition in the Ethics of Alasdair MacIntyre: Relativism, Thomism, and Philosophy* (Lanham, MD.: Lexington Books, 2004). 101.

28. MacIntyre, *After Virtue*, 200.

29. Lutz, *Tradition in the Ethics of Alasdair MacIntyre*, 103.

30. John Sabini and Maury Silver, "Lack of Character? Situationism Critiqued," *Ethics* 115, no. 3 (2005).

31. See Rebecca Gordon, *Letters from Nicaragua* (San Francisco: Spinsters/Aunt Lute, 1986).

‖ 1 ‖

Describing the Problem

The word itself has something repulsive and dangerous about it.... Both social conventions and the restrictions imposed on language by good manners make it difficult to speak of things as they really are. Torture is dirty and the language or writing used to describe it should also be dirty. If not, the screaming and the pain will always be missing....

—Pedro Castillo Yañez[1]

This is not a book about idiosyncratic acts of extreme violence perpetrated by some individuals on other individuals, the kind of crimes portrayed twenty times a night in television dramas. It is a book about an ongoing practice carried out over a long period of time by governments. It is a book about institutionalized state torture, a practice defined below. The definition has three parts: legal, phenomenological, and political. A legal definition covers laws and treaties on torture, in this case, specifically those binding the United States of America. A phenomenological definition outlines the mental, emotional, and social effects of torture on its targets. And a political definition treats the *purpose* of institutionalized state torture; it seeks to answer the question, Why do governments torture people?

An Introduction

A few introductory remarks are necessary before beginning a discussion of torture itself. Torture is difficult to write about for a number of reasons. First, there is its fascinating horror. Torture can have a simultaneously compelling and repellent effect on those who encounter its representations in picture or prose. Then there is the problem of credibility. We can have no direct experience of other people's pain. We cannot verify it by empirical observation. How then are we to treat the reports of those who have been tortured? How are we to evaluate the degree of suffering they say that they have experienced? How are we to evaluate the adequacy of the meanings that others attach to such experiences? As Elaine Scarry said in *The Body in Pain*, her classic meditation on physical pain and the human imagination, "To have pain is to have *certainty*; to hear about pain is to have *doubt*."[2] In the pages that follow, I hope to allay some of that doubt.

Scarry also warns that in writing about torture one is confronted with two conflicting imperatives: to convey the immediate reality of pain and to respect the agency of the sufferer. On one hand, a dry recitation will not convey to the reader the profound, world-destroying effects of torture. But, on the other, a too-vivid account risks arousing the reader's morbid fascination, even titillation—thus submitting the sufferer to further violation—rather than provoking reactions of sympathy, horror, or outrage. Writing about the difficulty that Amnesty International faces when attempting to stir to action those who receive its communications, Scarry says, "When, for example, one receives a letter from Amnesty in the mail, the words of that letter must somehow convey to the reader the aversiveness being experienced inside the body of someone whose country may be far away [and] whose name can barely be pronounced." The language of such a letter, Scarry continues

> must at once be characterized by the greatest possible tact (for the most intimate realm of another human being's body is the implicit or explicit subject) and by the greatest possible immediacy (for the most crucial fact about pain is *its presentness* and the most crucial fact about torture is that it *is happening*). Tact and immediacy ordinarily work against one another; thus the difficulty of sustaining either tone is compounded by the necessity of sustaining both simultaneously.[3]

I shall aim, as Scarry suggests, to "sustain both" tact and immediacy in this work. However, when it seems necessary to choose between the two, my inclination is to follow the admonition of Dr. Pedro Castillo Yañez and to err on the side of immediacy. Castillo, who is quoted at the beginning of this chapter, served as president of Chile's National Commission against Torture, constituted after the end of the Pinochet regime. He considers it an "ethical duty" to "discover the way in which this social blight may be most completely understood." Such an undertaking, he says "requires courage."[4]

But why should describing torture require courage? Accuracy, perhaps; discernment, maybe; careful attention to sources, certainly. But all of these are intellectual virtues, necessary to any successful scholarly undertaking. Why posit the need for a virtue from another realm, a moral virtue? Why should speaking, writing, or indeed reading about torture require courage? A few reasons come to mind.

Most obviously, there is the genuine physical risk run by those who denounce torture as it is happening—particularly those who are members of groups identified as enemies of the torturing state or who by their very denunciations invite such identification. This is a danger faced by human rights workers everywhere and most especially by those who investigate the doings of their own governments. It is not a danger generally encountered by American writers investigating U.S. practices.

There is however another lesser risk for writers about torture in this country, borne especially by those who spoke up in the early days of the "war on terror." This is the risk of being laughed at, not so much for *describing* torture as *naming* it, for the act of pointing to a particular public disclosure and saying, "This is torture." It is at the point of naming as torture practices that are officially described in other terms—as "counterintelligence,"[5] "enhanced interrogation methods,"[6] or "stress and duress"[7]—that the speaker or writer risks being denounced as cowardly and unpatriotic or unrealistic, foolish, and naive.

To name behavior as "torture," particularly when it is practiced by agents of a democratic state, is to break a tautological circle—one in which the state's self-definition includes the understanding that it does not practice torture. When a state that by definition "does not torture"[8] is accused of doing so, one of two things must be the case. Either there is something wrong with the definition of the state, or there is something wrong with the accusation. It requires a good deal less shifting of mental furniture to believe the latter explanation. Perhaps the accuser has misunderstood the character of the state (i.e., that by definition it does not torture) and has therefore mistaken the actions of a few for official policy. Or perhaps she is exaggerating the situation, indulging in a bit of hyperbole to make a point. In that case, the problem lies with her definition not of the state but of torture itself. What she is calling "torture" is really just aggressive interrogation. It has more in common with a fraternity hazing than with "real" torture.[9]

It is not surprising, for example, to hear Osvaldo Romo, a lower-echelon functionary of DINA, Chile's security police in the early years of the Pinochet dictatorship, claim that he never tortured anyone.

> "And applying [electrical] current?" a reporter asks him during a prison interview.
> "I don't believe applying current is torture," says Romo.[10]

Such "rhetoric of denial," as Talal Asad has called it, has not been limited, however, to apologists of dictatorships like Pinochet's. Because societies that consider themselves liberal or modern prohibit torture, their "authorities typically generate a rhetoric of public denial—of disclaiming that 'torture' has actually taken place within their domain of responsibility ('it was the unauthorized activity of undisciplined officials'), or of claiming that what appears to be 'torture' is really something less reprehensible ('reasonable pressure')."[11]

Similar arguments were advanced by functionaries of the U.S. executive branch under the George W. Bush administration. One example is the now-famous memo prepared in August 2002 for then-Counsel to the President Alberto Gonzalez by Jay S. Bybee and John Yoo, who were working in the Justice Department's Office of Legal Counsel. The memo provides an interpretation of the prohibition on "intentional infliction" of "severe physical or mental pain" found in the section of U.S. criminal code outlawing torture. In regard to physical pain, "in order to constitute torture" and hence to violate U.S. law, a victim's pain must be so great that it would "ordinarily be associated with a sufficiently serious physical condition or injury such as death, organ failure, or serious impairment of bodily functions."[12] Under this definition it seems quite possible that the Justice Department would have concurred with Señor Romo's contention that "applying current" is not torture.

Note that in June 2004, after this memo had became public, it was withdrawn and superseded in December 2004 by another opinion. "Questions have since been raised," the new opinion observes a bit wryly, "both by this Office and by others, about the appropriateness and relevance of the non-statutory discussion in the August 2002 Memorandum and also about various aspects of the statutory analysis, in particular the statement" defining severe pain or suffering.[13] The "non-statutory discussion" mentioned here refers to groundwork laid in the original memo for the legal exoneration of the president or other high officials should they find themselves accused of torture. In other words, this memo was written to shield members of the Bush administration from prosecution. "Because the discussion in that memorandum concerning the President's Commander-in-Chief power and the potential defenses to liability was—and remains—unnecessary," the new opinion explains that such discussion "has been eliminated from the analysis that follows."[14]

This is because such "consideration of the bounds of any such authority" is now irrelevant, as it "would be inconsistent with the President's unequivocal directive that United States personnel not engage in torture." The source cited for this presidential "directive" is a statement issued by President Bush on the occasion of the July 2004 United Nations International Day in Support of Victims of Torture. The portions quoted in the citation appear to be more assertion than directive:

America stands against and will not tolerate torture. We will investigate and prosecute all acts of torture . . . in all territory under our jurisdiction. . . . Torture is wrong no matter where it occurs, and the United States will continue to lead the fight to eliminate it everywhere.[15]

Here we enter the tautological circle drawn by the rhetoric of denial, in which the nation *by definition* does "not tolerate torture." Therefore any contention to the contrary must of necessity be false, a contradiction in terms. The state does not torture; therefore the state cannot torture; therefore the state does not torture.

We find examples of the full complement of Asad's "rhetoric of denial"—the implicit questioning of the accuser's loyalty to the nation or community, the displacing of responsibility onto people of lower rank, and the description of the state's actions as falling outside the definition of torture in the words of Roman Catholic Bishop Gillmore, then associated with the Chilean military, interviewed during the 1980s:

> Who is going to approve of torture? No one [. . .] but is there really torture? You know that sometimes things get exaggerated. It could be that there is a need for people in middle or lower ranks to extract in some way or other those secrets that might be of interest to the Community; not to the government, but to the community, to the tranquility of Chile. So those methods get exaggerated, and—it's not that anyone wants torture to happen—but sometimes a sloppy approach results.[16]
>
> But in the end, what has been done in Chile is almost nothing.[17]

But perhaps we have missed Dr. Castillo's point here. For he is claiming that what "requires courage" is not only the activity of describing and revealing torture but also of understanding it "as completely as possible." This is the "ethical duty" that he identifies.

Why would someone who wants to understand the reality of torture need to be brave? One obvious reason is what is sometimes called the "ick factor," the ordinary squeamishness that makes hearing the details of painful experiences unpleasant and even frightening to many people. Most people have little control over the immediate reactions of their own minds and bodies to images or descriptions of the real and profound agony of real human beings. Some people have unpleasant physical reactions to such psychic shocks: sweating, a racing heart, nausea. For others, the distress is more mental than physical: the intrusion of unwanted images, nightmares, the inability to get certain ideas "out of their heads." Other people may fear that they will discover or confirm something disturbing about themselves, for example, that they do not in fact experience the shock and discomfort that they believe they ought to. They may worry that they will exhibit fascination or even sexual arousal.

There is another reason why understanding the kind of torture contemplated in this book—institutionalized state torture—requires courage: once a person has understood it, there is no possible retreat into ignorance. She may find that Castillo's "ethical duty" of understanding torture has expanded in ways that she didn't bargain for, that she now carries a burden of responsibility she did not want, and that having understood something about torture she is now required to do something about it.

Institutionalized State Torture: A Definition

It might be argued that "torture" is too broad a category for definition. There are, after all, many kinds of torture, and the means and meanings of torture vary substantially across historical and geographical boundaries. This is certainly true. Understandings of the relationship between torture and truth-telling, for example, have changed substantially since the ascendancies of ancient Greece and Rome, regimes that practiced torture as a guarantor of truth. This is why, as Hannah Arendt points out, the Greeks reserved torture for slaves. Because it was believed that no one could invent a lie while under torture, the imposition of the necessity of telling the truth destroyed a person's freedom; torture must not therefore be applied to free persons.[18] Today, by contrast, the dependability of statements produced under torture is very much a matter of dispute.

St. Augustine felt most keenly the horror of the relationship that he believed exists between torture and truth-telling. He lamented the fact that to arrive at the truth about a crime, a wise judge was obligated to torture not only (possibly innocent) people accused of crimes but also (certainly innocent) witnesses to crimes. This, because "those who pronounce judgement cannot see into the consciences of those on whom they pronounce it." Augustine acknowledges that even torture is an imperfect remedy for human ignorance: "The witnesses may give false evidence, the defendant himself may hold out under torture with savage resistance and refuse to confess, and the accusers may be incapable of proving the truth of their charges, however true those charges may be; and the judge, in his ignorance, may condemn them."[19]

Torture, while an imperfect guarantor of truth, was the only possible remedy for a society's "indispensable" need to bring criminals to justice. The wise judge, Augustine said, "does not act in this way through a will to do harm, but because ignorance is unavoidable—and yet the exigences of human society make judgement also unavoidable." For this reason, he considered state torture a human evil but not a sin. He described the conflict between "unavoid-able ignorance and the unavoidable duty of judging," which required torture, "a mark of human wretchedness." This is why the judge, "if he has the wisdom of devotion . . . cries out to God, 'Deliver me from my necessities!' "[20]

While present-day defenses of state torture also make reference to the state's unavoidable need to ascertain truth, the nature of that necessary truth has changed in the intervening centuries. Most modern judicial systems rec-ognize that torture does not in fact guarantee the veracity of its victims' utter-ances. Rather than *requiring* evidence produced through torture, most modern criminal justice systems *exclude* it—in law if not always in practice. The indis-pensable need for "truth" met by torture in present-day liberal states lies in another realm, that of national security. It is the need to discover truth about future dangers to the state, rather than about past violations of its laws, that underlies present-day justifications of state torture.

It can also be argued that the nature of torture varies across national as well as historical boundaries, and so that we should not speak so much of *torture* as of *tortures*, each arising in its own national or ethnic setting. It may well be the case, for example, that we find certain specific techniques of torture (the "tea party"; the "tea party with toast") in Greece under its military dictator-ship,[21] while others ("stress positions"; "waterboarding") have become familiar to observers of the United States' "war on terror." It is even possible to track the migration of particular techniques over time from one location to another, as Darius Rejali has done admirably in *Torture and Democracy*.[22] The degree of official acknowledgement of torture may also vary from place to place, and similarly the self-understandings of those engaged in torture and of those who order it.

I would argue, however, that certain signal features characterize contempo-rary institutionalized state torture across a range of nations. The continuities are sufficient, I believe, to develop a description of state torture across several dimensions—legal, phenomenological, and political. Let us begin with a defi-nition of torture under U.S. law.

Legal Definitions

A good place to begin the legal description of torture under U.S. law is the defi-nition contained in the 1984 United Nations Convention against Torture and Other Cruel, Inhuman or Degrading Treatment or Punishment, to which the United States is a signatory. The Convention defines torture as

> any act by which severe pain or suffering, whether physical or mental, is intentionally inflicted on a person for such purposes as obtaining

from him or a third person information or a confession, punishing him for an act he or a third person has committed or is suspected of having committed, or intimidating or coercing him or a third person, or for any reason based on discrimination of any kind, when such pain or suffering is inflicted by or at the instigation of or with the consent or acquiescence of a public official or other person acting in an official capacity.[23]

When the U.S. Senate ratified this Convention a decade after its publication, it did so with a number of reservations. One of these restricts the U.S. understanding of "cruel, inhuman or degrading treatment" to that which is already "prohibited by the Fifth, Eighth, and/or Fourteenth Amendments to the Constitution of the United States."[24] Another reproduces language originally drafted by the Reagan administration's State Department, designed to remedy the perceived "vagueness" of the Convention's definition of mental torture.[25] The emendations recommended by the Reagan administration in 1988 appear in both the reservations with which the United States ratified the Convention in 1994 and in the enabling legislation passed in the same year. The relevant sections of that law are brief enough to reproduce in their entirety. Here is the first:

§ 2340. Definitions
   As used in this chapter—
   (1) "torture" means an act committed by a person acting under the color of law specifically intended to inflict severe physical or mental pain or suffering (other than pain or suffering incidental to lawful sanctions) upon another person within his custody or physical control;

This definition of torture appears to accord with the one contained in the UN Convention, with the additional exclusion of "incidental" pain or suffering (presumably of whatever severity) that arises out of otherwise lawful sanctions. It omits, however, the language found in the Convention describing the variety of contexts in which such pain might be inflicted: to obtain information, as punishment, or as a form of discrimination. One possible reading of this omission is a redefinition of torture as an activity whose primary objective or *specific intent* is the infliction of pain in and of itself. Such a reading of this section of the act is indeed contemplated in the 2002 Justice Department memo. The authors conclude, however, that while "as a theoretical matter, knowledge alone that a particular result is certain to occur does not constitute specific intent," a jury trying a torture case is likely to see things differently. "As a matter of practice in the federal criminal justice system," they conclude, "it is highly unlikely that a jury would acquit in such a situation."[26] In other words, ordinary people are unlikely to believe that the only behavior that counts as torture is an infliction of pain whose only purpose is the infliction of pain.

Section 2340 continues defining terms, focusing next on the question of what constitutes severe *mental* pain or suffering:

> (2) "severe mental pain or suffering" means the prolonged mental harm caused by or resulting from—
> (A) the intentional infliction or threatened infliction of severe physical pain or suffering;
> (B) the administration or application, or threatened administration or application, of mind-altering substances or other procedures calculated to disrupt profoundly the senses or the personality;
> (C) the threat of imminent death; or
> (D) the threat that another person will imminently be subjected to death, severe physical pain or suffering, or the administration or application of mind-altering substances or other procedures calculated to disrupt profoundly the senses or personality;

There are at least two problems with this definition. First, nothing in the Convention's definition of torture requires that the effects of "severe mental pain or suffering" be more "prolonged," more long-lasting, than those of physical pain and suffering. At what point do post-traumatic stress disorder or depression rise to the level of being "prolonged" harm? After six months? A year? If a form of treatment cannot be called torture until months or years afterward, how can the interrogator judge whether the things he is doing to a detainee amount to torture? (Of course, the target recognizes his own mental suffering as immediately as he would recognize physical pain, but the law does not ask his opinion about the matter.)

David Luban and Henry Shue call this maneuver the "substitution trick." In contrast to physical pain and suffering, which qualifies as torture in the moment, the framers of Section 2340 have substituted "a possible effect" (i.e., long-term psychological symptoms) "for its cause so that the cause itself ceases to constitute torture."[27] No such distinction is contemplated in the original language of the Convention, which speaks only of "severe pain or suffering, whether physical or mental."

Second, as Luban and Shue argue, Section 2340 arbitrarily limits the forms of mental torture to a specific set of four. "Why such an exclusive list?" they ask. "What about a threat of imminent rape? What about being prevented permanently from performing required religious observances—never [being] allowed to pray properly, for example? What about being required to perform sexual acts considered perverse and disgusting?"[28]

The historian Alfred McCoy has suggested that this legal interpretation of mental harm served the interests of the CIA, in that it implicitly "excluded sensory deprivation (hooding), self-inflicted pain (stress positions), and disorientation (isolation and sleep denial)—the very techniques the CIA had refined at such great cost over several decades." He suggests that the inclusion of this definition of mental suffering in the legislation is likely "the result of the CIA's clandestine maneuvering" and that this redefinition of mental harm would "if narrowly interpreted, exempt the agency's psychological methods from the UN Convention."[29]

McCoy refers here to a well-documented, decades-long secret CIA research program designed to identify and test effective means of inducing psychological "regression of the personality to whatever earlier and weaker level is required for the dissolution of resistance and the inculcation of dependence."[30] The particular techniques that he refers to, together with others such as exposure to loud, unremitting noises, excesses of heat and cold, and sexual and cultural humiliations, have indeed formed part of the arsenal of techniques employed by a variety of U.S. agencies in the context of the "war on terror" launched after September 11, 2001. I am not entirely convinced, however, that Section 2340 does permit all of these actions, which seem to me to fall into the prohibited category of "other procedures calculated to disrupt profoundly the senses or personality."

Luban and Shue offer a different explanation for the refined definition of mental pain or suffering found in Section 2340. They agree with McCoy that "narrowly defining mental torture did not begin in the George W. Bush administration—it has been the consistent U.S. government line for two decades through five presidencies including the ten years of two Democratic presidents, Bill Clinton and Barack Obama." In contrast to McCoy, they argue that the main reason for the redefinition of mental torture was not to give cover to the CIA but to provide legal protection for practices that are common within the U.S. penal system. They suggest that an examination of the legislative records "finds repeated concerns that unless the definition of mental torture is written narrowly, U.S. law enforcement officials might face accusations of torture. In other words, the definition of mental torture was narrowed for reasons of liability screening, not reasons of definitional accuracy."[31]

Finally, Section 2340 defines "United States":

(3) "United States" means the several States of the United States, the District of Columbia, and the commonwealths, territories, and possessions of the United States.[32]

This definition becomes relevant in the next section of the law, because the legislation only allows prosecution for actions taken *outside* the United States.[33] The framers of Section 2340 contended that existing federal and state laws already prohibit torture within U.S. borders. "Torture does not occur in the United States except in aberrational situations and never as a matter of policy." So the United States explained to the UN Committee against Torture in its initial report to the Convention's signing partners in 1999 (some four years after the report was due). "When it does," the report continues, "it constitutes a serious criminal offence, subjecting the perpetrators to prosecution and entitling the victims to various remedies, including rehabilitation and compensation." Hence, "although there is no federal law criminalizing torture per se, any act falling within the Convention's definition of torture is clearly illegal and prosecutable everywhere in the country, for example as an assault or battery, murder or manslaughter, kidnapping or abduction, false arrest or imprisonment, sexual abuse, or violation of civil rights."[34] The report goes on to cite specific instances of such prosecutions, for example, of "a sheriff in Gulf County, Florida was convicted of using his position to coerce five female inmates to engage in sexual acts with him."[35]

Here is Section 2340A:

§ 2340A. Torture

(a) Offense.—Whoever outside the United States commits or attempts to commit torture shall be fined under this title or imprisoned not more than 20 years, or both, and if death results to any person from conduct prohibited by this subsection, shall be punished by death or imprisoned for any term of years or for life.

(b) Jurisdiction.—There is jurisdiction over the activity prohibited in subsection (a) if—

(1) the alleged offender is a national of the United States; or

(2) the alleged offender is present in the United States, irrespective of the nationality of the victim or alleged offender.

(c) Conspiracy.—A person who conspires to commit an offense under this section shall be subject to the same penalties (other than the penalty of death) as the penalties prescribed for the offense, the commission of which was the object of the conspiracy.

The first and only prosecution to date under Section 2340A concluded in January 2009, when a federal judge sentenced Charles McArthur Emmanuel to 97 years in prison for torture and conspiracy to torture committed during his tenure as chief of Liberia's Antiterrorist Unit. Emmanuel, a U.S. citizen, is the son of former Liberian leader Charles Taylor, who has himself been indicted at The Hague on war crimes charges.[36]

Torture is also prohibited in other international conventions to which the United States is party, most important, the portion of the 1949 Geneva Conventions governing the treatment of prisoners of war. Congress passed enabling legislation for the 1949 Conventions in 1996.[37] These prohibitions are also incorporated into the U.S. Uniform Military Code of Justice.[38]

We can now summarize the legal definition of torture as *the intentional infliction of severe mental or physical suffering by an official or agent of a political entity.* It is important to remember, however, that the U.S.-enabling legislation for the UN Convention against Torture and the Geneva Conventions provides a much narrower definition of torture than that envisioned by the framers of those international documents. In other words, the legal definition of torture given in this book has much more in common with international law than with the much more constricted definition found in present-day U.S. law.

Phenomenological Definitions

A legal definition of torture is a beginning, but it hardly exhausts the meaning of the term. Elaine Scarry has offered a phenomenological description of torture as the intentional unmaking of a human being's world. To begin, profound physical pain, says Scarry, robs the victim of language and hence of his or her connection with any cognitive construction of the world.[39] Theologian William Cavanaugh elaborates on Scarry's description: "The immediacy of pain, its monopoly of attention and its incommunicability . . . shrinks the world down to the contours of the body itself; the enormity of the agony is the sufferer's only reality."[40] The world beyond the victim's body disappears, along with the victim's ability to communicate anything beyond the pain itself. In a similar way, torture forecloses its victim's sense of his or her life as extended in time. Past and future collapse into the unbearable present. Commenting on this phenomenon, Cavanaugh quotes an English doctor tortured by the Pinochet regime in Chile: "It was as though I was suspended over a pit," she said, so that "the past had no relevance and I could see no future."[41]

Scarry's analysis focuses on the effects of physical pain, but there is significant evidence that the terror and disorientation induced by psychological forms of torture can have the same world-destroying effect.[42] Indeed, the CIA's 1963 *KUBARK Counterintelligence Interrogation* manual sought to instruct potential interrogators in producing precisely this kind of "regression of the personality." In a section on "non-coercive" methods (which include measures taken to disrupt the target's perception of time and the administration of rewards and punishments unconnected to the target's behavior), the manual explains:

A subject who is cut off from the world he knows seeks to recreate it, in some measure, in the new and strange environment. He may try to keep track of time, to live in the familiar past, to cling to old concepts of loyalty, to establish—with one or more interrogators—interpersonal relations resembling those he has had earlier with other people, and to build other bridges back to the known. Thwarting his attempts to do so is likely to drive him deeper and deeper into himself, until he is no longer able to control his responses in adult fashion.[43]

Mock execution, waterboarding (in which the victim's physical sensations inform his brain that he is drowning), sleep deprivation, unrelenting exposure to unbearably loud noise—all of these have their own profound physiological, cognitive, and emotional effects. All act to reduce the victim's world to an eternal, incomprehensible here and now. In the section on "coercive" measures, the KUBARK manual advocates sensory deprivation and the avoidance of any sort of dependable routine. "Control of the source's environment permits the interrogator to determine his diet, sleep pattern, and other fundamentals. Manipulating these into irregularities, so that the subject becomes disoriented, is very likely to create feelings of fear and helplessness," thus producing what the manual calls a condition of "DDD": debility, dependency, and dread.[44] Nor are these effects "merely" psychological; recent research suggests that psychological torture also produces observable "neurobiological consequences."[45]

One method of torture that combines physical and psychological techniques has proved particularly effective—if the effect desired is mental and emotional breakdown. This is the use of so-called stress positions, in which the victim is required to remain motionless in an uncomfortable position. Discomfort quickly yields to agonizing pain, but it is a pain that appears to be self-inflicted, and is therefore psychologically as well as physically devastating. As McCoy observes, the 1963 CIA manual recommends such methods, as does a 1983 version used to train Honduran military and U.S.-backed Nicaraguan contras in the 1980s.[46] "It has been plausibly suggested," says the 1963 manual, "that, whereas pain inflicted on a person from outside himself may actually focus or intensify his will to resist, his resistance is likelier to be sapped by pain which he seems to inflict upon himself."[47]

The pain and accompanying physical damage produced by stress positions is far from negligible. When approving a list of "enhanced" interrogation techniques to be used at Guantánamo, then-Secretary of Defense Donald Rumsfeld famously wrote on the memo in his own hand, "I stand for 8–10 hours a day. Why is standing limited to 4 hours?"[48] But Scarry points out, "Standing rigidly for eleven hours can produce as violent muscle and spine pain as can injury from elaborate equipment and apparatus"—while leaving no marks on the tortured body.[49] Rejali calls torture that leaves no marks "stealth torture." He suggests that its effectiveness is also increased by the doubt it raises in the minds of those who hear claims of torture but can see no evidence that it has happened. Such claims "tangl[e] the victims and their communities in doubts, uncertainties, and illusions."[50]

Irishman Jim Auld describes being subjected to forced standing as one of a set of techniques tested on him and thirteen other men by British soldiers in Northern Ireland in 1971. Although he was severely beaten during his nine days' captivity, it was the use of these apparently nonviolent methods that drove him to attempt suicide by banging his head against a heating pipe. There were five methods in all: hooding, noise bombardment, food deprivation, sleep deprivation, and forced standing spread-eagled with hands pressing on a wall. These "later came to be known as the 'five techniques,'" says John Conroy, who has chronicled these events. "In combination, they induced a state of psychosis, a temporary madness with long-lasting aftereffects." Indeed the noise alone was so unbearable that several of those tortured described it as "the worst part of the ordeal."[51]

After some days of this treatment, Auld says, "I just felt so helpless and so isolated that I would have told anybody anything." As it happened, he had no connections with the Irish Republican Army, so "the interrogations were nothing for me because I wasn't in the position to tell them what they wanted to know." Nevertheless, he made confessions. "I admitted to being in everything but the crib [with the baby Jesus in Bethlehem], and if they had asked me I would have said, 'Yes, the crib as well. I'm in the background of it there,' because I was just so frightened." Some of his fellow prisoners recall being unable to spell their own names or count to ten. Others believed they were someone else.[52]

Years later, similar techniques produced a similar psychosis in a prisoner at Abu Ghraib. In that U.S.-run Iraqi prison, Saddam Saleh Aboud spent almost three weeks chained twenty-three hours a day in a sitting position while loud music played. "Every few days," reports the *New York Times*, "he was uncuffed for other treatments: douses of cold water, barking dogs, something called 'the scorpion,' in which his arms were cuffed to his legs, behind his back."[53] Finally, it was time for the questions.

> "They began talking to me," Mr. Aboud said. "They asked, 'Do you know the Islamic opposition?' I said, 'Yes.' They asked, 'Do you know Zarqawi?'" referring to Abu Musab al-Zarqawi, a Jordanian militant with ties to Al Qaeda. "I told them, 'I am his driver, I swear to God.'"

Having (falsely) confessed to being the driver for a man that the United States considered an elite terrorist, Aboud then made an even more startling admission:

"They asked me about Osama bin Laden," he said. "I said, 'I am Osama bin Laden but I am disguised.'"

He said he meant every word. "I was only afraid that they would take me back to the torture room," he said. "I would prefer to be dead."[54]

Eighteen days of torture produced not intelligence, but the ravings of a man who would say, and indeed believe, anything to make his abusers stop.

Not only does torture destroy the sufferer's sense of physical, temporal, and psychological reality, it also obliterates her social world, by forcing her to "betray" comrades and loved ones.[55] George Orwell provides a classic literary example of this phenomenon in the novel *1984*. After the Party has starved and tortured the rebel Winston Smith at the Ministry of Love and he has given up his hold on everything—principles, logic, reality—one last tie to his old world still remains to be severed. His tormentor O'Brien asks him if there is a single degradation that has not happened to him. Smith replies that there remains but one. He has not betrayed his sweetheart Julia. O'Brien acknowledges that this is true and sends him for a final session to Room 101, which contains, as everyone knows, "the worst thing in the world."[56] In Smith's case, the worst thing in the world is—rats.

Facing the imminent prospect of having his face devoured by slavering rats, Smith's world shrinks down to nothing: "There was a violent convulsion of nausea inside him and he almost lost consciousness. Everything had gone black." But in that blackness an idea presents itself to him: "There was one and only one way to save himself. He must interpose another human being, the *body* of another human being between himself and the rats." And at the moment before O'Brien springs open the cage and looses the rats on him, Smith realizes just *whose* body it is that can save him. "Do it to Julia!" he screams.[57]

It is tempting to believe that our own bonds to those we love—or to reality itself, for that matter—are stronger than Winston Smith's. In fact, such belief itself does part of the torturer's work; it further distances us from the victim. "There is," says Scarry, "not only among torturers but even among people appalled by acts of torture and sympathetic to those hurt, a covert disdain for confession."[58] But the truth is that almost everyone who is tortured confesses to something, whether or not it is something that ever happened.[59] We catch echoes of this inevitable speech and the disdain of those who produce it in the words of the Chilean torturer Osvaldo Romo. He describes the torture of two women leaders of a left-wing organization, the Movimiento de Izquierda Revolucionaria, known as the MIR: "Everybody talks under torture, everybody talks. . . . Some do it right away, others delay longer, but sooner or later they all sing like little birds."[60] He speaks with disgust of the weakness of "la Flaca Alejandra,"

MIR leader Marcía Alejandra Merino, saying, "She was one of the ones they tortured the least, who talked the most."[61] Afterward, he says that, like her fellow victim Luz Arce, she went to bed with her captors. "She slept with every-body just like Luz," he sneers, "that's how they bought their lives, they chose [to do] that."[62] He goes on to mention the others she gave up—*un montón de sus compañeros*—"a whole bunch of her comrades."[63]

Torture regimes understand that the pain they inflict is not primarily de-signed to produce information. Sometimes they even explain this to their vic-tims. Many who were tortured under Pinochet in Chile recall how after hours or days of resistance they finally let slip a word, a name, only to be told, "We already knew."[64] Lawrence Weschler reports a conversation with a plastic sur-geon who describes a similar experience during the years of military dicta-torship in Uruguay: "'And all of us,' he said 'were tortured for days on end, without even being interrogated at first. . . . Eventually they'd take us in for their interrogations—beatings, shocks, *submarino* immersions. They weren't really after any information—they knew everything already, had everybody's name. It was all just part of the process."[65]

That years of experience on several continents proves that interrogation by torture yields at best a mixed result—a few "facts" folded into mountains of confabulation—and that the institutions that practice torture know this; these realities suggest that extracting information may not in the end be torture's primary purpose. If a phenomenology of torture reveals a practice that destroys the victim's world and if the product of torture is not primarily information but an isolated, broken human being, we are left asking, what is torture for?

Political Definition

This question leads to a third definition of torture, a *political* definition. Tor-ture is a method of strengthening a regime through the destruction of persons and groups that might oppose it. It is a way of dismantling organized social bodies by violating the minds and bodies of the people who constitute them. Cavanaugh describes it this way: "With the demolition of the victim's affec-tive ties and loyalties, past and future, the purpose of torture is to destroy the person as a political actor . . . [and] to leave her isolated and compliant with the regime's goals."[66]

Michel Foucault named this relationship between the state and the indi-vidual an exercise of "pastoral power," which he sees as analogous to the power of religious leaders over the internal workings of the souls of their charges. He suggests that this is the defining relationship between individuals and the modern state. "Most of the time," says Foucault, "the state is envisioned as a kind of political power that ignores individuals, looking only at the interests of the totality or, I should say, of a class or a group among the citizens."[67] In fact, Foucault argues, the opposite is the case; the institutions of the modern state are deeply concerned with the regulation of the individual.

Foucault locates the historical origin of pastoral power in the rise of the institutional Christian church and its attention to the physical and spiritual well-being of its individual members. Pastoral power, says Foucault, "cannot be exercised without knowing the inside of people's minds, without exploring their souls, without making them reveal their innermost secrets. It implies a knowledge of the conscience and an ability to direct it."[68] Torture at the hands of the state is the apotheosis of pastoral power, the state's complete colonization of the prisoner's mind and soul. Through the process of interrogation, the torturer reconstructs the person, remaking the member of a union, a sewing cooperative, or a church into an atomized individual, whose only relationship is with those who are torturing her, with the representatives of the state.

The ritual of interrogation employs another power technique aptly described by Foucault—the "examination."[69] The examination, he says, occurs in a wide variety of settings, "from psychiatry to pedagogy, from the diagnosis of diseases to the hiring of labor."[70] It is a process by which the "observing hierarchy" turns its "normalizing gaze" on individuals, making it possible "to qualify, to classify and to punish."[71] In other words, by examining individuals in a legitimated, ritualized setting, the examiner deploys his power to establish what is true and what is right—and to sort the examinees on the basis of their conformity to the true and the right. This is precisely the task that the U.S. government openly proclaimed that it was performing at Guantánamo and in its other, more secret detention centers—interrogating the detainees to identify the "really bad guys."

It is its ceremonial nature that makes the examination so effective. "That is why," says Foucault, "in all the mechanisms of discipline, the examination is highly ritualized. In it are combined the ceremony of power and the form of the experiment, the deployment of force and the establishment of truth."[72] It is obvious that interrogation under torture involves the deployment of force. Unlike other forms of examination, torture does not hide the iron fist under a velvet glove. But Foucault's insight allows us to deconstruct the ritual of torture to reveal something else: the point of the interrogation is not to *reveal* the truth but to *establish* it. We will return to this point in a later chapter.

The isolation and subjection of the individual is only the beginning. The main target is the individual's social or political network and ultimately any locus of social cohesion outside the regime itself. The point, says Cavanaugh, is "to fragment the society, to disarticulate all the intermediate social bodies between the individual and the state—parties, unions, professional organizations"[73] as a means of retaining power. At the same time, the knowledge that people are being tortured—are confessing subversive activities real or imagined, are giving up names true or fictitious—creates suspicion and distrust within organizations and between friends and neighbors. Weschler describes a dinner party in Montevideo, Uruguay, years after the dictatorship's end. The guests recall how their social worlds had contracted in those days, how they loosened their connections to old friends and avoided making new ones. "You kept to yourself," explained one guest. "You stayed home, you kept your work contacts to a minimum."

The Uruguayan government had assigned every citizen a letter "grade" of A, B, or C. As were deemed good citizens and eligible for state employment; Bs were suspect and eligible only for private employment; and Cs lost all their rights and posed a danger to anyone who hired or associated with them. "And" says Weschler, "the point was that anyone at any time could suddenly find himself reclassified as a 'C'—because, after all, they knew everything."[74] Weschler quotes a description given by the Uruguayan sociologist Carina Perelli[75] of the climate of fear created by a regime engaged in torture:

> Fear exterminated all social life in the public realm. Nobody spoke in the streets for fear of being heard. . . . One tried not to make new friends, for fear of being held responsible for their unknown pasts. One suspected immediately those who were more open or were less afraid, of being "agents provocateurs" of the intelligence service. Rumors about tortures, arrests, mistreatments were so magnified by our terror as to take on epic proportions. . . . The fear of accountability loomed, larger than life, over every single activity in the public realm.[76]

This is the social and political effect of the use of torture: The victims' shame at their confessions and betrayals, the lasting physical and emotional effects of torture (which often include a profound aversion to any form of intimacy), serve to isolate them from former friends and comrades. At the same time, their mere presence in society, combined with the knowledge and imaginings about what has been done to them, the suspicion about what they may have done or said under torture, creates an atmosphere of distrust and terror that rends ordinary social and political bonds. As Cavanaugh puts it, "Torture breaks down collective links and makes of its victims isolated monads. Victims then reproduce the same dynamic in society itself, with the net result that all social bodies which would rival the state are disintegrated and disappeared."[77]

Rejali suggests that torture is effective at separating people from their communities even when it leaves no physical signs. Democratic governments favor "stealth torture" in part because the lack of marks on the body makes it harder

for others to understand what has happened to the person who was tortured—
and harder to understand the person herself:

> Stealth torture breaks down the ability to communicate. The inex-
> pressibility that matters here is the gap between a victim and his or
> her community. Stealth torture regimens are unlike other torture
> procedures because they are calculated to subvert this relationship
> and thereby avoid crises of [state] legitimacy.[78]

That torture produces in its victims terrible guilt and shame is well known to
those who practice it. The CIA's 1963 manual, for example, encourages the
torturer to make use of such feelings to render the victim "more compliant"
in the immediate present.[79] Even decades later, the social fissures opened by
betrayals under torture—real and imagined—remain as wide as ever. Former
comrades find they still cannot trust either themselves or each other. Costa
Rican journalist Nancy Guzmán describes how this process worked in Chile
under Pinochet and even after the end of his regime. "The perverse thing is that
the regression created by torture, the dependency on the torturer, continue
working after more than a quarter century," she says, "and there is no doubt
that there will be many ex-detainees who, when they read this interview, will
prefer to believe their tormentor, rather than a former comrade who suffered
the same fate they did."[80]

We have arrived, then, at a working definition of torture for the purposes of
this discussion. By institutionalized state torture, I mean *the intentional infliction of severe mental or physical suffering by an official or agent of a political entity,
which results in dismantling the victim's sensory, psychological, and social worlds,
with the purpose of establishing or maintaining that entity's power.* The following
chapter explores U.S. practices in the post-9/11 period and asks whether any of
these fit the definition of institutionalized state torture elaborated here.

Notes

1. Comisión Nacional contra la Tortura (Chile) and Pedro Castillo Yáñez, *Memoria, 1983–
   1990: Una Parte De La Historia De Chile* ([Santiago?]: La Comisión, 1999). Author's
   translation.
2. Elaine Scarry, *The Body in Pain: The Making and Unmaking of the World* (New York: Oxford
   University Press, 1985), 13; emphasis in original.
3. Ibid., 9; emphasis in original.
4. Comisión Nacional contra la Tortura (Chile) and Castillo Yáñez, *Memoria, 1983–1990:
   Una Parte De La Historia De Chile*, 8.
5. CIA, *KUBARK Counterintelligence Interrogation.*
6. Joby Warrick, "C.I.A. Tactics Endorsed in Secret Memos: Waterboarding Got White
   House Nod," *Washington Post*, October 15, 2008.

7. Dana Priest and Barton Gellman, "'Stress and Duress' Tactics Used on Terrorism Suspects Held in Secret Overseas Facilities," *Washington Post*, December 26, 2002.

8. Scott Stearns, "Bush Says America Does Not Torture," *Voice of America News*, November 1, 2009. http://www.voanews.com/content/a-13-2007-10-05-voa21/402318.html.

9. For an amplified description of this tautological circle as it relates to U.S. government pronouncements about torture in the post-9/11 period, see, for example, Rebecca Gordon, "Torture Comes out of the Closet," *Peace Review: A Journal of Social Justice* 18, no. 4 (2006).

10. "*¿Aplicar corriente?*" "Yo creo que aplicar corriente no es tortura." Author's translation.

11. Talal Asad, *Formations of the Secular: Christianity, Islam, Modernity* (Stanford: Stanford University Press, 2003), 105.

12. Office of Legal Counsel, *Memorandum for Alberto R. Gonzalez, Counsel to the President, Re: Standards of Conduct for Interrogation under 18 U.S.C. §§ 2340–2340a* 2002. Reproduced in Mark Danner, *Torture and Truth: America, Abu Ghraib, and the War on Terror* (New York: New York Review Books, 2004), 120.

13. Daniel Levin, *Legal Standards Applicable Under18 U.S.C. §§ 2340–2340a: Memorandum Opinion for the Deputy Attorney General*, December 30, 2004.

14. The United States offered the same explanation to the UN Committee against Torture in testimony about its 2006 report on compliance with the Convention against Torture. The Committee's minutes note that the U.S. representative explained that the "The first opinion had been withdrawn not because it purported to change the definition of torture, but because it addressed questions that need not have been addressed, namely the President's Commander-in-Chief power and the potential defences to liability, as clarified in the December 2004 memorandum." United Nations Committee against Torture, *Convention against Torture and Other Cruel, Inhuman or Degrading Treatment or Punishment: Thirty–Sixth Session Summary Record of the 703rd Meeting; Consideration of Reports Submitted by States Parties under Article 19 of the Convention; Seond Periodic Report of the United States of America*, May 5, 2006.

15. Levin, *Legal Standards Applicable Under18 U.S.C. §§ 2340–2340a: Memorandum Opinion for the Deputy Attorney General*, n. 7.

16. Comisión Nacional contra la Tortura (Chile) and Castillo Yáñez, *Memoria, 1983–1990: Una Parte De La Historia De Chile*, 134. "¿Quién va estar en acuerdo con la tortura? Nadie ... pero ¿habrá o no habrá tortura? Usted sabe que a veces se exageran las cosas. Puede que en los mandos medios o bajos haya esa necesidad de sacar en cualquier forma los secretos que pueden interesar a la Comunidad; no al gobierno, sino a la comunidad, a la tranquilidad de Chile. Entonces se exageran esos medios y—no es que se quiera la tortura—pero resulta una actitud torpe." Author's translation. I have been unable to discover Bishop Gillmore's first name.

17. Ibid. "Al fin y al cabo, lo que se ha hecho en Chile; casi no es nada." Author's translation.

18. Hannah Arendt, *The Human Condition* (Chicago: University of Chicago Press, 1958), 129.

19. St. Augustine, *Concerning the City of God against the Pagans*, trans. Henry Bettenson (New York: Penguin Books, 2003; reprint, 2003), 859–61.

20. Ibid.

21. Scarry, *The Body in Pain*, 44. A "tea party" was a beating with fists; a "tea party with toast" added clubs to the mix.

22. Darius M. Rejali, *Torture and Democracy* (Princeton: Princeton University Press, 2007).

23. United Nations, *Convention against Torture and Other Cruel, Inhuman or Degrading Treatment or Punishment*, December 10, 1984, http://www.un.org/ga/search/view_doc.asp?symbol=a/res/39/46.

24. U.S. Reservations, Declarations, and Understandings, Convention Against Torture and Other Cruel, Inhuman or Degrading Treatment or Punishment, Cong. Rec. S17486-01, October 27, 199.

25. Alfred W. McCoy, *A Question of Torture: CIA Interrogation, from the Cold War to the War on Terror*, 1st ed. The American Empire Project. (New York: Metropolitan Books/Henry Holt, 2006), 100–101.

26. Office of Legal Counsel, *Memorandum for Alberto R. Gonzalez, Counsel to the President, Re: Standards of Conduct for Interrogation under 18 U.S.C. §§ 2340–2340a*, 3–4.

27. David Luban and Henry Shue, "Mental Torture: A Critique of Erasures in U.S. Law," *Georgetown Law Faculty Publications and Other Works* (2011). http://scholarship.law.georgetown.edu/facpub/620.

28. Ibid.

29. McCoy, *A Question of Torture*, 100–101.

30. CIA, *KUBARK Counterintelligence Interrogation*, 41. For more about this research program, see also Naomi Klein, *The Shock Doctrine: The Rise of Disaster Capitalism*, 1st ed. (New York: Metropolitan Books, 2007).

31. Luban and Shue, "Mental Torture."

32. 18 USC, 113C, Section 2340 (2007).

33. The Bush administration argued that federal courts have no jurisdiction over the U.S. detention center in Guantánamo, Cuba, because it is located outside the United States, as were other U.S.-run detention centers, such as Abu Ghraib in Iraq and Bagram Air Force Base in Afghanistan. It would appear, however, that if for legal purposes these places lie outside the United States, activities taking place there would be of precisely the sort covered by Section 2340A.

34. United Nations, *Initial Reports of States Parties Due in 1995: United States of America. 09/02/2000. Cat/C/28/Add.5.(State Party Report)* 2000, Par. 11.

35. Ibid., Par. 53.

36. Carmen Gentile, "Son of Ex-President of Liberia Gets 97 Years,"*New York Times,* January 10, 2009.

37. The war crimes statute, 18 U.S.C. §2441; Luban and Shue, "Mental Torture."

38. Lisa Hajjar, "Torture and the Lawless 'New Paradigm,'" *Middle East Report on Line*, December 10, 2005. http://www.globalresearch.ca/torture-and-the-lawless-new-paradigm/1442.

39. Scarry, *The Body in Pain*, 35.

40. William T. Cavanaugh, *Torture and Eucharist* (Malden, MA: Blackwell, 1998), 37.

41. Ibid.

42. See, for example, Rona M. Fields, "The Neurobiological Consequences of Psychological Torture," in *The Trauma of Psychological Torture*, ed. Gilbert Reyes Disaster and Trauma Psychology (Westport: Praeger, 2008).

43. CIA, *KUBARK Counterintelligence Interrogation*, 77.

44. Ibid., 83. The separation between "coercive" and "non-coercive" methods appears to be a distinction without much difference.

45. Fields, "The Neurobiological Consequences of Psychological Torture"; Uwe Jacobs, "Documenting the Neurobiology of Psychological Torture: Conceptual and Neuropsychological Observations," in *The Trauma of Psychological Torture*, ed. Gilbert Reyes Disaster and Trauma Psychology (Westport: Praeger, 2008).

46. McCoy, *A Question of Torture*, 88–89.

47. CIA, *KUBARK Counterintelligence Interrogation*, 94.

48. Philippe Sands, *Torture Team: Rumsfeld's Memo and the Betrayal of American Values*, 1st ed. (New York: Palgrave MacMillan, 2008), 3.

49. Scarry, *The Body in Pain*, 45.

50. Rejali, *Torture and Democracy*, 31. Note that Rejali thinks that "Scarry is right to draw attention to the importance of expression in torture," but his emphasis is a different one. "The inexpressibility that matters politically is not the gap between the brain and the tongue, but between victims and their communities." This is, he says, "a gap that is cynically calculated, a gap that shelters a state's legitimacy."

51. John Conroy, *Unspeakable Acts, Ordinary People: The Dynamics of Torture* (Berkeley: University of California Press, 2000), 6.

52. Ibid., 7.

53. Ian Fisher, "Iraqi Tells of U.S. Abuse, from Ridicule to Rape Threat," *New York Times*, May 14, 2004.

54. Ibid.

55. I place the word "betray" in quotation marks here, because, as we shall see, torture rarely produces names that torturers do not already know. What is important to the torturers is not so much the *content* of the betrayal as the *fact* of it.

56. George Orwell, *1984* (New York: Harcourt, Brace, 1983), 253.

57. Ibid., 255–56.

58. Scarry, *The Body in Pain*, 29.

59. Ibid.

60. "En la tortura, todos hablan, todos hablan [...] algunos lo hacen antes y otros se demoran más, pero todos tarde o temprano cantan como pajaritos." Author's translation.

61. "Pero a la Flaca fue una de las que menos torturaron y que más habló." Author's translation.

62. "Después ella se acostó con todo el mundo, igual que la Luz, así compraron sus vidas, ellas eligieron eso." Author's translation.

63. Nancy Guzmán Jasmen, *Romo, Confesiones De Un Torturador*, 1st ed. (Santiago, Chile: Editorial Planeta Chilena, 2000), 100. Author's translation.

64. Cavanaugh, *Torture and Eucharist*, 28.

65. Lawrence Weschler, *A Miracle, a Universe: Settling Accounts with Torturers* (New York: Penguin, 1990), 125.

66. Cavanaugh, *Torture and Eucharist*, 38.

67. Foucault, Michel, *Essential Works of Foucault*. Vol. 3, *Power*, trans. Robert Hurley et al. ed. James D. Faubion. Paul Rabinow, series editor. (New York: New Press, 1994), 332.

68. Ibid, 333.

69. Michel Foucault, *Discipline and Punish: The Birth of the Prison* (New York: Vintage, 1995), 184.

70. Ibid., 185.

71. Ibid., 184.

72. Ibid.

73. Cavanaugh, *Torture and Eucharist*, 38.

74. Weschler, *A Miracle, a Universe: Settling Accounts with Torturers*, 91.

75. Perelli is perhaps better known to contemporary readers as a former director of the United Nations' Electoral Assistance Division.

76. Weschler, *A Miracle, a Universe: Settling Accounts with Torturers*, 91.

77. Cavanaugh, *Torture and Eucharist*, 34.

78. Rejali, *Torture and Democracy*, 8.

79. CIA, *KUBARK Counterintelligence Interrogation*, 83.

80. Guzmán Jasmen, *Romo, Confesiones de un Torturador*, 116–7. "Lo perverso es que la regresión creada por la tortura, la dependencia al torturador, sigue operando después de más de un cuarto de siglo y no cabe duda que habrá muchos ex detenidos que al leer esta entrevista preferirán creer a su verdugo que al ex camarada que sufrió su misma suerte." Author's translation.

2

Torture in the Conduct
of the "War on Terror"

The United States of America does not torture. And that's important
for people around the world to understand.
—President George W. Bush, *at a press conference*
on November 29, 2005

We tortured [Mohammed al-] Qahtani. His treatment met the
legal definition of torture.[1]
—Susan J. Crawford, *Convening Authority of U.S. military*
commissions, Guantánamo, 2009

Does the behavior of the United States in the post-9/11 period meet the definition of torture developed in the previous chapter? Sadly, the answer to this
question is an unequivocal yes. Nor is the voice of Susan J. Crawford (quoted
above) a lonely one. In the years since the Bush administration left power,
many observers across the political spectrum have stepped forward to say
the same thing. These include the European Court of Human Rights and the
Washington, D.C.-based Constitution Project, which issued a comprehensive report on the subject in 2013.[2]

The panel overseeing the Constitution Project's work was co-chaired
by former Republican congressman and Bush administration official Asa
Hutchinson and by James R. Jones, former chairman and CEO of the
American Stock Exchange, who was U.S. Ambassador to Mexico under Bill
Clinton. Among the others who served on the panel were former Ambassador to the United Nations Thomas Pickering, and former FBI Director
William Sessions. In what is perhaps "the most important or notable finding," the report observes "that it is indisputable that the United States engaged in the practice of torture." Going farther, the report assigns "some
responsibility for allowing and contributing to the spread of torture" to
"the nation's highest officials."[3]

What follows in this chapter is not a complete record of U.S. torture in the years since the attacks of 9/11. Nor does it necessarily focus on the most famous examples, such as the 183 times Khalid Sheikh Mohammed was subjected to waterboarding. My goal here is rather to compare the record of United States activities to the definition of institutionalized state torture developed in Chapter 1, which is *the intentional infliction of severe mental or physical suffering by an official or agent of a political entity, which results in dismantling the victim's sensory, psychological, and social worlds, with the purpose of establishing or maintaining that entity's power.*

The Intentional Infliction of Severe Mental or Physical Suffering by an Official or Agent of a Political Entity

The United States has indeed inflicted such suffering in a variety of venues over the course of the "war on terror."

Metropolitan Detention Center, Brooklyn, New York: Torture in the prosecution of the "war on terror" did not begin in Afghanistan, Abu Ghraib, or Guantánamo. The first such abuses appear to have taken place on U.S. soil, at the hands of local police and prison guards as well as of federal officials. Within weeks of the September 11 attacks, immigrant men were rounded up across the United States. Eighty-four of these were held, some for many months, in Brooklyn, New York. Here they were subjected to twenty-three-hour-per-day isolation, short shackling, beatings, sexual humiliation, and, in at least one case, anal rape with a police flashlight.[4] The *New York Daily News* reported in 2005:

> The detainees—none of whom were ultimately charged with anything related to terrorism—alleged in sworn affidavits and in interviews with Justice Department officials that correction officers:
> Humiliated them by making fun of—and sometimes painfully squeezing—their genitals.
> Deprived them of regular sleep for weeks or months.
> Shackled their hands and feet before smashing them repeatedly face-first into concrete walls—within sight of the Statue of Liberty.
> Forced them in winter to stand outdoors at dawn while dressed in light cotton prison garb and no shoes, sometimes for hours.[5]

Several of these techniques will appear familiar to anyone who has read accounts of overseas abuses by U.S. personnel as the "war on terror" progressed. Exposure to extremes of heat and cold, sexual humiliation, and sleep deprivation are among the approaches described as means of facilitating psychological regression in the CIA's 1960s KUBARK manual. They also appear on the list of "Counter-Resistance Techniques" approved in December 2002 by then-Secretary of Defense Donald Rumsfeld for use at Guantánamo.[6]

Afghanistan—Bagram and Kandahar: Indications that similar events were taking place under U.S. aegis overseas are found in a story that appeared in the *Washington Post* as early as December 2002. The piece describes the experiences of detainees being held at a U.S. air base in Bagram, Afghanistan, officially designated the Bagram Theater Internment Facility. "Those who refuse to cooperate inside this secret CIA interrogation center are sometimes kept standing or kneeling for hours, in black hoods or spray-painted goggles, according to intelligence specialists familiar with CIA interrogation methods. At times," said the *Post*, "they are held in awkward, painful positions and deprived of sleep with a 24-hour bombardment of lights." As we have seen, to be "kept standing or kneeling" in the same position "for hours" can produce excruciating pain.

Among those known to have been held by the CIA at Bagram is Omar al-Faruq, an alleged close associate of Osama bin Laden. Al-Faruq was captured in Indonesia and transferred to Bagram in June 2002. There, according to the *New York Times*, his "questioning was prolonged, extending day and night for weeks. It is likely, experts say, that the proceedings followed a pattern, with Mr. Faruq left naked most of the time, his hands and feet bound." A "western intelligence official" told the *Times* that "over a three-month period, the suspect was fed very little, while being subjected to sleep and light deprivation, prolonged isolation and room temperatures that varied from 100 degrees to 10 degrees."[7]

Another prisoner whose suffering has been well documented is Dr. Ghairat Baheer, an Afghan whose primary crime appears to have been that he is the son-in-law of an Afghan tribal leader who was responsible for the deaths of "dozens of American soldiers." Baheer had opposed the Taliban when they governed his country but became a U.S. target when he spoke out against the invasion of Afghanistan. He was captured by the CIA at his home in Pakistan in 2002 and transferred to Bagram. There, according to the London *Daily Telegraph*, "he claims he was held in a cell just two metres by two and a half, completely without light." The story continues:

> He said: "There were loudspeakers which played horrifying music 24 hours a day, and sounds of people shouting. I was hooked to the wall by handcuffs, with my feet shackled, and stripped naked. I was there for six months. But I didn't know where I was."
>
> Dr Baheer's ordeal lasted for years as he was shifted from one Afghan prison to another. Sometimes he was denied food; and in some facilities he was held in cells with al-Qaeda terrorists.[8]

Baheer was finally released from a Kabul, Afghanistan jail in 2005.

The most famous cases of torture at Bagram involve the deaths in captivity of two men. As is common among Afghans, each went by a single name. One, known as Habibullah, is believed to have been a Muslim mullah, or village expert on Islam. He was turned in to U.S. forces by an Afghan warlord in 2002. Like most prisoners who passed through Bagram in that time period, Habibullah was subjected to "standing restraints, sleep deprivation and peroneal strikes." The last is a punitive technique involving striking the peroneal nerve, which is accessible right below the knee joint. This causes unbearable nerve pain and, with repeated infliction, permanent nerve damage. Habibullah was found dead in an isolation cell in early December 2002, "tethered to the ceiling by two sets of handcuffs and a chain around his waist. His body was slumped forward, held up by the chains." He had died of a blood clot, which was most likely caused by the repeated blows to his legs. According to the autopsy, his body was covered with bruises. His death was eventually ruled a homicide.[9]

The other well-documented homicide at Bagram was that of a twenty-two-year-old taxi driver named Dilawar, from a small town in southern Afghanistan. His story has been chronicled in the 2007 documentary film *Taxi to the Dark Side*. Dilawar appears to have had no connection to the Taliban or to terrorism. He was captured in December 2002 near a U.S. base by a guerilla leader and turned over to U.S. soldiers. Five days later he was dead. Like Habibullah, his legs had been beaten so badly that, in the words of a coroner who later examined the autopsy report, they were "pulpified." Before he died, Dilawar was interrogated about a rocket attack outside the army base where he was picked up. (It was later determined that the attack was engineered by the militia leader who arrested Dilawar, so he might curry favor with the U.S. military by handing them some suspects.) "When he arrived in the interrogation room," according to the *New York Times*, "an interpreter who was present said, his legs were bouncing uncontrollably in the plastic chair and his hands were numb." There was a reason for this condition. "He had been chained by the wrists to the top of his cell for much of the previous four days." His legs had been beaten so badly over the previous days that when guards tried to make him kneel they would no longer bend. The interrogation produced nothing, so Dilawar was returned to his cell and once again chained to the ceiling. He was discovered there some hours later, dead, his body "already beginning to stiffen."[10]

The same *New York Times* story relies on the documents produced by an internal military investigation to conclude that, although these are the only acknowledged homicides at Bagram, the treatment received by Habibullah and Dilawar was common, even "routine." "The Bagram file includes ample testimony that harsh treatment by some interrogators was routine and that guards could strike shackled detainees with virtual impunity," reports the *Times*. "Prisoners considered important or troublesome were also handcuffed and chained to the ceilings and doors of their cells, sometimes for long periods." Nor were these the actions of a few poorly-supervised underlings. "Senior officers frequently toured the detention center, and several of them acknowledged seeing prisoners chained up for punishment or to deprive them of sleep."[11] Nor were Habibullah and Dilawar the only men to die in U.S. custody. On March 16, 2005, the Associated Press reported that of those detained in Iraq and Afghanistan by U.S. forces, 108 were known to have died.

No one above the rank of captain has been punished for any of the abuse at Bagram, the worst of which appears to have taken place from late 2002 through the spring of 2003. Army Captain Christopher Beiring received a reprimand, and Specialist Wille Brand, who admitted hitting Diliwar's legs over thirty times, was demoted to private. The person in charge of interrogations at Bagram during this period, Army Captain Carolyn Woods, was transferred to Iraq in the summer of 2003. In August of that year, she took charge of interrogations at Abu Ghraib prison.[12]

Similar events, and worse, took place at the detention center in Kandahar, Afghanistan, from which many prisoners were eventually sent to Guantánamo. Historian and journalist Andy Worthington has documented the Kandahar torture regime, which included constant beatings—especially on "sensitive areas, like the eyes, the nose and the genitals"—exposure to the bitter cold of Afghan winter nights, sleep deprivation, rape and other kinds of sexual humiliation, cigarette burns, electrical torture, being urinated on, being forced to walk barefoot over barbed wire, and being thrown face down onto broken glass. Testimonies from prisoners who passed through Kandahar include that of Jumah al-Dossari, whose civilian lawyers at Guantánamo passed his handwritten story on to Amnesty International while he was still imprisoned there. Al-Dossari describes, among other things, having his penis injected with petrol.[13] He begins his account this way:

> What I have seen is a huge tragedy and a weighty matter, far weightier than I can put to paper. Indeed, the enormous horrors that my eyes have seen have and continue to see renew my anxiety and pain and my very being and feelings are shaken at the mere thought or flash of them in my memory. How can my heart forget them and how can my soul who bore these horrors continue with life? As I hold my pen, my hand is shaking.[14]

"How I wish," he adds, "my memories and my thoughts could be forgotten. But for me, in forgetting it and its effects, there are still memories, lifelong evidence of what happened to me in my wounds, my afflictions, my pain and my sadness." In fact, that pain and sadness drove al-Dossari to attempt suicide several times while he was in Guantánamo.[15]

In March 2013, the United States transferred formal responsibility for the prison at Bagram to the Afghan government. The two parties had spent more than a year haggling over who would have final say over the release of prisoners. In the end, the United States ceded control over all but what the *New York Times* calls "a small number" of detainees. Who these are and what their fate might be remains unknown as of this writing.[16]

Guantánamo: A 1903 treaty with Cuba granted the United States a permanent lease on a piece of Cuban territory in Guantánamo Bay, "for use as coaling or naval stations only, and for no other purpose."[17] But 2001 and the following years have seen substantial expansion of the definitions of "coaling" (refueling) and "naval station." The detention center for prisoners seized in the "war on terror" opened at Guantánamo Bay in October 2001, and the first prisoners arrived in January of the following year. Guantánamo was selected primarily because of its peculiar geographical—and legal—position. "Officials chose the 45-square-mile base in southeastern Cuba," reported the *New York Times,* "because it was isolated from civilians and remote enough to allow them to control the prisoners and interrogate them." But there was a second reason for choosing Guantánamo. "The authorities also said they thought the base would be out of reach of American courts."[18] In August 2002, federal judge Colleen Kollar-Kotelly agreed with the administration and dismissed suits brought by two groups of detainees at Guantánamo. The Supreme Court reversed this position in June 2004 in *Rasul v. Bush,* reestablishing the judiciary's jurisdiction over claims of *habeas corpus* made by detainees held there. Much of what is known about operations at Guantánamo has been compiled in Worthington's excellent book, *The Guantánamo Files: The Stories of the 774 Detainees in America's Illegal Prison.* Another extensive compilation was produced at the Human Rights Center of the University of California–Berkeley and released in November 2008.[19]

In the first few months of operation, most of the brutality prisoners experienced came at the hands of five-member Extreme Reaction Forces (ERFs). So common were these attacks that detainees came to use the expression "ERFing" as a verb. Here is a description, from a detainee named Tarek Dergoul, of what it is like to be ERFed:

> They pepper sprayed me in the face and I started vomiting; in all I must have brought up five cupfuls. They pinned me down and attacked me, poking their fingers in my eyes, and forced my head into the toilet pan and flushed. They tied me up like a beast and then they

were kneeling on me, kicking and punching. Finally they dragged me out of the cell in chains, into the rec yard, and shaved my beard, my hair, and my eyebrows.[20]

As abusive and common as ERFing was in the early months at Guantánamo, its purpose was punitive and disciplinary; ERFing was not an adjunct to interrogations. It was an odd irony in that epoch that prisoners were less likely to be abused or tortured during actual interrogation than between sessions. That changed with the arrival in late 2002 of Major General Geoffrey Miller. Miller was brought in to replace Brigadier General Rick Baccus as commander of the Joint Task Force overseeing Guantánamo, because, it appears, the Pentagon was dissatisfied with the "negligible" amount of intelligence produced under Baccus's command.[21]

One reason for this apparent failure may well have been that the "the majority of the prisoners—the Taliban foot soldiers and those who were completely innocent" but had been sold to U.S. forces by Afghan and Pakistani bounty hunters—"had absolutely nothing to offer."[22] Miller, whose background was in artillery, not intelligence, set out to change that. In a decision that would have fateful consequences not only in Guantánamo but later at Abu Ghraib and other U.S. detention centers in Iraq, he "merged" the functions of two previously separate groups of personnel: the Joint Detention Group (the guards whose previous role was the maintenance of prison discipline and order) and the Joint Intelligence Group ("the interrogators and intelligence analysts"). Henceforth, the work of both groups would be dedicated to one purpose: wringing some kind of useful information from their prisoners. In this context, the guards became responsible for "setting the conditions" for interrogation— through the control and manipulation of "every aspect of the prisoners' physical existence."[23]

Under the new regime, prisoners were routinely beaten, not only by the ERFs but now also by regular guards. The Australian citizen David Hicks, who was released from Guantánamo in April 2007 reports having been beaten many times, "frequently while he was restrained and blindfolded," and once without interruption for eight hours. He also says his life was threatened "directly and indirectly" with weapons, both before and during interrogations. Others report repeated beatings with iron rods, or a plumber's wrench used to open water spigots.[24] Sami El-Leithi, an Egyptian national, became permanently paralyzed after interrogators broke two of his vertebrae and then refused him medical care.[25] It would seem then that some of the treatment at Guantánamo satisfies even the definition of "severe physical or mental pain" provided in the Bybee-Yoo memo mentioned in Chapter 1(i.e., as equivalent to the pain of organ failure or even death).

"Setting the conditions" for interrogation involved more than beatings, however. Under Miller, prisoners who were to be interrogated—those of supposed "high value" and others of no value whatsoever—often spent weeks or months in isolation first, sometimes naked in a tiny concrete cell devoid of furniture or blankets and with the air conditioning turned up high. One prisoner, Aryat Vakhitov, recalls being held in such an isolation cell for five months. "All of us," he says, "have problems with our kidneys because we slept on the iron [floor] with [the] air conditioning on."[26]

Often, too, detainees were subjected simultaneously to several of the measures identified in the CIA's manual as producing the "three Ds": debility, dependence, and dread. These, as has been noted above, include environmental manipulations designed to upset the prisoner's sense of ordinary time and space, together with sleep disruption and deprivation, and sensory deprivation or hyperstimulation. The words of one detainee convey very clearly the combination of mental and physical suffering common at Guantánamo:

> You lose track of time. . . . After a while—because you're confined to a really small room, you're tied down into this position, they've got the stereo banging out really loud with strobe lights flashing like ten times a second—it makes you hallucinate. At the beginning it doesn't really affect you, but after a while, after like 20 minutes, 10 minutes, you start getting cramps in your thighs, and your buttocks, and your calves, and slowly your legs, you know, just go numb. You're flimsy and you have no control. And when you move over, [the shackles] start cutting into you. . . . And even if you close your eyes you can still see the light and you start hallucinating. . . . Sometimes you'd get punched or kicked as well.[27]

Such short-shackling was common at Guantánamo, often accompanied by the additional humiliation of being watched and scolded by female interrogators while urinating or defecating in one's clothing, after enduring eight or ten hours in a stress position.

As late as 2006, prisoners were still being abused at Guantánamo. *Harpers* reporter Scott Horton reports that three "suicides" in that year may well have been homicides—accidental deaths brought on by harsh "interrogation" methods. Horton describes how on the night those three died, a fourth man, Shaker Aamer, a forty-two-year-old Saudi accused of serving as translator for Osama bin Laden, was tortured. Aamer, who is married to a British citizen, was in the process of receiving UK citizenship himself when he was picked up in Afghanistan in 2001. That night in Guantánamo seven naval policemen strapped him to a chair, gouged their fingers into his eyes, and "bent his nose repeatedly to the side so hard he thought it would break." There was more:

The MPs inflicted so much pain, Mr. Aamer said he thought he was going to die. The MPs pressed on pressure points all over his body: his temples, just under his jawline, in the hollow beneath his ears. They choked him.

None of this excruciating treatment left marks. But what Horton finds particularly "alarming" is that when Aamer screamed, the military police "cut off his airway, then put a mask on him so he could not cry out." Horton believes it very likely that this treatment is what killed the three men who died that same night.[28]

As of spring 2013, 166 prisoners remained at Guantánamo. Of these, eighty-six had been cleared for release three years earlier by a joint civilian–military task force appointed to review the cases of all remaining Guantánamo prisoners. None of these men has ever been convicted of a crime. Congressional action has "limited the president's options in releasing them" reports the *New York Times*, "through a statute that makes it very difficult to use federal money to transfer Guantánamo prisoners anywhere."[29]

The torment at Guantánamo has not ended. As of mid-May 2013, at least one hundred of Guantánamo's prisoners were once again on hunger strike, in a desperate attempt to draw the world's attention to their apparently endless detention. Many of them were being strapped twice daily to restraint chairs and force fed through nasal tubes. "Force" feeding is an appropriate term for this procedure, which, as one detainee's description shows, certainly causes "severe mental or physical suffering."[30] Samir Naji al Hasan Moqbel described the experience in a *New York Times* op-ed in April 2013:

> I will never forget the first time they passed the feeding tube up my nose. I can't describe how painful it is to be force-fed this way. As it was thrust in, it made me feel like throwing up. I wanted to vomit, but I couldn't. There was agony in my chest, throat and stomach. I had never experienced such pain before. I would not wish this cruel punishment upon anyone.[31]

Despite President Obama's promise to close the prison at Guantánamo Bay, steps taken by various government agencies point instead to a greater permanence. In January 2013 the State Department closed the office responsible for planning the shutdown of Guantánamo and permanently reassigned Daniel Fried, the special envoy in charge of the project, to other duties.[32] Six months later, Washington attorney Cliff Sloan was rumored to have been chosen to take Fried's place, after President Obama reiterated his intention to close Guantánamo, but no announcement has been forthcoming at this writing.

Meanwhile, in March 2013, the Pentagon requested almost $176 million to renovate Guantánamo, including $49 million to build a new facility to hold "special" prisoners.[33] In June of that year, the Southern Command announced plans to increase guard staff from 1,831 to 2,000, "including 15 extra public-affairs troops training 20 replacements."[34]

Abu Ghraib: By far the most famous, if not the worst, tortures of the "war on terror" are the outrages that took place in Abu Ghraib. One Wednesday night in April of 2004, CBS Television broadcast a series of shocking photographs. Image after image displayed U.S. soldiers gleefully engaged in the torture and ritual humiliation of captured Iraqis. The prisoners pictured were among the thousands held at Abu Ghraib, once Saddam Hussein's most notorious prison. The following day, the *New Yorker* magazine posted on its website an electronic version of a story by Seymour Hersh. His story amplified the CBS report and reproduced several of the photos shown on television the night before.[35]

These photographs are so well-known that there is no reason to describe them at length. Indeed, one of them, which depicts a hooded man draped in a blanket, standing with arms outstretched, trailing wires from hands and feet, has been reproduced in art, on book jackets, and in flyers, reports, and posters around the world. As we have seen, worse things than this have been done to prisoners held by U.S. forces, but this picture, and one of PFC Lynndie England leading a naked man on a leash, have achieved iconic status; these are the images that now spring to mind when the words "torture" and "United States" are heard together.

In the days following the revelations, U.S. government officials of the highest rank hastened to put the events at Abu Ghraib into what they considered to be a proper perspective. In various pronouncements, Chair of the Joint Chiefs of Staff Richard B. Myers, Secretary of Defense Donald Rumsfeld, and President Bush himself assured the world that the torture at Abu Ghraib was an aberration. It did not represent, as President Bush told the Arab press, "the America that I know. The actions of these few people," his interlocutors should understand, "do not reflect the hearts of the American people."[36]

In fact, although they were first revealed to the world at Abu Ghraib, many of the "interrogation techniques" employed there—isolation, environmental manipulation, stress positions, sleep deprivation, the use of military dogs, and sexual humiliation—were already in use in Afghanistan and at Guantánamo. Indeed, in August 2003 the Pentagon had dispatched General Miller from Guantánamo to Abu Ghraib to "GITMO-ize" the operation there. There he made the same structural changes he had introduced at Guantánamo, refocusing the work of military police on "setting the conditions" for interrogation by military intelligence.[37]

It would be almost another two years before even more horrifying photos and videos leaked out and appeared in the online magazine *Salon*. This later group of 297 photographs and 19 short videos were never as widely distributed as the first. Their images include a military dog attacking a naked man, leaving him bleeding from a deep bite on the leg. Videos taken with digital cameras reveal a prisoner apparently attempting to kill himself by banging his head over and over against an iron door.[38] Other photos and videos have never reached public view. Major General Antonio M. Taguba, whom the Pentagon assigned to investigate Abu Ghraib, told reporter Seymour Hersh that he had seen, in Taguba's words, a video depicting "a male American soldier in uniform sodomizing a female detainee."[39]

The Taguba report remains an important document in the history of U.S. torture in the "war on terror." In accordance with military protocol, General Taguba's writ ran only to the actions of individuals whose rank was lower than his own. Although he believed, as he later told Hersh, that responsibility for the torture that he documented lay at the highest level of government, his report describes only the actions of those he outranked. Nonetheless, and despite its dry, factual tone, it makes chilling reading. Among the abuses Taguba describes are these:

a. Punching, slapping, and kicking detainees; jumping on their naked feet;
b. Videotaping and photographing naked male and female detainees;
c. Forcibly arranging detainees in various sexually explicit positions for photographing;
d. Forcing detainees to remove their clothing and keeping them naked for several days at a time;
e. Forcing naked male detainees to wear women's underwear;
f. Forcing groups of male detainees to masturbate themselves while being photographed and videotaped;
g. Arranging naked male detainees in a pile and then jumping on them;
h. Positioning a naked detainee on a MRE Box, with a sandbag on his head, and attaching wires to his fingers, toes, and penis to simulate electric torture;
i. Writing "I am a Rapest" [*sic*] on the leg of a detainee alleged to have forcibly raped a fifteen-year-old fellow detainee, and then photographing him naked;
j. Placing a dog chain or strap around a naked detainee's neck and having a female Soldier pose for a picture;
k. A male military police guard having sex with a female detainee;
l. Using military working dogs (without muzzles) to intimidate and frighten detainees, and in at least one case biting and severely injuring a detainee; and
m. Taking photographs of dead Iraqi detainees.[40]

In addition, the report continues, "several detainees also described the following acts of abuse, which under the circumstances, I find credible based on the clarity of their statements and supporting evidence provided by other witnesses." These include:

a. Breaking chemical lights and pouring the phosphoric liquid on detainees;
b. Threatening detainees with a charged 9 mm pistol;
c. Pouring cold water on naked detainees;
d. Beating detainees with a broom handle and a chair;
e. Threatening male detainees with rape;
f. Allowing a military police guard to stitch the wound of a detainee who was injured after being slammed against the wall in his cell;
g. Sodomizing a detainee with a chemical light and perhaps a broom stick; and
h. Using military working dogs to frighten and intimidate detainees with threats of attack, and in one instance actually biting a detainee[41]

For his pains, General Taguba was forced into early retirement in 2007 after thirty-four years of military service.

At least one prisoner died during interrogation at Abu Ghraib. Manadel al-Jamadi arrived there in November 2003, a transfer from a CIA site. Autopsy results suggest he died of asphyxiation—the combined effect of several broken ribs, blunt force trauma to the head and torso, and having hung by the wrists for hours with feet barely touching the ground—while in the company of CIA interrogators at Abu Ghraib. The Army ruled al-Jamadi's death a homicide. A member of the Navy SEAL team that captured him was tried and acquitted for lack of evidence in a court martial. No CIA operative was ever charged, although the Justice Department convened a grand jury about the case in 2012. No indictments were handed down, however, and Attorney General Eric Holder announced that no further charges would be sought, because there is insufficient evidence to make a conviction likely.[42]

CIA agents working at Abu Ghraib were known to the military as OGA's—"other government agencies." There was, however, another locus of U.S. torture—the unknown number of secret prisons, or "black sites" where the CIA *was* the government agency that interrogated prisoners it kidnapped from many countries, including Indonesia, Italy, Pakistan, and Macedonia.

The CIA black sites: As the name suggests, the number and location of these sites is a secret. It is generally acknowledged, however, that the CIA has used the U.S. Air Force base in Bagram and facilities on the British-owned island of Diego García.[43] Other sites include the "Dark Prison" near the airport in Kabul, so-called because of "its absolute lack of light." The "Salt Pit" is located in an abandoned brick factory north of the same city.[44]

It is well-known that the CIA used waterboarding on a number of "high value detainees" at these sites, including Khalid Sheik Muhammed, who is believed to have planned the September 11 attacks. Bush administration memos declassified in 2009 reveal that Muhammed was waterboarded 183 separate times.[45] Other CIA methods are perhaps less spectacular in the public imagination but just as painful and frightening to the victims. These include enforced standing for excruciating lengths of time. Detainees who had been held in CIA custody described to the International Committee of the Red Cross "not just standing, but being kept on their tiptoes with their arms extended out and up over their heads, attached by shackles on their wrists and ankles, for . . . eight hours at a stretch." The whole time, "they were kept stark naked and often cold." Nor was this a one-time event. "This process was repeated every day or two for three months in some cases."[46]

Sleep deprivation—sometimes for as long as ninety-six hours—and sensory insult were also routine. As at Guantánamo, CIA prisoners have "described being bombarded by bright lights and eardrum-shattering sounds twenty-four hours a day for weeks on end." People who have been exposed to both report that this kind of "noise stress" is worse than waterboarding.[47]

In autumn 2006, President Bush announced he was transferring the remaining prisoners in CIA custody to Guantánamo. The move came in response to the Supreme Court's June 2006 ruling in *Hamdan v. Rumsfeld* that all detainees in U.S. custody, even those held by the CIA, were covered by the Geneva Convention. The transfer of these fifteen or so prisoners did not necessarily mean the end of the CIA program, however. According to reporter Jane Mayer, the Bush administration took steps to ensure its capacity to continue torturing. "In late July," says Mayer, "the White House issued an executive order promising that the C.I.A. would adjust its methods in order to meet the Geneva standards." However, she adds "Bush's order pointedly did not disavow the use of 'enhanced interrogation techniques' that would likely be found illegal if used by officials inside the United States." The executive order appears to be an attempt at an end run around *Hamdan*. It "means that the agency can once again hold foreign terror suspects indefinitely, and without charges, in black sites, without notifying their families or local authorities, or offering access to legal counsel."[48] Shortly after taking office, President Obama issued his own executive order, which among other things, prohibited the use of torture and ordered the closing of the CIA's black sites. The order was however "crafted to preserve the CIA's authority to detain terrorist suspects on a short-term transitory basis prior to rendering them to another country for interrogation or trial."[49]

Extraordinary rendition: Article 3 of the UN Convention against Torture prohibits transferring a detainee to "another State where there are substantial grounds for believing that he would be in danger of being subjected to torture." Such grounds must be evaluated using "all relevant considerations including, where applicable, the existence in the State concerned of a consistent pattern of gross, flagrant or mass violations of human rights." In other words, the Convention prohibits the United States—or indeed any signatory—from sending a prisoner to be tortured in another country.[50] Nevertheless, this is precisely what has happened repeatedly during the "war on terror." I mention only a few examples—two well-known cases and a third because of the egregious nature of the torture involved.

In late September 2002, Canadian citizen Maher Arar cut short a family vacation in Tunisia to begin a consulting job. His flight to Montreal took him through JFK International Airport in New York, where he was seized by the FBI and members of the New York Police Department. After a few days in the Metropolitan Detention Center, the CIA flew Arar to Jordan. The ultimate destination, however, was Syria, where Arar was born but had not lived since he was fifteen years old. He had asked repeatedly not to be sent there, because he believed he would be tortured. And that is exactly what happened. Arar was held for more than ten months in Syria, where he was repeatedly beaten with thick electrical cords until he (falsely) confessed to being a member of Al Qaeda. His captors kept him in a grave-like cell. In Arar's own words:

> We went into the basement, and they opened a door, and I looked in. I could not believe what I saw. I asked how long I would be kept in this place. He did not answer, but put me in and closed the door. It was like a grave. It had no light.
>
> It was three feet wide. It was six feet deep. It was seven feet high. It had a metal door, with a small opening in the door, which did not let in light because there was a piece of metal on the outside for sliding things into the cell.
>
> There was a small opening in the ceiling, about one foot by two feet with iron bars. Over that was another ceiling, so only a little light came through this.
>
> There were cats and rats up there, and from time to time the cats peed through the opening into the cell. There were two blankets, two dishes and two bottles. One bottle was for water and the other one was used for urinating during the night. Nothing else. No light.
>
> I spent 10 months, and 10 days inside that grave.[51]

Maher Arar was not a member of Al Qaeda. He was not a terrorist of any kind. The Canadian government has officially apologized for its complicity in his original arrest at JFK and in 2007 paid him $10 million dollars in compensation for its role in his ordeal.[52] But suppose Arar had been a terrorist? Would his deportation to Syria then have been legal? Not according to the UN Convention. At the time of his rendition, the State Department knew that Syria's government exhibited a "consistent pattern of gross, flagrant or mass violations of human rights." Nonetheless, according to the *Washington Post,* "Syria, where use of torture during imprisonment has been documented by the State Department, maintains a secret but growing intelligence relationship with the CIA, according to intelligence experts."[53]

Nor can the U.S. actions in the Arar case be blamed on ignorance of what happens in Syrian jails. "The U.S. government officially rejects the assertion that it knowingly sends suspects abroad to be tortured," says the *Post,* "but officials admit they sometimes do that. 'The temptation is to have these folks in other hands because they have different standards,' one official said. 'Someone might be able to get information we can't from detainees,' said another." Nor was Arar's case an isolated excess. Since September 11, 2001, "There have been 'a lot of rendition activities'" a "senior U.S. intelligence official" told the *Post.* "'We are doing a number of them, and they have been very productive.'"[54]

Another well-documented example of rendition involved the kidnapping and torture of a Lebanese-born German citizen named Khaled el-Masri. Masri was picked up while traveling by bus to Macedonia in December 2003, apparently because "his name was similar to that of an associate of a 9/11 hijacker." Macedonian police handed him over to the CIA in the capital, Skopje.[55] There, as the European Court of Human Rights found almost a decade later, he was "severely beaten, sodomised, shackled and hooded, and subjected to total sensory deprivation"—treatment the court described as torture. Then he was sent to Afghanistan, where he spent four months being held in a small, dark cell while periodically being kicked, beaten, and interrogated.[56] Eventually the CIA released him, essentially dumping him on a country road in Albania, where he was eventually picked up by the Albanian police.[57]

What happened to Binyam Mohammed al-Habashi (generally known as Binyam Mohammed) was much worse. Mohammed was an Ethiopian citizen in his early twenties who had indefinite permission to live in United Kingdom, where his father had sought asylum in 1995. He was arrested in Karachi, Pakistan, and turned over to U.S. agents, who for reasons that remain unclear had decided he was an "accomplice" of José Padilla. Padilla is an American Muslim convert whom the United State at one time accused of planning to explode a "dirty bomb" in a U.S. city. Padilla became famous as the first U.S. citizen to be designated by President Bush an "illegal enemy combatant." He was never tried on the dirty bomb charges. However, after several years in U.S. military prisons, where it seems likely that he was tortured, Padilla was tried and convicted on a lesser charge of conspiracy to murder and sentenced to seventeen years and four months in prison in the United States.

Binyam Mohammed was tortured in Pakistan, and then the Americans sent him to Morocco, because "the Pakistanis can't do exactly what we want them to." In Morocco, his jailers cut the clothes off his body with a scalpel, then applied it to his bare chest. He screamed. Next, "one of them took my penis in his hand and began to make cuts. He did it once, and they stood still for maybe a minute, watching my reaction. I was in agony." So they kept going. "They must have done this 20 to 30 times, in maybe two hours. There was blood all over." This happened once a month for eighteen months. Between these sessions, Mohammed experienced psychological tortures that will be familiar to the reader: "He was shackled and made to listen to Meat Loaf and Aerosmith" (not the average Moroccan musical choices), "played at full volume through earphones for days on end." There were, says Mohammed, "even worse things" that were "too horrible to remember, let alone talk about." For a year and a half, Mohammed never saw daylight and was never permitted to sleep through the night.[58]

As many as fifty-four different countries are thought to have participated in the U.S. program of extraordinary rendition. Nor is it clear that the practice ended with the close of the Bush adminsitration. President Obama's executive order issued immediately after his inauguration prohibits CIA use of "enhanced interrogation" techniques and requires that the CIA's black sites be shut down. It does not, however, end the practice of rendition. The matter was referred to an inter-agency task force, whose report, if it has been completed, has never been made public as of this writing.[59]

I believe that the foregoing pages have established that United States actions under the rubric of a "war on terror" satisfy the first part of our expanded definition of institutionalized state torture (i.e., the infliction of severe mental or physical suffering by agents of the state). But what of the remaining of the criteria?

Which Results in Dismantling the Victim's Sensory, Psychological, and Social Worlds

"We're going to change your brain."
—Remark of a Moroccan interrogator to Binyam Mohammed al-Habashi[60]

"Plenty [of people] lost their minds. I could hear people knocking their heads against the walls and the doors, screaming their heads off."
—Binyam Mohammed al-Habashi[61]

The destruction of detainees' sensory worlds has been a regular feature of U.S. treatment in every detention center described in this chapter. It forms the core of the "enhanced interrogation" techniques approved in the Rumsfeld memo of 2002. Methods used range from sensory deprivation—keeping prisoners in permanently darkened cells—to the sensory overload caused by constant exposure to loud noise and bright lights. Nor are the effects of such methods an unintentional byproduct; they are designed, as General Miller said about their use at Guantánamo and Abu Ghraib, to "set the conditions" for visits to the interrogation room.

The same methods were used against detainees in Afghanistan. The *New York Times* explained the approach in 2003. In U.S. detention centers, "disorientation is a tool of interrogation and therefore a way of life," reported the *Times*. "To that end, the building [at Bagram]—an unremarkable hangar—is lighted 24 hours a day, making sleep almost impossible," according to "Muhammad Shah, an Afghan farmer who was held there for 18 days." A U.S. spokesman explained to the *Times* that "it was legitimate to use lights, noise and vision restriction, and to alter, without warning, the time between meals, to blur a detainee's sense of time." He also acknowledged that "sleep deprivation was 'probably within the lexicon'" of techniques available to interrogators.[62]

For human beings, the stability of our psychological worlds depends in part on the reliability of our sensory worlds.[63] "Indeed," says a physician who has studied the subject for many years, "there is a long history to the use of isolation and perceptual deprivation by interrogators as a means of destroying an inmate's sense of identity and his will to resist." Isolation from sensory and human contact has empirically observable effects on a prisoner. In fact, "even a few days of solitary confinement" can produce predictable "shifts" in a person's electroencephalogram pattern "towards an abnormal pattern characteristic of stupor and delirium."[64]

This is what happened to José Padilla, who was held in isolation for almost five years in military prisons. His cell at the Naval Brig, the only one occupied on that entire tier of the prison, was eight feet by ten feet and contained only a metal bed, a sink, and a toilet. For weeks at a time he had no human contact. Meals were slid into his cell through a slot in the bottom of the door. The door itself had a small window, which was painted over. The cell was lit twenty-four-hours a day, and a video camera observed his every move. The only people he ever saw were guards, who were forbidden to speak to him, and interrogators.[65]

The psychological effects of this confinement were profound. Several physicians diagnosed him with post-traumatic stress disorder (PTSD), whose symptoms include "hypervigilance" and "physiological reactivity when reminded of his trauma [in the Brig] (his eyes start blinking wildly, and he begins making odd, eerie facial grimaces)." This "reactivity" included a "tendency to identify with his captors rather than his own attorneys." But Padilla's condition was more profound than PTSD alone would account for. "He has become profoundly suspicious, apparently paranoid at times (e.g., his conviction that his mother's letter was a forgery)." He perseverates, repeating the same irrational thought "over and over again. . . . In short, his presentation suggests not simply a reaction to fear and trauma, but really a *disorganizing, psychotic* reaction."[66] The Guantánamo ordeal of Mohammed al-Qahtani, described in a "meticulous" record of his treatment, which was leaked to *Time* magazine in 2005, had similar effects. After enduring "intense isolation over three months" he also suffered psychological disintegration evidenced by his "talking to nonexistent people, reporting hearing voices," and "crouching in a cell covered with a sheet for hours on end."[67]

Isolation and sensory manipulation are two methods that encourage psychological disintegration, but there are others in the U.S. interrogator's arsenal. These include sexual humiliations, like the ones pictured in the photos from Abu Ghraib, and sexual approaches by female guards and enforced homosexual behaviors. Indeed, when I had occasion in Jordan in 2006 to meet an Iraqi sheik who had been tortured by U.S. forces, his first question to our little group was whether all American women were "promiscuous sluts," like the ones who had tormented him by forcing him to look at their naked breasts during his detention. This was a somewhat surprising conversational gambit, given the circumstances of our meeting. I was traveling as part of a group of American human rights activists, visiting Jordan and Syria to speak with Iraqi refugees. Our meeting took place in the offices of the Iraqi human rights organization where the sheik himself was employed. But the psychological trauma of sexual humiliation had damaged this man sufficiently so that polite conversation with American women, even those who were likely to be sympathetic, was beyond him.

The steps involved in the CIA's "takeout" procedure for those it arrests or kidnaps are designed to induce psychological regression. This procedure has been described by a former member of a CIA transport team as "a carefully choreographed twenty-minute routine, during which a suspect [is] hog-tied, stripped naked, photographed, hooded, sedated with anal suppositories, placed in diapers, and transported by plane to a secret location."[68] When it was revealed that the CIA had been using European airports for the transport of its prisoners, the Parliamentary Assembly of the Council of Europe made an inquiry. To knowingly permit such activity would violate the charter of this pan-European human rights organization, to which forty-nine nations belong. The Council concluded that the immediate objective of the CIA's methods is to induce psychological debilitation in those it detains:

A person involved in the Council of Europe inquiry, referring to cavity searches and the frequent use of suppositories during the take-out of detainees, likened the treatment to "sodomy." He said, "It was used to absolutely strip the detainee of any dignity. It breaks down someone's sense of impenetrability. The interrogation became a process not just of getting information but of utterly subordinating the detainee through humiliation." The former C.I.A. officer confirmed that the agency frequently photographed the prisoners naked, "because it's demoralizing."[69]

That U.S. torture has produced psychological debility is also demonstrated by the number of suicides attempted and completed at Guantánamo. At least five detainees are known to have killed themselves, and scores of attempts have been reported. For many detainees, it is the open-ended nature of their incarceration that has been most terrible. Lost in a legal fourth dimension, U.S. detainees held outside the United States have had no reason to believe that their captivity will ever end.[70]

Just as human beings' sensory and psychological worlds are intertwined, our psychological and social worlds are inextricably linked together. There is no social world without social interaction. And, as observers from Aristotle to modern social scientists have remarked, human beings are social animals. In the most immediate sense, solitary confinement, which most prisoners taken in the "war on terror" have experienced at some point in their captivity, reduces a person's social world to the few contacts, all of them hostile, he or she has with other people. Isolation also has well-documented effects on a person's later ability to interact with other persons. Suspicion, distrust, and hypersensitivity to emotional or physical stimuli persist long after isolation has ended.

With the Purpose of Establishing or Maintaining that (Political) Entity's Power

This last part of our definition is the most difficult to demonstrate. The U.S. program differs from other torture regimes described in the first part of this chapter, in that most of its targets were captured outside U.S. borders and do not represent an internal political threat to the U.S. government. In fact, most are not U.S. citizens and even those who are citizens have been presented to the U.S. public as foreign, alien others, not really "Americans." Nevertheless there are similarities between classic torture regimes' targeting of internal "enemies" and actions of the United States in its conduct of the "war on terror."

These include the quality of the information given up under torture and torture's other political purposes.

What is the nature of the intelligence that has emerged from the thousands of interactions between torturers and their prisoners in the "war on terror?" Just as interrogation has served as the pretext, if not the purpose of torture under the other torture regimes described in this chapter, interrogation through torture has produced very little "actionable intelligence" for the United States. Put bluntly, most of it is worse than useless. President Bush made repeated claims to the contrary, arguing that, as a Defense Department press release put it, "the best source of information about [future attacks] has proven to be the terrorists themselves." Speaking at the White House in 2006, the then-president said, "Captured terrorists have unique knowledge about how terrorist networks operate. They have knowledge of where their operatives are deployed and knowledge about what plots are under way." This information has "become so critical to U.S. security that the United States must ensure they have the means at their disposal to get information from these detainees."[71]

President Bush often asserted that intelligence gathered through such necessary "means" had forestalled terrorist attacks on U.S. soil. Perhaps this is true, but ordinary citizens have no way of knowing. What we do know is that many detainees have made false confessions and false accusations against other detainees. To take one example, Al-Qahtani, after "months of isolation, torture and abuse, during which he was nearly killed" eventually falsely identified thirty photographs of fellow prisoners as those of Osama bin Laden's bodyguards.[72] Even if the information had been true, it is far from clear how identifying men who had guarded bin Laden some years before would serve any useful purpose in the present.

The abuses at Abu Ghraib were initially excused by apologists on the grounds that the prisoners had information that might save U.S. soldiers' lives. No such information has reached the public, which is not entirely surprising, given that the shelf life of battlefield intelligence is very short, far shorter than the time that detainees were held at Abu Ghraib. Some were tortured at Abu Ghraib without even a token attempt to extract information. The victims in these cases had already been identified by prison authorities as not being intelligence targets at all but "common criminals."[73]

The United States cannot be unaware that their interrogation programs have produced very little actionable intelligence. Yet until its last days, the Bush administration continued to argue that it needed complete latitude in the treatment of its prisoners to protect the nation and its people. Former Vice President Cheney continues to make similar claims in speeches and in his autobiography, published in 2011.[74] Perhaps advocates of "enhanced interrogation" really do believe that if they can just be "enhanced" a little bit more our inter-rogation programs will bear real fruit. These claims were revived after the as-sassination of Osama bin Laden in 2011 and again with the release in 2012 of the film *Zero Dark Thirty,* which portrays the raid on bin Laden's hideout in Pakistan. After the raid in Abbottabad, then-CIA Director Leon Panetta told NBC News that the CIA's "enhanced interrogation techniques" had produced the information that ran bin Laden to ground.

This view is disputed by many knowledgeable people, including Ali Soufan, a former FBI agent who himself has interrogated al Qaida suspects, using the FBI's standard methods, which involve the gradual gaining of a suspect's confi-dence. (Indeed the conflict between FBI and the CIA over interrogation meth-ods has been a running battle in the "war on terror.")[75]

Nor is Soufan the only one to argue that bin Laden could have been found without the use of torture. In response to the release of *Zero Dark Thirty,* Senator Dianne Feinstein joined Senator Carl Levin in making public the text of a letter addressed to the film's producers. The accompanying press release reads in part:

> The senators described the movie as "grossly inaccurate and mislead-ing," particularly graphic scenes of CIA officers torturing detainees that "credits these detainees with providing critical lead information" on the courier who led to the bin Laden compound.
>
> The senators wrote: "Zero Dark Thirty is factually inaccurate, and we believe that you have an obligation to state that the role of torture in the hunt for Usama Bin Laden is not based on the facts, but rather part of the film's fictional narrative.[76]

Dictatorships like those in Central and South America used torture to terrify their citizens with the belief that the same thing could happen to them if they were to step out of line. I believe that the United States' use of torture has a similar symbolic function in relation to the rest of the world. The sheer geo-graphical reach of the CIA's black sites; the assistance, voluntary or otherwise, of dozens of nations in the rendition program; and the obvious impunity with which U.S. operatives seem to act all signal to the world at large that the United States can do whatever it wants. A national torture regime threatens those who oppose its power within its own borders. In a sense, the United States torture regime does the same thing but beyond its borders. Targeted killings using unpiloted aircraft further reinforce the message.

The belief that our democratic government has had to resort to torturing the "really bad guys" also uses citizen fears to reinforce government power in this country. It makes the erosion of civil liberties in this country—the war-rantless wiretaps, the "no-fly" lists, the special interviews with legal residents who are Muslim or of Middle Eastern descent, and the National Security Agency's massive surveillance of telephone and Internet activity revealed in 2013—seem like minor irritations by comparison to the dangers U.S. citizens are supposed to face.

With the identification of "foreigners" as an imminent danger (including, perhaps U.S. citizens who are Muslim or of Middle Eastern or South Asian descent), we see another similarity to the paradigmatic torture regime. Those who are deemed members of the class of beings who may properly be tortured are defined as falling outside a circle of belonging. Those who may be tortured are not like "us." They don't belong to "our" people, or even perhaps, to the human species itself. This is dangerous territory, especially when we consider what John Conroy calls "one of the central aspects of torture, that the class of people whom society accepts as torturable has a tendency to expand."[77] That class has in fact expanded to include Muslim men living in the United States, including U.S. citizens. Journalist and former U.K. *Guardian* editor Victoria Brittain describes how "special administrative measures" make it "possible for the government to pre-convict and in many cases pre-punish a small set of Muslim men," by holding them for months and even years in pretrial solitary confinement. I will argue in Chapter 7 that there is already a larger group of U.S. citizens whom society accepts as torturable: prisoners in state and federal jails.

We now have a clear idea of what is being debated when people argue about torture and to what extent contemporary U.S. practices fit that definition. It is time to take a look at the state of those debates, both in the academic world and in the more popular discussions, such as those found in daily newspapers. That is the focus of the next chapter.

Notes

1. Bob Woodward, "Detainee Tortured, Says U.S. Official: Trial Overseer Cites 'Abusive' Methods against 9/11 Suspect," *Washington Post,* January 14, 2009.
2. Constitution Project, *The Report of the Constitution Project's Task Force on Detainee Treatment* (Washington, DC: Constitution Project, 2013).
3. Ibid., 3.
4. Larry Cohler-Esses, "Brooklyn's Abu Ghraib," *New York Daily News,* February 20, 2005.
5. Ibid.
6. Philippe Sands, *Torture Team: Rumsfeld's Memo and the Betrayal of American Values,* 1st ed. (New York: Palgrave MacMillan, 2008), 2–3.
7. Don Van Natta Jr., Raymond Bonner, and Amy Wandman, "Threats and Responses: Interrogations; Questioning Terror Suspects in a Dark and Surreal World," *New York Times,* March 9, 2003.
8. Ben Farmer, Philip Sherwell, and Dean Nelson, "Afghanistan's 'Guantanamo' Poses New Prison Problem for Barack Obama," *The Telegraph,* January 24, 2009.
9. Tim Golden, "In U.S. Report, Brutal Details of 2 Afghan Inmates' Deaths" *New York Times,* May 20, 2005.

10. Ibid.

11. Ibid.

12. Tim Lasseter, "U.S. Abuse of Detainees Was Routine at Afghanistan Bases," *McClatchy Newspapers*, June 16, 2008. http://www.mcclatchydc.com/259/story/38775.html.

13. Andy Worthington, *The Guantánamo Files: The Stories of the 774 Detainees in America's Illegal Prison* (Ann Arbor: Pluto Press, 2007).

14. Amnesty International, "Days of Adverse Hardship in US Detention Camps–Testimony of Guantánamo Detainee Jumah Al–Dossari," December 16, 2005. http://www.amnesty.org/en/library/asset/AMR51/107/2005/en/98c38595-d477-11dd-8743-d305bea2b2c7/amr511072005en.html; Ibid.

15. Josh White, "A Detainee Speaks: I'm Home, but Still Haunted by Guantanamo," *Washington Post*, August 17, 2008.

16. Rod Norland, Michael R. Gordon, and Alissa J. Rubin, "Karzai Has Nothing but Praise for U.S. upon Bagram Prison Transfer," *New York Times*, March 26, 2013.

17. "Agreement between the United States and Cuba for the Lease of Lands for Coaling and Naval Stations; February 23, 1903," Article II.

18. Neil A. Lewis, "Traces of Terror: The Prisoners; Judge Rebuffs Detainees at Guantánamo," *New York Times*, August 1, 2002.

19. Laurel E. Fletcher and Eric Stover, *Guantánamo and Its Aftermath: U.S. Detention and Interrogation Practices and Their Impact on Former Detainees* (Berkeley: University of California at Berkeley, 2008).

20. Worthington, *The Guantánamo Files*, 133.

21. Ibid., 191.

22. Ibid.

23. Ibid., 192.

24. Ibid.

25. Ibid., 193.

26. Ibid., 195.

27. Fletcher and Stover, *Guantánamo and Its Aftermath*, 43–44.

28. Scott Horton, "The Guantánamo 'Suicides': A Camp Delta Sergeant Blows the Whistle," *Harper's Magazine*, March 2010. http://harpers.org/archive/2010/03/the-guantanamo-suicides/.

29. Editorial Board, "Hunger Strike at Guantánamo," *New York Times*, April 5, 2013.

30. Force feeding as a form of punishment has a long history. Women suffragists in England suffered similar treatment in the early twentieth century,

31. Samir Naji al Hasan Moqbel, "Gitmo Is Killing Me," *New York Times*, April 15, 2013.

32. Charlie Savage, "Office Working to Close Guantanamo Is Shuttered," *New York Times*, January 29, 2013.

33. Charlie Savage, "Money Requested for New Prison at Guantánamo," *New York Times*, March 21, 2013. http://atwar.blogs.nytimes.com/2013/03/21/pentagon-wants-to-build-new-prison-at-guantanamo/.

34. Carol Rosenberg, "Guantánamo Prison Getting Guard Reinforcements," *Miami Herald*, June 19, 2013. http://www.miamiherald.com/2013/06/05/3434821/guantanamo-prison-getting-reinforcements.html.

35. Seymour M. Hersh, "Torture at Abu Ghraib," *New Yorker*, May 10, 2004; Ibid.

36. David Stout and Terence Neilan, "Bush Tells Arab World That Prisoner Abuse Was 'Abhorrent,'" *New York Times*, May 5, 2004.

37. Jane Mayer, *Dark Side: The Inside Story of How the War on Terror Turned into a War on American Ideals* (New York: Doubleday, 2008), 241–42.

38. Joan Walsh, "The Abu Ghraib Files," *Salon*, March 14, 2006. http://www.salon.com/news/abu_ghraib/2006/03/14/introduction/.

39. Seymour M. Hersh, "The General's Report: How Antonio Taguba, Who Investigated the Abu Ghraib Scandal, Became One of Its Casualties," *New Yorker*, June 25, 2007.

40. Maj. Gen. Antonio M. Taguba, *Article 15–16 Investigation of the 800th Military Police Brigade* (U.S. Department of Defense, 2004).

41. Ibid.

42. Constitution Project, *Moving Forward*, 392–93.

43. Van Natta Jr., Bonner, and Wandman, "Threats and Responses."
44. Jane Mayer, "The Black Sites: A Rare Look inside the C.I.A.'S Secret Interrogation Program," *New Yorker*, August 13, 2007.
45. Scott Shane, "Waterboarding Used 266 Times on 2 Suspects," *New York Times*, April 20, 2009.
46. Mayer, *Dark Side*, 168.
47. Ibid., 168–69.
48. Mayer, "Black Sites."
49. Amrit Singh, *Globalizing Torture: CIA Secret Detention and Extraordinary Rendition* (New York: Open Society Foundations, 2013), 8.
50. United Nations, Convention against Torture and Other Cruel, Inhuman or Degrading Treatment or Punishment (1987).
51. Maher Arar, "This Is What They Did to Me," *Counterpunch*, November 5, 2003. http://counterpunch.org/arar11062003.html.
52. Ian Austen, "Canada Reaches Settlement with Torture Victim," *New York Times*, January 26, 2007.
53. DeNeen L. Brown and Dana Priest, "Deported Terror Suspect Details Torture in Syria; Canadian's Case Called Typical of C.I.A.," *Washington Post*, November 5, 2003.
54. Ibid.
55. Dana Priest, "Wrongful Imprisonment: Anatomy of a C.I.A. Mistake; German Citizen Released after Months in 'Rendition,'" *Washington Post*, December 4, 2005.
56. Richard Norton-Taylor, "CIA 'Tortured and Sodomised' Terror Suspect, Human Rights Court Rules," *The Guardian*, December 13, 2012. http://www.guardian.co.uk/law/2012/dec/13/cia-tortured-sodomised-terror-suspect.
57. Amy Davidson, "Torturing the Wrong Man," *The New Yorker*, December 13, 2012. http://www.newyorker.com/online/blogs/closeread/2012/12/khaled-el-masri-torturing-the-wrong-man.html.
58. Worthington, *The Guantánamo Files*, 230–31.
59. Singh, *Globaliazing Torture*, 8–9.
60. Cited in Worthington, *The Guantánamo Files*, 231.
61. Ibid.
62. Van Natta Jr., Bonner, and Wandman, "Threats and Responses."
63. M.D. Grassian, Stuart, "Neuropsychiatric Effects of Solitary Confinement," in *The Trauma of Psychological Torture*, ed. Gilbert Reyes Disaster and Trauma Psychology (Westport, Connecticut: Praeger, 2008), 124.
64. Ibid., 115.
65. Ibid., 122–23.
66. Ibid., 124.
67. Worthington, *The Guantánamo Files*, 206.
68. Mayer, "Black Sites."
69. Ibid.
70. The indefinite nature of their detention has led Guantánamo's prisoners to undertake several organized hunger strikes. The most recent of these began in February 2013 and, as of this writing, included at least 100 of the prison's remaining 166 detainees.
71. Donna Miles and Jerry J. Gilmore, "Bush: Successful Programs Have Prevented Further Attacks," *Defense Link*, December 6, 2006. http://www.defense.gov/news/NewsArticle.aspx?ID=724.
72. Worthington, *The Guantánamo Files*, 209.
73. "Hearing: Top Generals Accept Responsibility for Iraq Abuses," in Senate Armed Services Committee (Washington, DC: National Public Radio, 2004).
74. See, for example, Dick Cheney, "Text of Dick Cheney's National Security Speech at AEI," May 21, 2009. http://www.foxnews.com/politics/2009/05/21/raw-data-text-dick-cheneys-national-security-speech-aei/(accessed 5/21/2009). Also see Richard B. Cheney and Liz Cheney, *In My Time: A Personal and Political Memoir* (New York: Threshold, 2011).
75. Ali Soufan, "Torture, Lies and Hollywood," *New York Times*, February 24, 2013.

76. Dianne Feinstein, "Feinstein Releases Statement on *Zero Dark Thirty*, December 19, 2012. http://www.feinstein.senate.gov/public/index.cfm/press-releases?ID=b5946751-2054-404a-89b7-b81e1271efc9.

77. John Conroy, *Unspeakable Acts, Ordinary People: The Dynamics of Torture* (Berkeley: University of California Press, 2000), 27. Indeed, we may be seeing a similar expansion a related realm: the use of unpiloted aircraft to assassinate targeted individuals. Under the Obama administration such assassinations were of questionable legality (and morality) when the targets only included foreign nationals. The category of legitimate targets of assassination has now expanded to include U.S. citizens—essentially applying a death penalty without benefit of the due process provided for in the U.S. Constitution.

3

The Current Discussion

Suffocating our terror fighters with excessive legal caution can only
impair the difficult task of defending a free society that believes in
the rule of law from terrorists who believe in neither freedom nor law.
—Wall Street Journal *editorial, January 10, 2009*

This chapter deals with the ethical debates about torture that have arisen since
the terrorist attacks of September 11, 2001. Here I examine arguments found
in academic books and journals addressed to professional students of ethics. I
also look at how two newspapers of record approached the issue over a number
of years. Readers who are not philosophers may be tempted to skip the first part
of this chapter. In fact, the arguments that academic ethicists make are not difficult to follow, and they will be familiar to anyone who has thought about the
ethics of torture. The scholarly arguments will be clearer, however, if we first
define two technical terms. These are "consequentialism" and "deontology."

Consequentialism is a kind of ethics in which an action is judged right or
wrong depending on its consequences. Good actions have good consequences;
bad actions, bad ones. This raises two obvious questions: What makes a consequence good or bad? And, consequences for whom? The answer to each of
these depends on the kind of consequentialism being considered. The best-
known form of consequentialism is utilitarianism, which is often expressed in
the formula "the greatest good for the greatest number." "Good" in this case
has been defined differently by different utilitarians. For John Stuart Mill,
good was "happiness," by which he meant very simply "pleasure and the absence of pain."[1] For Mill's utilitarian mentor, Jeremy Bentham, the good to be
maximized was less well defined, perhaps because to him its nature was obvious. In any case, it is important to note that utilitarians seek to maximize
benefits and to minimize detriments *for the largest possible number of people.*
There are other forms of consequentialism. Nationalism, for example, seeks
to maximize benefit for a particular nation rather than for people general. The
consequentialist ethics expressed by Niccolo Machiavelli in *The Prince* judge a
ruler's actions by whether the ruler succeeds in what the ruler has set out to do.

Deontology is often described as the opposite of utilitarianism, because it judges an action based not on its consequences but on the motives behind the action. Good actions in this view are those that are motivated by a devotion to duty, and the word deontology is derived from *deon*, the Greek for "duty." The best-known deontologist is Immanuel Kant. Kant believed that reason unadulterated by either emotion or concern for a particular outcome is the best guide to identifying a person's duty and, therefore, the best and only trustworthy guide to ethical action. Unless we rely only on rational thought, he argued, it is very easy to be led into believing that what we *want* to do is also what we *ought* to do.

Kant argued that rational beings' ability to use reason to discern our duty makes us uniquely valuable creatures, creatures with moral worth. Because of this moral worth, rational beings should not be treated as things. Rather, we should always treat that rational capacity in ourselves and other people as an end in itself and never merely as a means to achieve some other purpose. When the ethicists in this chapter say they are taking a deontological or Kantian approach, this is what they usually mean.

Much of the literature examined in this chapter in fact takes either a consequentialist or deontological approach—and occasionally a combination of the two—to the question of whether torture is ever morally justified. A smaller group of academic writers consciously advance arguments that fall outside the general rubrics of these two methods. Some of the authors presented here write in favor of a general prohibition on torture; others, against one. However, with one or two exceptions, they all treat torture as *episodic incidents*—unique, temporally and socially isolated behaviors—about which it is possible to make similarly isolated ethical judgments. I argue that insofar as they do not address torture as it is actually practiced, such approaches to torture as a moral problem, however internally consistent, will necessarily remain incomplete.

To bring some order to a wide-ranging discussion, I have divided this chapter into several sections. It begins with the academic literature, as found in books and in articles appearing in secular and religious peer-reviewed journals of ethics. This material is presented in three subsections: consequentialist arguments, deontological arguments, and those that do not fall neatly into either category. The section on consequentialist approaches to torture begins by addressing an approach that arises so frequently that it has been given its own name—the "ticking-bomb" problem. This hypothetical problem appears in numerous guises: as an imminent threat to innocent schoolchildren (Jean Bethke Elshtain);[2] as a kidnapped child with a limited oxygen supply; or as a suitcase full of plague germs in the hands of a terrorist (the latter two posited by Richard Posner)[3]. The classic version is the ticking time-bomb that a government official knows will explode very soon, killing and injuring many people, if he or she fails to torture a captive who knows the location of the bomb. Because the ticking-bomb problem underlies so many consequentialist arguments in favor of torture, it receives special attention here.

The last section of this chapter contains a survey of the arguments about real-world torture appearing in two U.S. newspapers with national readership—the generally liberal *New York Times* and the decidedly conservative *Wall Street Journal*. For the most part, these editorials address actual events rather than theoretical questions. Perhaps for that reason, the majority of the arguments found in both papers are of a consequentialist bent.

I have limited my research almost entirely to work published since September 11, 2001.[4] I do not make this restriction because there is no earlier work of interest on the subject; however, official U.S. response to the terrorist attacks of that day has given the discussion a new immediacy, especially for citizens of this country. Revelations of actual torture and its implementation at the highest official levels have taken the discussion beyond the realm of the hypothetical, despite a strong speculative current of ticking-bomb theorists who seek to drag it back in that direction.

The Academic Debate

Consequentialist Arguments for Torture

In general, consequentialist arguments about torture turn on the utilitarian goal of bringing about the greatest good for the greatest number. In some cases, however, advocates of torture base their consequentialist arguments not on the *number* of lives to be saved but on the *innocence* of those lives however few these might be. So, while most who would permit torture on consequentialist grounds speak in terms of a situation in which many lives are at risk, we find Richard Posner, a Justice of the U.S. Court of Appeals for the Seventh Circuit, arguing that it is "proper" to torture a single (presumably guilty) "kidnapper" to save a single (innocent) child.[5]

Most consequentialists who argue in favor of torture specify that they are only speaking of what political philosopher Henry Shue has called "interrogational torture," whose purpose is eliciting lifesaving information, rather than "terroristic" torture, which aims to intimidate "people other than the [immediate torture] victim."[6] Shue points out, however, that the distinction between "interrogational" and other types of torture is easier to maintain in the pages of scholarly journals than it is in prison cells.[7]

Let us begin then with the ticking-bomb problem, as we will find some version of it at the heart of most consequentialist arguments for torture. The approach of moral philosopher Fritz Allhoff is a good place to begin this discussion. In 2003, Allhoff argued on utilitarian grounds that some instances of torture are morally permissible. Specifically, one may legitimately torture another if "the use of torture aims at acquisition of information, the captive is reasonably thought to have the relevant information, the information corresponds to a significant and imminent threat, and the information could likely lead to the prevention of the threat."[8] In other words, torture is permissible to save the lives of innocent people, as long as it is "reasonable" to think the tortured person knows something that is "likely" to help the torturer save those lives. This is the quintessential utilitarian argument for torture.

In the same article, Allhoff also points out that a strictly Kantian deontology "would, in all cases, reject" torture. Although he himself rejects Kantianism out of hand, he does argue that some versions of rights theory also justify torture on two grounds: either that by entering a terrorist plot, one forfeits the right not to be tortured, or that even if the right not to be tortured is absolutely nonderogable (i.e., that people cannot voluntarily surrender it), there will still be cases of conflicting rights, in which situation, one should act so as to "to minimize the overall violation of rights."[9] This last approach is sometimes called a "utilitarianism of rights," because while it acknowledges the existence of rights as properties inherent in persons, it adjudicates among conflicting rights claims by exercising utilitarian principles of seeking the greatest good (or the least evil).

In a 2005 follow-up article, Allhoff uses the ticking-bomb case to present a formal argument, based on a method called separation of cases, to prove specifically that not only is torture morally permissible but also that Kantianism is wrong in general. He derives this conclusion on the grounds that Kantianism and any other theory that rejects torture even in the paradigm ticking-bomb case "simply cannot be plausible moral views."[10] He frames the problem so that those deciding whether to torture a captive have "epistemic certainty" (i.e., that they know without any doubt) that the captive is responsible for the bomb and possesses the information necessary to prevent its detonation.[11] Later in the article, he amends his original framing such that "millions or billions" of people stand to die and that "the necessary torture to elicit the preventative information could be comparatively minor."[12] Allhoff's point is that no plausible moral theory will reject torture in this ideal case. The argument that such conditions never occur in actual experience is irrelevant, he says, because it cannot be shown logically that they could not occur. Therefore, whether one argues from any ethical position—utilitarian, non-Kantian deontological, virtue ethics, or social contractarian—one must accept that at least in this one ideal case, torture is morally permissible.

Allhoff is careful to remind the reader that his argument is a piece of formal moral theory and that "nothing (pragmatically) important hangs on accepting the intuition in the ticking time-bomb case."[13] His interest in the problem of torture is entirely formal. "As a moral philosopher," he says, "the question of real-world justifiability [of torture] is really not one on which I have much to say; I am more interested in the theoretical arguments that can be rendered on either side of this debate."[14] I find this claim more than a little disingenuous. While he argues that the main burden of his article is an attempt to eliminate Kantian deontology as a plausible moral theory in general, he has hardly chosen the problem of torture at random. Indeed, he claims in the abstract of his article that "even if this paper has dealt with idealized cases, it paves the way for the justification of torture in the real world."[15]

One is tempted to respond to Allhoff in the words of G. E. M. Anscombe, written fifty years earlier: "The point of considering hypothetical situations, perhaps very improbable ones," says Anscombe, "seems to be to elicit from yourself or someone else a hypothetical decision to do something of a bad kind." The danger of such hypothetical argumentation, as Allhoff's efforts demonstrate, is that it "has the effect of predisposing people—who will never get into the situations for which they have made hypothetical choices—to consent to similar bad actions, or to praise and flatter those who do them, so long as their crowd does so too, when the desperate circumstances imagined don't hold at all."[16]

This is precisely what has happened with hypothetical arguments justifying torture that begin with Allhoff's "epistemic certainty" about the target's guilty knowledge and devolve into former Vice President Cheney's moral imperative to employ "enhanced interrogation methods" whenever the failure to do so might "make the American people less safe." Anything else, says Cheney is "recklessness clothed in righteousness."[17]

Henry Shue has written eloquently of the problems that we are likely to encounter as soon as we start down the "way" that Allhoff believes that he has helped to pave. The problem with unanchored speculations like Allhoff's is that "justifications for torture thrive in fantasy" and that, in practice, people tend to recast reality to fit the fantasy. "We imagine," he says, that

> we have exactly the person we need—not some poor devil who looks like him to agents who have parachuted in from another culture. We imagine that the person we hold knows exactly what we need to know—not out-of-date information overtaken by events. We imagine that the person will reveal exactly what we need—not simply vomit and die, or descend into a psychotic state (of course torturers become better at it when they have more practice). We imagine that the information that will be revealed will be sufficient to prevent the terrible catastrophe—not that the catastrophe will simply be re-scheduled for a different time or place.[18]

We will return to Shue's role in this discussion in the section on deontological approaches to torture.

If Allhoff has chosen to locate his consequentialist justifications in the land of theory, others have argued forcefully for the actual use of torture on consequentialist grounds. Perhaps the most famous of these positions is the proposal of Harvard legal scholar Alan Dershowitz that the United States should institute a formal procedure for granting torture warrants. Dershowitz believes that in the context of the "war on terror" it will become necessary at some point to use torture to save civilian lives from terrorist attack. Therefore, Dershowitz argues that although he is "generally against torture as a normative matter" and "would like to see its use minimized," given that torture will in fact used, that use should be legally regulated.[19] To do otherwise is, in Dershowitz's view, hypocrisy, and it leaves the decisions and form of the actual torture in the hands of low-level functionaries. Dershowitz also has opinions about the form torture ought to take; he favors the use of "a sterilized needle underneath the nail."[20]

Several scholars have responded to Dershowitz's proposal, either directly or implicitly. Legal scholar Oren Gross, for example, prefers to retain an absolute ban on torture, while allowing for the possibility of "catastrophic cases" in which "state agents" might act outside the law and seek "ex post ratification of their conduct." In other words, should a government official resort to torture, even though it is prohibited by law, the official might seek an "ex post" or after-the-fact legal sanction for those actions. Where Dershowitz advocates prior legal permission (in legal terms, an ex ante approval), Gross would prefer to rely on a "sense of self-indignation when rules are violated (which is the result of the social, political, and legal ethos of the community), coupled with uncertainty about the chances of ratification" to restrain what might otherwise become "a too easy rush to use extralegal powers."[21]

Federal Judge Richard Posner agrees with Dershowitz that torture will be necessary in some extreme cases but takes issue with the proposal for torture warrants on several grounds. First, he wonders whether a warrant will really provide the sort of restraint that Dershowitz envisions, especially in view of the latter's "well-known distrust of judges' competence and probity." Further, he worries that regularizing a procedure makes it more "likely to become regular." Posner's solution is to place the decision to torture in executive, rather than judicial hands. Leave the prohibitions in place, "with the understanding that they will not be enforced in extreme circumstances." On the question of whether the ex post ratification advocated by Gross should be available, Posner remains silent. He does acknowledge that civil libertarians might rightly be concerned that legal justifications of torture such as Dershowitz's could easily lead to the acceptance of torture in progressively less extreme cases. He does not say why locating the power of decision in the hands of the executive branch makes such a slide down a slippery slope any less likely. In any case, Posner prefers to "stick with our perhaps overly strict rules, trusting executive officials to break them when the stakes are high enough to obtain political absolution for their illegal conduct."[22] Experience, however, suggests that such trust does not appear to have been well-placed in recent years.

Sanford Levinson, also a legal scholar, is the editor of the well-regarded anthology, *Torture: A Collection*. Levinson leans toward a Dershowitz-style of ex ante regulation of torture through warrants, in preference to Gross's and Posner's ex post sanctioning of torture. He adds an additional twist, however, suggesting that the U.S. government should pay off those it tortures. Thus, "anyone against whom a torture warrant is issued [would] receive a significant payment as 'just compensation' for the denial of his or her right not to be tortured." Furthermore, "the compensation could be increased if it turned out that the person tortured had no significant information to give to the authorities."

Here we have stepped well beyond Allhoff's "epistemic certainty" into an epistemological quagmire: How are we to know with sufficient certainty to warrant increasing the "compensation" whether the torture victim truly had no significant knowledge or was simply able to withhold such knowledge? This is not an idle question; it goes to an essential assumption entailed by moving the ticking-bomb case beyond the hypothetical realm (i.e., that torture will inevitably produce the required information). Levinson thinks it likely that knowing that "substantial" compensation will be "paid to *everyone* who is tortured" will actually "serve to limit the incidence of torture."[23] Unless by "substantial" Levinson is suggesting that the government pay out sums in the billions of dollars for each occurrence, the limiting effect of such "compensation" strikes me as minimal. After all, this "compensation" is not coming out of the torturer's pocket, even though it might strain the torturer's government department's annual budget. Furthermore, a compensation scheme that proposes to pay "everyone" who is tortured would seem to imply that torture will be used with some frequency, certainly more frequently than a ticking-bomb case is likely to arise. The offer of a generalized compensation thus would seem to contradict Levinson's position that a ticking-bomb case is the only legitimate occasion for torture.

To be fair to Levinson, he appears horrified by the directions of his own thinking and concludes the article by citing two strong arguments against torture: that it renders this country too like those we seek to defeat through torture and that torture by a liberal democracy like the United States produces a "moral contagion" that might infect other nations. He ends with the observation that in contemplating torture we are indeed "staring into an abyss."[24] Levinson has since made it clear in interviews that he believes that torture is equally wrong whether practiced by dictatorships or democracies and should be reserved only for cases in which "it could save, say, thousands of lives."[25]

Consequentialist Arguments against Torture

Because the ticking-bomb problem presents the paradigm case in favor of torture, this is also where consequentialist arguments against torture generally begin. Many of these challenge the empirical validity of the proposition that torture produces good information. Experience demonstrates that the quality of statements made under torture is uneven at best.[26] Proponents of torture often brush this objection aside, as Richard Posner does, by observing that the use of torture is "too common" to "suppose that it doesn't work."[27] I find this argument less than convincing. One might also argue that the use of leeches to treat paralysis was "too common" in medieval Europe to suppose that it did not work.[28]

Others who reject the argument that torture does not work contend that history proves that it does. While this book's major concern is with arguments in the post-9/11 context, so many of these arguments (both pro and con) make reference to the French experience in Algeria that it is worth addressing here. Among the most frequently cited cases is the use of torture in colonial France's campaign against the National Liberation Front (FLN) in the city of Algiers. Historian Alfred McCoy has addressed this question, specifically examining the case of Algiers, where the French army arrested between 30 and 40 percent of all the men living in the Arab quarter of that city and tortured most of them. This campaign of torture did indeed succeed in breaking the FLN's operation in Algiers. McCoy's conclusion from examining this history and that of the U.S. Phoenix program in Vietnam (under which tens of thousands were tortured) is that "the choices are clear. Major success from limited, surgical torture is a fable, a fiction." However, "mass torture of thousands of suspects, some guilty, most innocent, can produce some useful intelligence." However, such mass torture also has "long-term political consequences that subvert the effort's larger aims."[29] In other words, the French victory over the FLN proved only temporary, while the barbarity of its torture campaign horrified the world and ultimately increased the resolve of the Algerian independence fighters.

Alistair Horne, author of *A Savage War for Peace*, is probably the best-known English-language historian of the war between France and colonial Algeria. In an introduction to the 2006 edition of *A Savage War*, he has described some of the long-term consequences mentioned by McCoy. "In the Algerian War what led—probably more than any other single factor—to the ultimate defeat of France was," he says, was "the realisation in France and the world at large, that methods of interrogation were being used that had been condemned under the Nazi Occupation."[30] Furthermore, his study has convinced him that "history teaches us that, in the production of reliable intelligence, regardless of the moral issue, torture is counter-productive."[31]

British scholar Neil MacMaster, who has written extensively on European racism in general and the French Algerian population in particular, also believes that U.S. academics and journalists could learn something about the efficacy of torture from the French experience in Algeria. He is particularly appalled by what seems to him the insular nature of the post-9/11 discussion in the United States. Those who advocate torture, he says, have "developed their arguments *de nouveau,* reinventing the wheel as it were, without any reference to the huge field of historical, ethical, philosophical and legal knowledge that exists in relation to the practice of torture." In particular, he contrasts the discussions in the United States to "the major and concurrent French debate during 2000–04 on torture during the Algerian war." The French discussion, he suggests "highlighted the profound dangers of such forms of violence which, like a gangrene, threatened to corrupt the entire social and political order."[32] Like McCoy and Horne, MacMaster also argues that despite its apparent short-term successes, widespread torture eventually "served to drive most of the Algerian population into the arms of the FLN," thereby subverting France's own objectives.[33]

MacMaster also suggests that specific techniques employed by the French in Algiers have affected U.S. tactics in Vietnam and elsewhere. One bit of "elsewhere" to which we know that they have migrated is Latin America, through the U.S. School of the Americas, which was located in Panama in the 1970s. The Chilean torturer Osvaldo Romo proudly told his interviewer that in his counterinsurgency training there he had learned "how to make organigrams and decide this person goes here, and this person goes there, and to know who had more information and who didn't have much to say."[34] Such an "organigram," or organizational diagram, will be familiar to anyone who has seen the *Battle of Algiers,* in which the fictional French Colonel Mathieu uses information derived from torturing thousands of Arab men to fill in the little pyramids on the chalkboard at his headquarters.

MacMaster writes that in the twenty-first-century French debate on torture, a "consensus," shared from mainstream left to center-right parties and by many former soldiers of the Algerian campaign, was that "the use of torture had constituted an unspeakable catastrophe." This was true not only because France ultimately lost the war as a result but also because of the cost to France itself in literally hundreds of thousands of cases of psychiatric trauma among former military personnel. For France, torture, which MacMaster says is "widely referred to as 'la gangrene,' [had] led to the degeneration of the liberal democratic state, its institutions (particularly the army and the judiciary), its core values and fundamental respect for human rights and dignity."[35]

MacMaster's observation of the French debate would appear to contradict Richard Posner, who maintains that "torture is uncivilized, but civilized nations are able to employ uncivilized means, at least in situations of or closely resembling war, without becoming uncivilized in the process."[36] Let us give one last word on this matter to Horne, who describes how the tortures used in Algiers found their way back to France. In 1962 at the height of the Algerian war, he reports that dozens of Algerian immigrants were tossed into the Seine river and drowned and others hanged from trees, while "the *gégène* [a torture device that uses electricity generated by a field telephone] made its ugly appearance on the Paris scene" in French police stations dealing with ordinary French crime.[37]

It might be observed at this point that we have strayed a bit from perfectly utilitarian arguments for or against the use of torture. Nonetheless, we are still discussing torture in terms of its consequences, which brings us to another condemnation of torture, made by philosophers Vittorio Bufacchi and Jean Maria Arrigo in an article entitled "Torture, Terrorism and the State: A Refutation of the Ticking-Bomb Argument." Bufacchi and Arrigo contend that the ticking-bomb argument depends upon a number of suppositions that empirical observation reveals are often counterfactual: that the "intelligence" that the bomb exists is itself reliable and that the captive actually has the knowledge to prevent its detonation; that torture will work quickly enough to prevent detonation; that the information produced by the captive will be truthful; and that the captive will not, while speaking truthfully, nevertheless unintentionally give false information.[38]

Bufacchi and Arrigo's larger point, however, is that the ticking-bomb argument is actually a stand-in "for a more complex thesis, one about the best method for maximizing welfare." And if that is the case, they argue, an adequate consequentialist examination must weigh all the costs and benefits to a nation of torturing and of maintaining the capacity to torture persons suspected of threatening the nation's welfare. They conclude that "the ticking-bomb argument ultimately fails as a consequentialist argument because it ignores the intensive preparation and larger social consequences of state-sponsored torture."[39]

Such "social consequences" include distortions in scientific scholarship (as in the fifty-year history of secret and often illegal research on human subjects carried out at U.S. and Canadian universities, which is documented by Alfred McCoy);[40] distortions in the roles of medical and psychological professionals and institutions; damages to the military including "demoralization of personnel, destabilization of the institutional structure, and loss of honour;" damages to the legal system, and even to the "core values on which the liberal democratic state rests;" and the great difficulty with which any of these damages can be repaired.[41] "Part of the difficulty of social repair," they contend, "is the high proportion of innocents who are tortured." In fact, a realistic "moral calculus of the ticking-bomb argument should weigh (a) the evil of the murders of innocent victims of the bomb against (b) the corruption of key social institutions, the evil of torture of many innocents mistakenly tortured, and the ruination of many torturers."[42]

Bufacchi and Arrigo close by reminding readers of the "the tremendous institutional support required for any rational hope of extracting [a] terrorist's plan under torture." Effective torture cannot be achieved by a solo operator making things up as he or she goes along. It requires an infrastructure of prisons, guards, doctors, psychologists, torturers, and trainers of torturers. Even marginally effective torture is not something that can be used once in a unique emergency. "A skilled torturer is like a skilled surgeon, requiring frequent practice."[43]

Lest the reader doubt this last contention, consider a regular pedagogical technique of the Brazilian police in the time of the military regime in the 1970s. In Brazil, ordinary prisoners were often tortured in front of classes in interrogation that police cadets attended; in effect, they were used as "instrument[s] for practical demonstrations." A comprehensive report issued by the Roman Catholic Archdiocese of Saõ Paolo says that "one of the first officials to introduce this practice into Brazil was Dan Mitrione, an American police officer. As a police instructor in Belo Horizonte during the early years of the Brazilian military regime, Mitrione regularly took beggars off the streets and tortured them in classrooms."[44]

In contrast to most ethicists, both MacMaster and Bufacchi and Arrigo treat torture as an ongoing practice anchored in larger institutions, rather than as isolated incident or incidents. In so doing, they begin to address what appears to me to be a significant shortcoming of much of the rest of this discussion.

Deontological Arguments against Torture

Deontology, whether of the strictly Kantian or a more general variety, has also been called into service on both sides of the torture debate. Deontological arguments against torture are perhaps the more straightforward, and so let us begin there.

In his 1978 essay "Torture," Henry Shue argues that part of the reason that torture evokes a response of moral disgust is that it does not represent the "fair fight" contemplated in the laws of warfare, which enjoin careful distinction between combatants and noncombatants. In torture, as opposed to combat, one participant is necessarily both unwilling and defenseless. Shue makes a distinction to which writers on torture continue to refer: between "terroristic" torture, whose purpose is to frighten people other than the victim, and "interrogational" torture, whose purpose is "extracting information."[45] The first, he says, is "the purest possible case" of a violation of Kant's prohibition on treating humanity merely as a means to some other end. He therefore sees no problem with disallowing terroristic torture on Kantian grounds.

He then asks whether interrogational torture might be "less objectionable" because, although the victim remains defenseless, he or she has, like a combatant in lawful war, the option of surrender (i.e., compliance with the torturer's demands). Might such a "constraint"—the requirement that the victim have the possibility of escape through compliance—make torture a "fairer" fight? Shue concludes that, in fact, it does not. If the captive is a willing collaborator with his or her captors or an innocent bystander, there is no reason to torture the captive in the first place. If, on the other hand, the captive is a dedicated and loyal adherent of a cause, compliance signifies "in a word, betrayal; betrayal of one's ideals and one's comrades." Such betrayal, says Shue, cannot "be counted as an escape" from torture because it constitutes a deep violation of personal integrity, of what Kant might call one's "humanity."[46]

Shue acknowledges that in the face of a profound threat and perfect knowledge that the person to be tortured can prevent disaster (his version of the ticking-bomb is a nuclear device poised to destroy the city of Paris with all its inhabitants and cultural artifacts), it would be right to torture. However, he concludes by rejecting this kind of quandary ethics, pointing out "how unlike the circumstances of an actual choice about torture the philosopher's example is."[47] In a 2006 article, Shue renounces his earlier support of torture even to prevent such a hypothetical disaster as the obliteration of Paris. He raises two objections to the ticking-bomb argument, which he calls "idealization" and "abstraction." Idealization, he says, is "the addition of positive features to an example in order to make the example better than reality, which lacks those features."[48] Allhoff's "epistemic certainty" that the person whom we propose to torture has, and will surrender, information necessary to defuse a ticking bomb is an example of such a positive feature. The ticking-bomb case simply does not exist in nature as it does in the laboratory of the ethicist's mind.

More important, in my view, is what Shue calls "abstraction." Here, rather than adding positive features like certainty and timeliness to the ticking-bomb scenario, we "delete" negative features whose presence would render it less ideal. Chief among these negative features is one of the key arguments of this book: Real-world torture is not an activity. It is a practice. It is not possible, Shue now argues, to torture effective only once or only once in a very rare while. Shue explains:

> For torture is a practice. Practitioners who do not practice will not be very good at what they do. Who are we imagining that they will

practice on? Practitioners without the best equipment will also not be very good. Where will they obtain their "cutting edge" equipment? How will they test it in order to be sure it will work when the catastrophe looms?

Shue concludes, "The moderate position on torture is an impractical abstraction—it is torture in dreamland."[49]

In a frequently quoted 2005 article, Princeton philosopher David Sussman extends the Kantian argument begun by Shue in 1978. Like Shue, Sussman is not prepared to rule out torture in every conceivable circumstance, but he does argue "that it bears an especially high burden of justification, greater in degree and different in kind from even that of killing." His approach is "broadly Kantian," but his argument transcends the Kantian objection to violating a person's "capacities for rational self-governance." There is a particular evil in torture, because it "forces its victim into the position of colluding against himself through his own affects and emotions, so that he experiences himself as simultaneously powerless and yet actively complicit in his own violation."[50]

Whereas Shue points to the enforced betrayal of comrades or cause as a source of torture's moral evil, for Sussman, the betrayal goes deeper still. In torture one is forced to substitute the torturer's will for one's own. The betrayal is of one's very self. "So construed, torture turns out to be not just an extreme form of cruelty, but the pre-eminent instance of forced self-betrayal." This is because "despite his conscious commitments, the victim experiences within himself a dialectic where some part of him serves as the eager agent of his tormentor. Even if," says Sussman, "the victim is not in a position to provide the information or denunciations wanted, he still finds a part of himself taking his torturer's side."[51] Sussman's point is that, to end the torment, the torture victim adopts the torturer's goals as his own, thus reshaping the victim's own will into the image of the torturer's will.

Sussman also rehearses a number of utilitarian objections to torture, touching on most of the points made by other authors quoted here. He argues that that while they are indeed legitimate in themselves, these utilitarian arguments against torture fail to capture "the moral significance of the social and intentional structure of the 'drama' that torture enacts." Here is where Sussman believes that Kantian moral theory can make a unique contribution to the discussion. The most "orthodox" Kantian objection is that torture violates the humanity or autonomy of the victim, by using her "as a mere means to purposes she does not or could not reasonably share."[52]

This, says Sussman, is part of the moral problem with torture but not the whole story. He introduces a second objection, which is that intense physical pain not only bends the victim's agency in directions that are the torturer's and not the victim's own, it actually annihilates, "if only temporarily or incompletely," that very agency by "crowding out every other aspect of his mental life." He proposes an extension of Kantian thought to argue that because pain is the product of the action of one's own body, to cause pain in one who has not consented to it is a unique kind of attack on human agency and dignity. As we have seen in Chapter 1, those who design tortures have seized on this aspect of the experience, seeking to design methods of amplifying the awareness that the torture is something the victim is doing to herself. This line from the CIA's 1963 KUBARK manual is worth repeating here: "It has been plausibly suggested that, whereas pain inflicted on a person from outside himself may actually focus or intensify his will to resist, his resistance is likelier to be sapped by pain which he seems to inflict upon himself."[53] Here Sussman is arguing, as has Elaine Scarry whom he quotes in this section, that in torture even pain that is inflicted "from outside" is perceived by the victim as something the victim's own body is doing to him or her.

"What is distinct about torture," Sussman continues, "is that it does not just traduce the value such dignity represents by treating its subject as a mere means. Rather torture, even in the 'best' case, involves a deliberate perversion of that very value, turning our dignity against itself." Thus torture causes the victim to become what Sussman calls "a moral abomination," that is, "a free and accountable agent whose freedom nevertheless belongs to the will of somebody else."[54] As we have also seen in Chapter 1, the CIA spent several decades studying techniques—both physical and psychological—designed to produce complete "regression" in victims precisely so that their wills might be reconstructed in conformity with the torturer's will.[55]

Amartya Sen addresses the issue of torture in the context of an effort to establish a basis for human rights claims in general. His purpose is to provide a foundation for the very concept of human rights and an adequate explanation of how such rights arise—including some more recently articulated, or "second generation," rights such as food security or health care. Sen argues that human rights are first "ethical demands."[56] These demands are related to underlying freedoms, the need to protect which gives rise to both perfect and imperfect obligations. He takes as his paradigmatic example the ethical duties associated with the human right not to be tortured, which he uses to explicate the difference between these two kinds of duties. It is in this context that Sen considers an issue that receives less attention than it deserves. What are the duties and responsibilities of people who become aware that torture is being practiced?

He argues that in general, *rights* that inhere in persons generate in other persons *duties* to preserve those rights. Like other human rights, "the human right of not being tortured springs from the importance of freedom from torture for all. But it includes, furthermore, an affirmation of the need for others to consider what they reasonably do to secure the freedom from torture for any person." The obligation is "obviously straightforward" for anyone planning to torture or already engaged in torture, "to wit, to refrain and desist. The demand," says Sen, "takes the clear form of what Immanuel Kant called a perfect obligation."

But others also have obligations in this context, which, although "imperfect," are still real. "The perfectly specified demand not to torture anyone is supplemented by the more general, and less exactly specified, requirement to consider ways and means through which torture can be prevented and then to decide what one should, thus, reasonably do." Sen's approach to the problem of torture is rare, in that he is concerned with the obligations of ordinary persons whose connection to torture is indirect—for example, citizens of a country known to be practicing torture—rather than with the moral quandaries faced by those with the power and authority to order torture or those who practice it directly.[57]

Sen provides no simple answers, but at the same time he does not consider it impossible to devise a reasonable adjudication of the imperfect obligation to confront torture that is ongoing. Such an imperfect obligation is one among many that a person inevitably must face. He does not intend, he says, to plunge us into "a pandemonium of practical reasoning. . . . To accept that one has a duty to consider many different types of actions is not an agreement to tie oneself up in hopeless knots." A number of parameters come into play, not least among them the likelihood of successful action. What is required is that one not ignore what one knows, that one "be willing to seriously *consider* what one should reasonably do."[58] And then, presumably, to do it.

The bioethicist and theologian Peter A. Clark, S. J. also addresses the question of the responsibility of those whose relationship to ongoing torture is less direct than that of torturers themselves. In a 2006 article, he takes up the question of the proper role of medical personnel in military interrogations, generally condemning those physicians who have assisted in, or turned a blind eye to, torture at U.S. detention centers. Clark argues that providing such assistance is as much a violation of Kant's categorical imperative never to treat persons as means to other ends as is torture itself. In referring to Abu Ghraib and Guantánamo, he says, "The detainees were used as means to an end in an attempt to gain results that would help win the war against terrorism. Human rights and the basic dignity and respect that every person deserves became the casualty."[59]

Equally important for Clark is his contention that medical involvement in torture represents a serious violation of the fundamental principle of beneficence, in that the "ethical duty of every medical professional is to maximize comfort and minimize pain and suffering." But doctors—and one might add psychologists—working in interrogation at U.S. detention centers have done the opposite. "These medical professionals," says Clark, "had direct knowledge that detainees had been abused, because they treated their burns, broken bones and other assorted injuries and then allowed these detainees to be placed back into harm's way."[60] It might be argued that for a military doctor to actually attempt to obstruct a detainee's further interrogation would require extraordinary courage—and might also have little chance of success. To this argument I imagine that Immanuel Kant would answer, as he does in the *Foundations of the Metaphysics of Morals,* that what matters is that they would have made an all-out effort:

> The good will is not good because of what it effects or accomplishes or because of its competence to achieve some intended end; it is good only because of its willing. . . . Even if it should happen that . . . this will should be wholly lacking in power to accomplish its purpose, and even if the greatest effort should not avail it to achieve anything of its end, and if there remained only the good will—not as a mere wish, but as the summoning of all the means in its power—it would sparkle like a jewel all by itself. . . . Usefulness or fruitlessness can neither diminish nor augment its worth.[61]

In addition to violating the principle of beneficence, says Clark, physician-assisted torture violates its corollary, that of nonmaleficence, which is perfectly stated in the words of the Hippocratic Oath: "First, do no harm." Physicians who assist in torture do so in violation of the oath. Finally, Clark addresses the problem of competing duties, articulated by some medical professionals who are also members of the military. He argues that the principle of justice, which he defines as recognizing "that each person should be treated fairly and equitably, and be given his or her due," trumps the duty to obey illegal or unjust orders. It seems fair to say, as Clark does, that this view has historic precedent; it underlay, for example, the judgments of Nazi doctors that were made at Nuremburg.[62]

Deontological Arguments Supporting Torture

In general then, the deontological arguments against torture appear to be quite straightforward applications of imperatives of duty, justice, and respect for humanity in self and others. Deontological arguments offered *in favor* of torture tend to be framed in the context of some version of the ticking-bomb case and the competing duties that arise in that context for the person who must decide whether to use torture. The most interesting of these argue for a decision in the affirmative, while attempting to retain a commitment to the idea that torture is a moral evil, even in this extreme case. These arguments differ from legal arguments like those of Dershowitz and Posner, which seek either ex ante or ex post legal justification for those who torture in extreme circumstances. Here what is sought for the torturer is not, or not only, legal justification but forgiveness. Two examples suffice to illustrate this current of thought.

A version of Michael Walzer's classic 1973 essay, "Politics and the Problem of Dirty Hands" appears in *Torture: A Collection*. Its argument combines deontological and consequentialist thought in an unusual way. It is deontological, in that it advocates that a political leader has a duty in some circumstances to dirty his own hands (and soul) to protect the hands and souls of those he or she leads. It is consequentialist in that such dirtying is undertaken to promote the well-being of the larger society.

Walzer draws on Weber and Machiavelli to make the point that the duty of a good politician includes a willingness, when necessary, to acquire "dirty hands." He reminds us of the distinction Weber makes in "Politics as a Vocation" between an "ethic of ultimate ends" and an "ethic of responsibility."[63] To take up his or her vocation, the politician, the great leader, must sacrifice any absolutist ethic in favor of one that accepts the responsibilities inherent in a position that permits the legitimate use of violence. This is a genuine, heroic, and "tragic" sacrifice, says Walzer. And it is the same sacrifice Machiavelli asks of the Prince, who must learn, if he is to be a good ruler, "how not to be good."[64]

Walzer offers two examples to illustrate his thesis. The first is a good, honest politician who must decide whether to make a deal with "an unscrupulous ward boss" involving the awarding of contracts for school construction in return for make-or-break electoral support. The second is a version of the ticking-bomb problem, set in the context of an anti-colonial war. In the first case, says Walzer, we want the politician to make the deal, "precisely" because he is the kind of politician who "has scruples about it." In the second case, a nonviolent anti-colonial leader who has taken advantage of chaos to seize power chooses to order the torture of a "captured rebel leader who knows or probably knows" the location of hidden bombs. He gives the order despite a firm belief that "torture is wrong, indeed abominable, not just sometimes, but always."[65]

Walzer's argument is that in these cases, and others like them, it is evident that the good politician must sometimes be willing to violate not only laws but moral principles—thus bearing personally the responsibility for an evil choice—while protecting the people from some greater evil. This, he says, is what "we" want in political leaders: the willingness to make wrong moral choices while acknowledging—at least to themselves—their wrongness, and perhaps repenting and doing penance in some way. The issue of dirty hands cannot be resolved through legal penalties; these will not even be enforced "against the sort of actor I am considering," says Walzer, "largely because he acts in an official capacity." In fact, if the actor does his or her work properly (e.g., in the case of the candidate who makes an illegal deal for votes), we will never know that a crime has been committed. So we are left to trust that the political leader who does evil to do good will work out his or her own proper punishment and expiation—or seek it from "the priest and the confessional."[66]

I believe that Michael Walzer is describing something very real: the fact that people in general, and political leaders in particular, often confront situations in which their duties compete or in which every choice results in profoundly painful outcomes for someone. And I agree with him and his interlocutors that in such situations, a refusal to choose is itself a choice and an abdication of responsibility that is itself culpable.

However, I think that something is missing from Walzer's characterization of the problem, and it is the same thing that I believe is also missing from most ethical discussions of torture. Walzer treats the decision to commit particular necessary "crimes" as if they were separable from the rest of the politician's life. "It is not the case," he says, that when the politician "does bad in order to do good he surrenders himself forever to the demon of politics. He commits a determinate crime, and he must pay a determinate penalty."[67] But anyone who has ever been involved in electoral politics will tell you that the deal for votes posited by Walzer cannot be severed from the rest of the politician's career. It will inevitably have further ramifications, not least of which will be the hold the ward boss now has over the politician because the boss knows the politician's secret.

Furthermore, and just as important, having made one deal, our politician with scruples may well find that similar deals must be made in the next election cycle, and it may well cost the politician less moral anguish to make that next deal, and the next. It would not be unreasonable to suppose that a disposition to accept such deals could become a moral habit. While Walzer acknowledges that we don't want our leaders to override moral rules "too quickly or too often," he certainly envisions them doing so repeatedly in the course of a life of political leadership.

This possibility is troubling when we consider Walzer's treatment of his second example—that of the anti-colonial leader who must decide whether to torture someone who only "probably" knows the location of possible bombs. Here Walzer's formulation deviates from the classic ticking-bomb case, in that he acknowledges that the certainty prescribed in other versions is unattainable. Indeed, this is part of the politician's challenge, the fact that "political action is so uncertain that politicians necessarily take moral as well as political risks, committing crimes that they only think ought to be committed." As we have seen, however, torture, like accepting graft illegal political favors, has its own logic, one that renders it a crime that is very difficult to commit only once and about which, in any particular instance, it becomes progressively easier to believe that it "ought to be committed" again.[68]

Jean Bethke Elshtain's essay in the same collection is a reflection on Walzer's meditation on dirty hands. She says that before "the watershed event of September 11, 2001," she was one of the many people who listed torture in the "category of 'never,'" because it had seemed unlikely to her until then that the United States would ever confront the kind of quandary "favored by moral theorists in their hypothetical musings on whether torture could ever be morally permitted." It is not clear to me whether Elshtain means to say, as so many have said, that September 11 "changed everything" or just that those terrible events led her to imagine for the first time situations in which torture might be justified.

In any case, the reference to September 11 appears a bit odd, because her version of the ticking-bomb problem involves a situation that might have happened at any time in this or any other country, at least since the invention of high explosives and timing devices. Someone has hidden a bomb scheduled to explode within an hour in one of several hundred elementary school buildings in a city. The local authorities have apprehended a "known member of a terrorist gang" (presumably the gang responsible for the bomb) and are "as close to one hundred percent certain as human beings can be in such circumstances" that he knows which building has the bomb. Like Allhoff, Elshtain believes this dilemma brings into relief the contrast between deontology and utilitarianism. While the deontologist clings to the Kantian principle of not using a person as a means to an end, the utilitarian says torture "the creep." So, asks Elshtain, "where do you stand? With Kant or with Bentham?"[69]

Elshtain replies that she would prefer to locate herself beside neither philosopher, looking instead to a Christian theological tradition that "is not primarily a deontological ethic." I would suggest, however, that the position Elshtain describes shares with orthodox deontology a commitment to duty—if not an understanding of how that duty is best discerned. Elshtain is referring here to what Christianity considers to be "the concrete responsibility of neighbor-love and neighbor-regard." But where does that responsibility lie in this case? With the "innocent" children or the—presumably guilty—prisoner? Elshtain proposes to use the Roman Catholic tradition of casuistry to discern the answer to this question. One begins with a moral guideline in the form of a rule and follows that rule, unless an unanticipated situation arises in which the consequences of clinging to the rule are "so dire" that one must make the "least bad" choice of overriding the rule in this rare case.[70] Elshtain suggests that the reader ask him- or herself who he or she would want to be making the decision about whether to torture the prisoner: a leader who values his or her own conscience and moral "purity" over the lives of hundreds of children or one who refuses to become "complicit" in their deaths?

For Elshtain, the answer is obvious; the responsibility of Christian love and concern for one's neighbor demands that the leader order the torture. Elshtain maintains that although the leader ought to order torture, torture itself remains wrong. "Remember," she says, "the political leader who has approved torture as a way to elicit information that may save the lives of hundreds of children does *not* thereby sanction or normalize torture."[71]

Note that in both Walzer's and Elshtain's formulation of the ticking-bomb dilemma, the leader "orders" the torture done; the leader does not literally dirty his or her own hands with the prisoner's blood. I would suggest that there is at least one other "neighbor" and probably several, to be taken into consideration here—those who carry out the torture ordered by the leader and who must live with the same stains on their consciences. Nor is this an inconsequential detail; both Walzer and Elshtain have presented the moral problem of torture as the tragic drama of an individual leader with the power and authority to make the torture happen. But torture does not "happen" by itself. It is done by human beings who are themselves moral agents, not levers and cogs, and who, if they are to get the job done within that precious hour, must have the necessary training, skill, and institutional infrastructure. The willingness to torture *in extremis* presupposes the preparations necessary to be in a position to do so should the need arise: the availability of an appropriate location, the necessary equipment, and previously trained torturers.

Other Ethical Approaches

Utilitarianism and deontology do not of course exhaust the store of available ethical methods. Let us look at a few other approaches, both secular and theological.

Michael Ignatieff adopts a position that is fairly similar to those of Walzer and Elshtain in *The Lesser Evil: Political Ethics in an Age of Terror*, published in 2004. What differentiates Ignatieff from the other two is that he approaches the question of torture as part of the general problem of how a liberal democracy ought to balance the sometimes competing demands of liberty and security in a time when terrorism is common. Thus, as the subtitle of his book suggests, his interest is in political rather than personal ethics. He argues that both utilitarian and deontological approaches are essential to maintaining a democratic society, but that "neither a morality of consequences nor a morality of dignity can be allowed exclusive domain in public policy decisions." His alternative is a "lesser evil morality," one that refuses to privilege any of three goods—rights, dignity, and public safety—above the other two. In fact, he says, it is precisely "privileging one to the exclusion of the others—that produces moral error." In cases of terrorist emergency, says Ignatieff, all of these concerns "must be weighed in the balance equally," and none should automatically "trump" the others. "This," he says, "is an ethics of prudence rather than first principles," whether utilitarian or deontological.[72]

Perhaps surprisingly, this prudential ethics produces for Ignatieff an explicit answer to the question of whether a liberal democracy should permit torture. His answer is a fairly unequivocal "No." Not only is torture wrong for all the reasons of human dignity advanced by deontologists but also because "liberal democracy's very history and identity is tied up with an absolute prohibition of torture."[73] Furthermore, Ignatieff recognizes the long-term effects of torture both on victim and torturer. Part of the value of an absolute prohibition is that it "relieves a state's public servants from the burden of making intolerable choices, ones that inflict irremediable harm both on our enemies and on themselves, on those charged with our defense."[74]

But Ignatieff's absolute prohibition comes at a price; only "the deliberate infliction of physical cruelty and pain" counts as torture. All the psychological techniques whose profound and enduring effects are described in Chapter 1 Ignatieff prefers to name "coercion." If interrogations of prisoners "include nothing worse than sleep deprivation, permanent light or permanent darkness, disorienting noise, and isolation" then "there might be a lesser evil justification for it."[75] Given the deontological basis of Ignatieff's prohibition on torture, it is not unreasonable to suppose that if he understood the devastating physiological and psychological effects of such treatment, he might change his mind.

In the pursuit of an ethics of the lesser evil, Ignatieff counsels his readers to keep their eyes on the prize, which, he says, "is preserving the identity of liberal society itself and preventing it from becoming what terrorists believe it to be." "Terrorists," he says, "seek to strip off the mask of law to reveal the nihilist heart of coercion within, and we have to show ourselves and the populations whose loyalty we seek that the rule of law is not a mask but the true image of our nation."[76] If one accepts the premise—that the rule of law is the true image of our nation—Ignatieff's conclusions would seem to follow. (One might argue, however, that the characterization of the United States as unwaveringly devoted to the rule of law is at the very least overstated. From its inception and certainly over the eight years of the George W. Bush administration, any "true image" of the United States would have to have include, if not a heart, at least a fist or two of coercion.)

Sumner B. Twiss, Florida State University's Distinguished Professor of Human Rights, Ethics, and Religion, has written extensively on issues of human rights and international human rights law. In "Torture, Justification, and Human Rights: Toward an Absolute Proscription," he seeks a grounding for a universal proscription on torture that takes into account the problem of cultural relativism. "This approach," he says, "involves elements of moral intuitionism, a minimal natural law position, and consequentialist arguments that ought—taken together or independently—to be convincing to all people of good will, regardless of their cultural location."[77] Although Twiss does not stress this point, it would seem that to be successful, such an approach could not, like Ignatieff's, rest on appeals to the values of liberal democratic states alone.

Twiss is inspired in part by a 1966 article in which Philip L. Quinn suggests a "divide and conquer approach" to the problem that no society seems willing to impose an absolute ban on torture—at least in the case of a ticking-bomb emergency. Twiss takes up Quinn's challenge in the hope that, while no single argument will convince everyone or every society, for all persons there exists *some* argument that will do the job.[78]

In considering likely candidates for grounding an absolute ban, Twiss reexamines the first and fourth articles of the 1948 Universal Declaration of Human Rights and the conversations that attended their drafting. In considering the wording of Article 1 ("All human beings are born free and equal in dignity and rights. They are endowed with reason and conscience and should act towards one another in a spirit of brotherhood."), he observes that the drafters made reference to prelogical, "practical moral apprehensions, apperceptions, or convictions shared by people belonging to diverse, even somewhat antagonistic, moral traditions."[79] In addition to this implicit moral intuitionism, Twiss also finds "a very spare natural law position," which holds that human beings share a common nature that makes the "protections and conditions" described in the Declaration "good for us." This despite the fact that the framers of the Universal Declaration rejected any "Thomistic" appeal to a Christian natural law, which could not be embraced by all nations.

In the section of his paper entitled "Towards an Absolute Proscription," Twiss argues that there is now more empirical evidence available than there was in 1948 about the permanent, personality-annihilating effects that torture has on its victims. As a result, subsequent treaties have included language that makes it clear that no exceptional circumstances—such as war or insurrection—may be invoked to justify torture:

> It is now known that the harm for the victim of torture, no matter the length of time it is administered, is both severe and permanent. The harms include not only permanent physical injury and disability (what we usually think of) but also chronic anxiety, inability to trust others, subsequent deliberate self-injury, violent behavior toward

others, substance abuse, depression (often leading to suicide), paranoia, severe insomnia, uncontrollable nightmares and flashbacks,
self-loathing, psychosomatic illness, shortened life-span, permanent
alterations of brain patterns, and so the list continues. The empirical
evidence is overwhelming that for most survivors of torture, the rest
of their lives is a sort of living death.[80]

Twiss argues that this new understanding gives rise to two justifications for
an absolute prohibition of torture. One is based on a deepening of the initial
"moral intuition" that torture is wrong. Such newly "informed reflection, to
put it this way, so deepens and extends the primary moral intuition about torture that it converts it into an intuition that torture is always wrong." The same
"considerations" also strengthen consequentialist arguments on the grounds
that we now understand "that the harmful consequences for the victims of torture (and in the aggregate they number in the hundreds of thousands) by far
outweigh whatever benefits government elites may derive from the use of such
practices to hang onto their positions of political power."[81]

More is now known, Twiss continues, about the effects of torture on the
familial, friendship, and social networks of the tortured and on the society in
general where institutional torture is practiced. These effects are revealed, he
says, in "well-documented case studies and empirical data that the torture of
primary victims inflicts extreme hardship and trauma on the victims' relatives
and does serious long-term damage to family relationships, in addition to im-
posing devastating effects on the wider community, not only fomenting hatred
and spirals of violence, but also resulting in the breakdown of civilian institutions amounting to a kind of collective trauma for the entire community."[82]

Torture does further damage to a society, he argues, in that its systematic
use "in any society makes that society morally and historically dysfunctional."
This, he continues, is because "such torture is invariably accompanied by vigorous public government denial of its use," which produces a "false history" in
the society where it takes place. These systematic social damages of torture,
says Twiss, deepen both the initial moral intuition that torture is wrong and
shore up the "ancillary" consequentialist argument against torture.[83]

Twiss then considers the large body of evidence that institutionalized torture "has a tendency to metastasize and spread into ever more horrorific [sic]
forms, even when there are supposed countervailing checks internal to a society and its subcultures. Moreover," he says, "practices of torture also tend to
become routinized—to become routine administrative procedure—whatever
its specific type." Not only does torture spread—as is demonstrated in the
recent history of metastasis of U.S. torture techniques from Bagram to Guantánamo to Abu Ghraib—but "interrogational" torture often slips into "punitive"

torture and even displays "an irreversible tendency" to devolve into what Twiss calls "recreational" torture, torture for fun.[84] We have certainly seen evidence of this in the photographs of gleeful torturers that emerged from Abu Ghraib.

People know intuitively that "recreational" torture—torture performed on an unwilling victim for the enjoyment of the torturer—is "transparently" wrong. Hence, argues Twiss, it follows that insofar as institutional torture has an "irreversible tendency" to produce torture for fun and we know that torture for fun is absolutely wrong, "this particular intuition is so strong and obvious that anything inevitably leading to its violation, especially on a routine basis, must itself be co-implicated as wrong." Therefore, Twiss states, "we have an intuitionally grounded case for an absolute prohibition of torture."[85]

Twiss concludes that his three-part argument (moral intuition, natural law, and consequentialism) is sufficient to convince all persons of good will that torture ought to be absolutely prohibited. He summarizes his several reasons. First, a fuller understanding of what torture is deepens the original moral intuition that it is wrong, an intuition that underlay the prohibition included in the Universal Declaration of Human Rights. Second, if that is not enough, the consequentialist argument becomes much more compelling once the full consequences of torture are understood. Third, these arguments are founded on "empirically based unshakable premises" about the reality of torture. These premises are not hypotheses. They are established "facts" that "are not going to be overturned by new studies." Finally he refers to his own and other cross-cultural comparisons of ethical systems to reach the inductive conclusion that "the world's moral systems all include prohibitions of assault on the innocent, defenseless, and vulnerable as a kind of moral primitive." Because this "intuition" appears to be universal, Twiss is convinced that the convergence of the two streams of reasoning—intuitional and consequentialist—have already produced a Rawlsian-style "overlapping consensus" for an absolute prohibition.[86]

In an epilogue, Twiss briefly—and devastatingly—addresses the ticking-bomb problem, arguing that the scenario presented is so unrealistic, that "rather than sharpening our moral intuitions about the wrongness of torture, it tends to dim or otherwise obscure them by injecting fear and anxiety into the equation." Furthermore, by focusing our attention on fictional scenarios, it "deflects" us from recognizing the real and "well-known facts about the nature of torture, its tendency to slide into ever worse forms, and its tendency to grow."[87]

There is much to admire in this article, which is why I have treated it at some length. In particular, I respect Twiss's insistence on the observable fact that state torture is an expanding and enduring institutionalized practice, rather than an isolated and isolatable episode.

Theological Approaches

Rabbi Edward Feld serves as rabbi-in-residence at New York's Jewish Theological Seminary. He is also the North America director of Rabbis for Human Rights. In a 2006 article that probably originated as a Sabbath sermon, he draws on two parts of Jewish scriptural tradition, the Torah and the Mishnah, to address the ethical problem of torture. In this context he reprises many of the arguments described above: that torture is an attempt to "take away" a person's will, that when we torture people, "we want them to betray themselves, to betray what they most believe in, to betray what they hold sacred, to betray their own sense of honor."[88]

Feld observes that the version of the Decalogue (the Ten Commandments) found in Deuteronomy closes by reminding the Jews that they were once slaves in Egypt. Thus, one purpose of the Sabbath is to remind us of what it is to be a slave, to be a person without power. Jews are commanded to keep the Sabbath not only by refraining from work ourselves, but by providing rest for everyone, even the least powerful among us. Thus we understand that the command to remember the Sabbath is a command to remember the value of every person.

Furthermore, to observe the Sabbath teaches us that we may not always do exactly as we desire. "Indeed," says Feld, "the Jewish commitment to law is fundamentally based on an understanding of the need for limits." And those limits involve our response and responsibility to the other, as Emmanuel Lévinas has suggested. "Lévinas argues that all of Jewish religious law is a way of channeling our raw emotions and directing us toward an appreciation of otherness." Such an appreciation does not allow for torturing the other.

Feld also reminds us that the Sabbath is a memorial of the creation of the world. He quotes a passage from the Mishnah, which I find strikingly modern in its insistence on the unique value of each human being:

> Why was Adam created singly: to teach you that if anyone destroys one soul, scripture considers it as if a whole world was destroyed, and if anyone save a person's life then scripture considers it as if a whole world was maintained. Also, for the sake of peace between peoples, that no person could say my ancestry is greater than yours and so that no one should say that there is more than one creator.
>
> How great is the Holy One, for a person creates many coins from the same mold and they are all similar to each other, but the sovereign of the universe, the Holy One forms each human in the mold of that first person but no human being is like another. Therefore every human being must say: the world was created for me.[89]

The context of this portion of the Mishnah, says Feld, is the warning a court should give to witnesses in a capital case, to remind them that the person on trial is, like the witnesses, an image of the Holy One, one for whom the world was created. The honor due the human being, says Feld, extends beyond the soul to the very body, even the executed body of a convicted criminal. "What the rabbis of the midrash and the Mishnah formulated were behaviors that would honor human beings in both body and spirit. They defined this as a principle of Jewish law: *kavod habriot*, the need to honor all living beings. What torture seeks to do," Feld says, "is the opposite of the application of this principle. Rather than honoring the prisoner as a fellow human being, the prisoner is to be broken, and the means to do this is the infliction of pain and degradation."[90]

Feld concludes his essay by reminding his listeners that human beings are asked to look into the face of the other and to recognize there the face of God, "even in the person you suspect of being your enemy, even in the face of the criminal."

William Cavanaugh is best known for his 1998 book *Torture and Eucharist: Theology, Politics, and the Body of Christ,* which chronicles the role of the Roman Catholic church in Pinochet's Chile. In it he argues that whereas the Eucharist constitutes and reconstitutes the body of Christ, which is composed of the people living together in solidarity, torture does the opposite. Torture attacks the body of Christ and the social bodies that comprise it by attacking the individual bodies of human beings.

In a more recent article, Cavanaugh speaks of another aspect of torture, its capacity for the "production" of enemies. The Eucharistic liturgy both reminds Christians of, and enacts in the moment, a certain narrative about who they are: they are living members of the body of Christ. Torture also serves, says Cavanaugh, a quasi-liturgical purpose. It imposes a different narrative on human beings, not one of their own making. "Torture, in other words, is the most acute example of the ability of the state to impose its narrative on an individual." But this imposition does not end with that one person's body. "Torture is a social, one might say 'liturgical,' enactment of the imaginative power of the state."[91]

The liturgy of the Eucharist rehearses a narrative in which the communicants represent a single body, and in the process it recreates that body. Torture, says Cavanaugh, operates in a similar way. "Torture is both a product and a reinforcement of a certain story about who 'we' are and who 'our' enemies are." In the process, the very meaning of the state is created and imposed on the people. Thus, "the state is not just the agent of torture but the effect of torture as well."[92]

Cavanaugh believes that both defenders and opponents of torture accept too readily as fact the contention that most torture is designed to extract information. This, he says, is the fallacy that lies behind the ticking-bomb scenario and various other utilitarian arguments for or against torture. He reminds us that "torture victims tell of finally relinquishing a piece of information after withstanding days of brutal treatment, only to be told by their interrogators, 'We already knew.' "[93]

The main function of torture, says Cavanaugh, is to alter the imaginations of the people—first, by inducing fear and, second, by constructing enemies. Speaking of Chile under Pinochet, he says, "The regime desperately needed the monstrous enemies its propaganda spoke of, and such enemies were produced largely in the torture chamber." In other words, torture produced false confessions of terrible evil and corruption, thus justifying the regime.[94]

Cavanaugh acknowledges the differences between Chile under Pinochet and the present-day United States, allowing that "neither the United States nor US-occupied Iraq is the same kind of authoritarian regime imposed in Chile under Pinochet." People in this country are not generally afraid to speak, nor is "direct government reprisal . . . yet a significant concern for most." Nevertheless, says Cavanaugh, the U.S. government "constantly" works to keep its people afraid. In this case, "it is not the fear of the state but of the enemies of the state against whom the state protects us." This is an important point; Cavanaugh asserts that the torture conducted by the United States would not have its intended effect if the citizens of this country did not know it was happening. In other words, knowing that the government is willing to do something as extreme as torture reminds U.S. citizens that they are in serious danger from which the government alone can save them.[95] Thus, torture plays an important role in what Cavanaugh calls a "theater of fear."

There is another, somewhat more benign "theater of fear" that Americans attend every time they fly. This is the security check ritual—liturgical in its ordered, predictable stages, with its proper actions performed in the proper order and manner. Flyers, who are both actors and audience, experience the long, snaking line, the removal of the shoes and jacket, the emptying of the pockets, the careful presentation of tubes and bottles in their one-quart Ziploc bag. The whole performance is constructed to convince travelers both that they should be afraid and that the government will save them from their enemies.

Torture is also justified by describing its targets as less than human (the Pinochet regime called their victims "humanoids," to distinguish them from "real" human beings). Today's "terrorists" serve a similar role. Cavanaugh argues that torture does more than turn human beings into monsters in the public imagination. "It also helps to *create* the enemies that we need," by forcing people to play the role of degraded, filthy creatures, as happened at Abu Ghraib, where prisoners were captured in photographic tableaux that presented them as "depraved sub-humans." Thus, "the imagination of the war on terror is inscribed on their bodies in a kind of ritual drama, or antiliturgy."[96]

Indeed, there are several photos from Abu Ghraib that appear to anyone familiar with Christian iconography like images of a "degraded, filthy" cruci- fied Christ. One is the famous picture (described in the previous chapter) of the hooded, blanket-covered man standing with arms outstretched on a box of soldiers' rations. Another less familiar series of photos illustrates Cavanaugh's "antiliturgy" even more explicitly. We see a naked prisoner in a wide hallway separating rows of cells. He stands upright, arms outstretched, head thrown back, one foot behind the other, obviously posed by someone else. In the back- ground a smiling soldier holds a baton. The prisoner could easily be a sculptor's model for a crucifix—except for the fact that his body is covered in what ap- pears to be human excrement.

It is striking that the image created in this "ritual drama" is faithful to biblical descriptions of Jesus' crucifixion, down to the presence of a laughing soldier. It is ironic that the laughing soldier is Sgt. Charles Graner, leader of the Army torturers at Abu Ghraib, a man who pointedly describes himself as a Chris- tian.[97] Of course, crucifixion as the Romans practiced it was itself a torturous death, one reserved for slaves, rebels, and other "depraved sub-humans." And like modern torture, crucifixion signaled to the people who observed it the degraded and filthy nature of the one who was crucified. This degradation is what Paul refers to with mingled horror and wonder in Philippians 2:8, where he speaks of Jesus as "obedient to death, even death on a cross."

For Cavanaugh, the use of torture in the "global war on terror" serves not so much in the destruction of enemies as in their "production." It is part of a grand narrative of "a clash of civilizations, of progress and democracy versus archaic oppression, of the beacon of freedom and light versus those who hate our freedoms, of all that is good versus an implacable evil, of Captain America versus the humanoids." Such an undertaking requires a clean division in the public imagination between friends and enemies, leaving no middle ground between those who are with us and those against us. "Torture," says Cavana- ugh, represents "this drama of friend and enemy brought to its most height- ened realization."[98]

In what appears to be a challenge to views of torture such as Walzer's and Elshtain's, Cavanaugh points out that "torturers sometimes imagine their acts as a kind of self-sacrifice on their part: 'What terrible things I must do in order to defend my beloved people!'" It is a dirty business, the reasoning goes, "and those who 'take the gloves off' and 'get their hands dirty' do so for a higher moral purpose." Cavanaugh does not say it, but one might even imagine the good politician who tortures as a sort of inverted Christ figure. Rather than an innocent person whose sacrifice redeems the guilty, we have a guilty figure whose sacrifice protects the innocent. The torturers, Cavanaugh continues, justify their actions on the grounds that only the most terrible threat could have driven such good people to such extreme action. Thus torture—because it represents a terrible sacrifice on the part of the *torturer*—is "invested with high moral seriousness." Furthermore, "only the most morally righteous nation could be trusted with the capacity to use torture for a good purpose."[99]

In the next section, Cavanaugh addresses similarities that he observes between American and Chilean exceptionalisms, the belief that the uniquely important virtues of the nation justify whatever might be necessary to protect it. He points out that, as Chile did under Pinochet, the United States today engages in what he calls a "striptease of power," in which torture is simultaneously denied and revealed:

> On the one hand, denying that we torture is crucial to maintaining the imagination of the United States as morally exceptional. On the other hand, retaining the prerogative to torture is essential for maintaining the imagination of the American nation-state as protector from the subhuman forces that threaten us. The drama of torture must never be played out on a fully public stage. At the same time, the widespread imagination of torture is important for fostering both the dire sense of emergency and exception in which we live and the sense that the state will do whatever is necessary to protect us from the threat it helped create.[100]

Cavanaugh's references to a "theater of fear" and a "striptease of power" raise an important question: To what extent has the U.S. government intentionally orchestrated the various disclosures of detainee mistreatment?[101] This question is not an easy one to answer. For one thing, a government is not a monolithic entity. Any government is composed of people with competing personal and institutional interests. This is perhaps even more true when some of those people must periodically stand for election. But even an explicitly authoritarian regime will contain conflicts and tensions, no matter how much it may strive to present a single face to its citizens.

The history of U.S. torture in the last decade is a good example of a government's lack of uniformity. Even within the executive branch, we have heard public differences of opinion about acceptable "interrogation" methods, differences between the CIA and the armed forces, between the presidency and some members of congress, between the presidency and the judiciary, and between the civilian leadership of the Department of Defense and the armed forces.

Government positions also change over time. I expect that the Bush administration was less than pleased when the photographs from Abu Ghraib first became public in 2004. (For one thing, to the naïve observer they looked, as many commentators have observed, like something out of the 1950s television show *Amateur Hour*.) The Bush administration sought simultaneously to downplay the photos' importance and to distance itself from responsibility for what they showed. However, three years later, when stories about the CIA's use of waterboarding began to appear in the press, the administration took a different stance. Waterboarding was indeed important; it was a serious and necessary means of protecting the American people. (It was not, of course, torture.)

It is fair to say that the Bush administration never publically announced (or admitted) that it was torturing people. In fact, there is evidence that at least one government agency, the CIA, even destroyed videotapes of some of its interrogation sessions, ostensibly "to protect the identities of CIA employees who appear on them." (Whether such protection was to be from enemy attack or prosecution remains unclear.)[102] However, top-level administration officials, including then-President Bush and Vice President Cheney, robustly and publicly embraced the methods used at Guantánamo and in CIA black sites as necessary measures taken to protect the nation.

My answer to the question posed above is not a simple one. I think that outside the United States, knowledge about the torture of detainees in the "war on terror" was expected to serve its usual purpose of terrifying potential enemies. To that extent, the U.S. government was happy for information about what was happening in Abu Ghraib, Bagram, or Guantánamo to make its way into the world. Inside this country, things were more complicated. Some government officials had personal motives (such as fear of prosecution) for keeping torture a secret; others may have welcomed the release of some details as a means of reminding Americans of the lengths to which they were going to protect us. I suspect that the answer is different for each individual revelation. In a sense, however, it doesn't matter whether government officials consciously set out to reveal specific details of its activities. Power need not always be exercised intentionally to have its effects. Regardless of the complex of motivations surrounding each disclosure about the treatment of detainees, the result has been the "striptease of power" that Cavanaugh describes.

Cavanaugh concludes his 2006 article with a theological call to Christians to deny, by an open resistance to torture, that we live in "exceptional" times, to step out of the "theater of fear" and "create spaces to live in God's imagination" rather than in our own tortured nightmares.

It seems appropriate to end this section of the chapter with Cavanaugh's contribution; it was his *Torture and Eucharist* that first led me to think about torture as an extended practice that helps to shape the people by and among whom it is practiced. In the previous pages, I have explored the recent academic literature on the ethics of torture. I have observed that those who argue that torture is sometimes morally justified—whether their arguments are consequentialist, deontological, or a combination of the two—generally do so in the context of some version of the hypothetical case of the ticking bomb. Those who argue for an absolute prohibition however—and who are often accused of being unrealistic—are in fact more likely than their opponents to examine torture empirically, rather than as a hypothetical puzzle to be solved.

One similarity stands out in almost all these academic arguments about torture: They treat it as if it were an isolated episode—a rare, perhaps even unique, event in the life of an individual or a nation. In the following chapters, I shall argue that this is an inaccurate view of torture. Torture is not a discrete *action* that can be judged by itself—whether by evaluating its consequences or by examining its adherence to duty and respect for human dignity. Torture is a continuing, socially embedded *practice*. It has its own history and traditions, its own culture and rituals of initiation, its own goods and evils, its own virtues and vices.

Torture on the Editorial Pages

Academics are not the only people who argue about torture. Those arguments can be observed in many aspects of contemporary culture. Implicit arguments abound, in places as diverse as Gary Trudeau's comic strip *Doonesbury* and the Fox television show *24*. Explicit arguments have appeared in online news sites, in individual blogs, and in a variety of other Internet venues. An extensive examination of how these sources treat torture in the post-9/11 period is an important piece of research that remains to be done. It is, however, beyond the scope of this book.

I have chosen to focus instead on one particular nonacademic locus of explicit argument about the ethics of torture—the editorial pages of daily newspapers. While the physical form of the daily newspaper may be shrinking, editorial pages still serve as a reliable barometer of opinion among various segments of the political class in this country. I have chosen two nationally read newspapers, the generally liberal *New York Times* and the conservative *Wall Street Journal*.

I examined the 158 unsigned editorials dealing with torture published by these two papers from the day after the attacks of September 11, 2001 through February 2009. Of these, 121 appeared in the *Times* and 37 in the *Journal*. That the *Times* published more than three times as many editorials about torture as the *Journal* is not perhaps surprising; from the *Journal's* point of view, there was nothing to write about. Twenty-nine of their editorials contain explicit language to the effect that none of the abuse experienced by prisoners held by the United States in the "war on terror" has constituted torture. For example, a

June 6, 2004 editorial reads in part, "The latest hubbub concerns a December 2002 list of interrogation techniques approved by Defense Secretary Donald Rumsfeld for prisoners at Guantanamo Bay and similar to those used at Abu Ghraib. They include forcing prisoners to stand for a maximum of four hours, the use of hoods, and quizzing them in 20-hour stretches. These 'stress positions,' as they're called, aren't torture either." If torture is occurring, the *Journal* jokes in the same piece, the victim is the Bush administration:

> The subject of Wednesday's Senate hearing was the "torture" memos produced by the Justice Department early in 2002 and used as the basis for a Defense Department report a year later. The government hasn't released these private communications, but they have been leaking out in dribs and drabs in a kind of Beltway political torture.

On May 5, 2004, a few days after the pictures from Abu Ghraib appeared in public, the *Times,* by contrast, describes the abuses there as something that "any reasonable person would view as torture" and chastises Secretary of Defense Donald Rumsfeld for clinging "to euphemisms." The paper repeatedly takes similar positions on revelations of the mistreatment of U.S.-held prisoners in Afghanistan, Guantánamo, and in secret CIA prisons.

What ethical approaches do we find embedded in these editorials? A content analysis suggests that consequentialist arguments predominate in both newspapers—although the actual arguments presented in each are very different. I choose the term "consequentialist" rather than "utilitarian" in this context, because both papers make arguments about torture (or in the case of the *Journal* "aggressive interrogation") based on its potential consequences for the United States. But neither paper makes the more general utilitarian appeal to the ethical requirement to bring about the greatest good for the greatest number, regardless of nationality or location.

Eighteen of the *Times* editorials raise the clearly consequentialist concern that U.S. violations of detainees' rights or of the Geneva Conventions places U.S. soldiers at risk of retaliatory actions, should they be captured. Here, for example, is the *Times* on August 30, 2007:

> The need to be honest about Abu Ghraib and correct the abuses at military and C.I.A. prisons is not only about upholding the law and American values. It is about the safety of American soldiers. Every right the United States denies to its detainees may one day be denied to Americans captured in wartime. Every abuse the United States visits on detainees increases the risk of American soldiers being abused in foreign prisons.

The *Journal*, conversely, focuses on the consequentialist demands of "protecting a free society that believes in the rule of law from terrorists who believe in neither," as a June 25, 2004 editorial puts it in a phrase that recurs frequently in its editorials. It is important to note that the *Journal*'s justifications for "aggressive questioning" extend beyond the protection of U.S. citizens from imminent terrorist attack to the gathering of "actionable intelligence" for use on the battlefield in Iraq. Acknowledging that regular combatants would be protected by the Geneva Conventions, the *Journal* argues that such protections do not extend to Iraqi detainees held at Abu Ghraib. "In other words," they contend, "the Geneva Conventions do not speak specifically to the interrogation treatment of non-uniformed Baathist or jihadi guerrillas detained in connection with attacks on U.S. forces or Iraqi civilians." The real danger, they say, "is that all of this [revelation about Abu Ghraib abuses] will result in the collection of less actionable intelligence to stop the roadside bombs and mortar attacks that are killing American soldiers and Iraqi civilians."

It is worth noting that the editorials appearing in both papers differ from the academic writing on torture reviewed in this chapter in an important way: In most cases they do not ask whether torture is morally permissible. They assume that, with the exception of the ticking-bomb case, it is not.[103] Where the two papers differ is in their definition of torture. The *Times* repeatedly refers to methods such as stress positions, hooding, isolation, and exposure to extremes of heat and cold as torture. The *Journal,* although it acknowledges in a September 21, 2006 editorial that the Canadian Maher Arar "actually appears to have been tortured" when the CIA "rendered" him to Syria, does not consider the same treatment—beatings, isolation, and sensory deprivation—torture when applied to detainees in U.S. custody. "Opponents of interrogating al Qaeda detainees," they say in the same editorial, "keep slandering the Bush Administration by equating all aggressive questioning techniques with 'torture.'" In a September 8, 2006 editorial defending "aggressive questioning aimed at saving [U.S.] lives," the *Journal* offers a partial definition of torture, one it asserts is shared by "most people": Torture in this understanding is defined by the infliction of "grievous bodily harm," but *only* if it is meted out as "punishment or retribution" and not, apparently, in the course of interrogations.

Almost every year from 2001 through 2008 an increasing number of *Times* editorials warn about the threat that torture, and the institutional apparatus supporting it, might represent to the rule of law and democracy. One such editorial about the rule of law appeared in 2001 and two in 2003. In 2008 the *Times* addressed this theme twenty-four times—about twice a month. Table 3.1 illustrates this development:

Table 3.1 **New York Times Editorials Warning of Dangers of U.S. Torture**
Apparatus

	To Rule of Law	*To Democracy*
2001	1	0
2002	0	1
2003	2	0
2004	10	4
2005	18	4
2006	15	5
2007	22	5
2008	24	6
Total	**93**	**25**

The *Times* refers thirty-eight times to its concern about damage to the international image of the United States as a result of revelations of prisoner abuse.
The trajectory of these editorials is a sad one. For the first few years, the concern expressed is that events like those at Abu Ghraib present an inaccurate
reflection of the "real" United States but one that will be embraced by many
around the world and used by its adversaries for their own purposes. Thus,
an editorial appearing on May 1, 2004, a few days after the pictures from Abu
Ghraib became public, suggests that the abuse "hands America's enemies in
and out of Iraq a gratuitous propaganda victory at the worst possible moment."
Six days later we read: "The abuses in Abu Ghraib and throughout the military detention system stain this country's reputation and play into Osama bin
Laden's portrait of an evil America. The Bush administration has given a gift
to Al Qaeda's worldwide recruitment efforts." But by December of the same
year, the *Times* is speaking of damage to "American values" and not only to
"America's image."

By 2007, we see a real shift. The lament about the damage to the image of the
United States in the world has become a tacit admission that this image reflects
a genuine, demoralized reality. On March 1, 2007 the *Times* says of José Padilla, who was brutalized and held in complete isolation in a darkened cell for
over three years, "We will probably never know if Mr. Padilla was a would-be
terrorist. So far, this trial has been a reminder of how Mr. Bush's policy on prisoners has compromised the judicial process. And it has confirmed the world's
suspicions of the United States' stooping to the very behavior it once stood
against."

Again, in a June 6, 2007 editorial demanding the closing of the detention camp at Guantánamo (one of many such pieces), the editors write that such a closure is the only "path likely to lead to a result that would allow Americans to once again hold their heads high when it comes to justice and human rights." Again on December 31, 2007, looking toward the 2008 presidential election, the editors say, "We can only hope that this time, unlike 2004, American voters will have the wisdom to grant the awesome powers of the presidency to someone who has the integrity, principle and decency to use them honorably. Then when we look in the mirror as a nation, we will see, once again, the reflection of the United States of America." And on March 8, 2008, the *Times* wonders if the United States has broken in a grave way with the intentions of its founders. "The founding fathers," the *Times* says, "knew that when you dispensed with the rule of law, the inevitable outcome was injustice. Now America is becoming the thing they sought to end."

Of the two papers, only the *New York Times* regularly makes arguments that one might call deontological, but unlike those reviewed in the section above on academic writing, these are not arguments for the general wrongness of torture. For the most part they concern the specific duty of the United States to abide by treaties to which it is signatory, especially the Geneva Conventions, and of U.S. officials, both legislative and executive, to abide by U.S. law.

The *Times* alone addresses the moral duties of the general U.S. public in the face of revelations of torture, observing that "the broad outlines of this disaster have long been visible." This, they suggest, "is shocking in itself," as is "the fact that average citizens have not risen up to demand that these abuses come to an end."

The *Wall Street Journal*, however, appears hostile to any form of moral argumentation that is not in some way consequentialist. On several occasions it decries both "moralizing" and the "moralists" who do it. The *Journal* closes a June 11, 2004 editorial about interrogation methods at Guantánamo and Abu Ghraib with the observation that "we sure wish the moralizing critics would keep in mind that this is also a debate over how to protect the United States." Six months later, another editorial denounces the "hypocrisy" of "torture moralists" who by opposing waterboarding refuse to "admit that protecting Americans takes more than denouncing 'torture' at the top of one's lungs."[104] Of course, the *Journal* is itself arguing a moral position, but it is one that judges actions based on whether they produce the outcomes that the editors desire and thus, in their view, is a piece of grown-up realism, rather than puerile "morality."

To the extent that the *Journal* addresses moral issues in the context of duty, these revolve around the nation's duty to protect CIA operatives and members of the Bush administration from facing any possible legal penalties for their interrogation practices and policies. Twelve editorials touch on this subject, including two within the first two months of 2009, which expressed worry that the Obama administration and the new Congress might pursue further investigations of such practices and policies. This is quite different from the view of ethicists such as Elshtain and Walzer, who argue that torture may sometimes be necessary but that those who accept the necessity ought also accept the moral, and perhaps legal, guilt.

The *Times*, by contrast, has called for investigations of interrogation practice and policies in eleven editorials, including three in 2008 and one in 2009. As early as February 5, 2005, an editorial demands a full investigation of all U.S. detention centers:

> We strongly agree with the American Bar Association, which wrote to President Bush on Feb. 1 to urge the appointment of an independent, bipartisan commission with subpoena power. The bar association talked about Iraqi civilians in military custody, but we believe that a panel should look at all prisoners, all detention centers and all involved government agencies.

The *Journal* prefers to see each revelation of torture as an isolated incident. They are at pains to demonstrate that there is no link, for example, between the policies of the Defense Department or the presidency and the events at Abu Ghraib. So, we see in a May 24, 2005 editorial the *Journal's* contention that, "yes, there were abuses in Iraq beyond what was pictured at Abu Ghraib, but abuses happen in war and in civilian prisons too." Furthermore, these abuses were the aberrant actions of a few sadists on "the night shift," say the editors. "No evidence has been produced to support allegations that the abuses were 'systematic' or that they were inspired or condoned by superiors up the chain of command."

The *Times,* however, appears to consider torture an institutional problem. Writing in August of the same year, after the release of two reports about Abu Ghraib, the *Times* observes:

> For anyone with the time to wade through 400-plus pages and the resources to decode them, the two reports issued this week on the Abu Ghraib prison are an indictment of the way the Bush administration set the stage for Iraqi prisoners to be brutalized by American prison guards, military intelligence officers and private contractors.
>
> The Army's internal investigation, released yesterday, showed that the torture of prisoners at Abu Ghraib went far beyond the actions of a few sadistic military police officers—the administration's chosen culprits. . . . Another report, from a civilian panel picked by Defense

Secretary Donald Rumsfeld, offers the dedicated reader a dotted line from President Bush's decision to declare Iraq a front in the war against terror, to government lawyers finding ways to circumvent the Geneva Conventions, to Mr. Rumsfeld's bungled planning of the occupation and understaffing of the ground forces in Iraq, to the hideous events at Abu Ghraib prison.

Table 3.2 summarizes the ethical approaches taken by each paper:

What do we learn by studying and comparing these editorials? First, it appears that an almost unbridgeable chasm separates the views of the two editorial pages. (That chasm continues to exist today, as a sampling of each paper's response to the release of the film *Zero Dark Thirty* indicates.) I suspect that a similar chasm also separates the views of many ordinary Americans. It would also seem that the *Journal* has succeeded in setting the terms of the debate, by defining the primary issue not as torture but as the safety of U.S. civilians and soldiers. The *Journal* has certainly been assisted in this task by the long reach of Fox news media, — which is not surprising given that Rupert Murdoch's News Corp owns both. The *Times* appears in many cases to accept the terms of debate set by the *Wall Street Journal* and also frames its own objections to torture in instrumental terms. So we see the *Times* emphasizing, for example, the danger that torturing detainees represents for any captured U.S. soldiers and the propaganda victories that it provides to U.S. adversaries. Unlike some of the philosophers discussed in this chapter, however, neither newspaper is willing to argue in favor of any practice it actually calls "torture."

Proponents of torture, whether scholars or journalists, share an inability to examine torture as it is actually practiced. As a result, they persist in treating torture as isolated and morally isolatable actions taken by relatively isolated individuals. Among the academics, those who would countenance torture generally locate their arguments in the hypothetical world of the thought

Table 3.2 **Ethical Approaches to Torture in *New York Times* and *Wall Street Journal* Editorials**

Ethical Method	New York Times	Wall Street Journal	Total
Consequentialism	49	25	74
Deontology	16	1	17
Elements of both	25	0	25
Other or none	31	11	42
Total	**121**	**37**	**158**

experiment. Allhoff, for example, is frankly derisive about attempts to drag empirical considerations into the purely "theoretical" argument that he says interests him. The *Wall Street Journal,* whose editorialists pride themselves on a certain hard-nosed realism, appear to have examined less carefully than the "moralizing" *New York Times* the actual practices of the U.S. government, in particular the roles of those in its upper echelons.

I think there is a quality missing from the arguments of both the *Journal* and the academic proponents of hypothetical torture. Michael Ignatieff makes reference to it in his consideration of an ethics of a lesser evil. I would call it "practical wisdom" or "prudence." This is, in the thinking of Aristotle and his theological descendant St. Thomas Aquinas, the specific *intellectual* excellence that allows us to make good ethical decisions. It is "right reason" about things to be done. Practical wisdom involves a reasoned consideration of one's empirical knowledge of the world. It is formed and informed by good moral habits. And when it is missing, we tend to think and do silly and wrong things like, for example, separating our ideas about torture from the empirical evidence available about the kind of practice torture really is.[105]

This discussion of prudence brings us to our next chapter, in which I examine a different way of thinking about moral problems, using the concepts of practice, virtue, and tradition elaborated by the contemporary virtue ethicist Alasdair MacIntyre.

Notes

1. John Stuart Mill, *Utilitarianism and on Liberty* (Malden, MA: Blackwell, 2003), 186.
2. Jean Bethke Elshtain, "Reflection on the Problem of 'Dirty Hands,'" in *Torture: A Collection,* ed. Sanford Levinson (New York: Oxford University Press, 2004).
3. Richard A. Posner, "Torture, Terrorism, and Interrogation," in *Torture.*
4. The one exception is Henry Shue's classic 1978 article "Torture," which appeared in *Philosophy and Public Affairs.* Shue has written on torture since 2001, but contemporary scholars make frequent reference to this earlier piece, so I include it in this review.
5. Posner, "Torture, Terrorism, and Interrogation," 293. Note that Posner appears to contradict himself at the end of this same essay, when he suggests that torture to save the single kidnap victim might indicate that one has taken a wrong step "down the balancing path," 297.
6. Henry Shue, "Torture," *Philosophy and Public Affairs* 7, no. 2 (1978): 132.
7. Ibid.
8. Fritz Allhoff, "Terrorism and Torture," *International Journal of Applied Philosophy* 17, no. 1 (2003): 115.
9. Ibid., 110.
10. Fritz Allhoff, "A Defense of Torture: Separation of Cases, Ticking Time-Bombs, and Moral Justification,"*International Journal of Applied Philosophy* 19, no. 2 (2005): 243.
11. Ibid., 246.
12. Ibid., 252. One might legitimately object here that Allhoff has fallen into a logical contradiction of terms. Torture, by definition, is not "minor."
13. Ibid., 248.

14. Ibid., 260.
15. Ibid., 243.
16. G. E. M. Anscombe, "Modern Moral Philosophy,"*Philosophy* 33, no. 124 (1958).
17. Dick Cheney, "Text of Dick Cheney's National Security Speech at AEI," May 21, 2009. http://www.foxnews.com/politics/2009/05/21/raw-data-text-dick-cheneys-national-security-speech-aei/.
18. Henry Shue, Richard H. Weisberg, and Sanford Levinson, "The Debate on Torture; War against Virtual States; Responses," *Dissent* 50, no. 3 (2003): 90.
19. Alan Dershowitz, "The Torture Warrant: A Response to Professor Strauss," *New York Law School Law Review* 48, no. 1–2 (2003).
20. Wolf Blitzer, "Dershowitz: Torture Could Be Justified," March 4, 2003. http://edition.cnn.com/2003/LAW/03/03/cnna.Dershowitz/.
21. Oren Gross, "The Prohibition on Torture and the Limits of the Law," in *Torture: A Collection,* ed. Sanford Levinson (Oxford: Oxford University Press, 2004), 244.
22. Posner, "Torture, Terrorism, and Interrogation," 298.
23. Sanford Levinson, "The Debate on Torture; War against Virtual States," *Dissent* 50, no. 3 (2003): 88; emphasis in original.
24. Ibid., 90.
25. Cary Federman, "Interview with Sanford Levinson," September 1, 2007. http://writerinterviews.blogspot.com/2007/09/sanford-levinson.html.
26. This is an argument commonly found in less scholarly venues like newspaper editorials, but see also William T. Cavanaugh, *Torture and Eucharist* (Malden, MA: Blackwell, 1998); Alfred W. McCoy, *A Question of Torture: CIA Interrogation, from the Cold War to the War on Terror,* 1st ed. The American Empire Project. (New York: Metropolitan Books/Henry Holt, 2006); ElaineScarry, *The Body in Pain: The Making and Unmaking of the World* (New York: Oxford University Press, 1985).
27. Posner, "Torture, Terrorism, and Interrogation," 294.
28. Thomas Oswald Cockayne, ed., *Leechdoms, Wortcunning and Starcraft of Early England: The History of Science before the Norman Conquest,* 3 vols. (Bristol, UK: Thoemmes, 2001), 65.
29. McCoy, *A Question of Torture,* 198.
30. Alistair Horne, *A Savage War of Peace: Algeria, 1954–1962* New York Review Books Classics (New York: New York Review Books, 1977; reprint, 2006), 18.
31. Ibid., 19.
32. Neil MacMaster, "Torture: From Algiers to Abu Ghraib," *Race & Class* 46, no. 2 (2004), 2.
33. Ibid., 9.
34. Nancy Guzmán Jasmen, *Romo, Confesiones de un torturador,* 1st ed. (Santiago, Chile: Editorial Planeta Chilena, 2000), 109. "Yo había hecho cursos de contrainsurgencia in Panamá y tenía la formación para poder hacer los organigramas y decidir este p'acá y este p'allá y saber quiénes tenían más información y quiénes no tenían mucho que decir." (Author's translation.)
35. MacMaster, "Torture: From Algiers to Abu Ghraib."
36. Posner, "Torture, Terrorism, and Interrogation," 294–95.
37. Horne, *A Savage War of Peace,* 500.
38. Vittorio Bufacchi and Jean Maria Arrigo, "Torture, Terrorism and the State: A Refutation of the Ticking-Bomb Argument," *Journal of Applied Philosophy* 23, no. 3 (2006), 361–62. In 2007, Dr. Arrigo served on the American Psychological Association's Psychological Ethics and National Security task force, which investigated the role of psychologists in assisting interrogations of detainees held in the "war on terror."
39. Ibid.
40. McCoy reports, for example, that "between 1953 and 1963, [the CIA's "mind–control" project] MKUltra and allied projects dispensed $25 million for human experiments by 185 nongovernmental researchers at eighty institutions, including forty-four universities and twelve hospitals." McCoy, *A Question of Torture,* Chapter 2.
41. Bufacchi and Arrigo, "Torture, Terrorism and the State," 364–65.
42. Ibid., 367.
43. Ibid., 368.

44. Archdiocese of São Paulo, *Torture in Brazil: A Shocking Report on the Pervasive Use of Torture by Brazilian Military Governments, 1964–1979*, trans. Jaime Wright. Special Publications (Austin: University of Texas Institute for Latin American Studies, 1998), 14.
45. Shue, "Torture," 132–33.
46. Ibid., 135.
47. Ibid., 142.
48. Henry Shue, "Torture in Dreamland: Disposing of the Ticking Bomb," *Case Western Reserve Journal of International Law* 37, no. 2–3 (2006), 231.
49. Ibid., 237.
50. David Sussman, "What's Wrong with Torture?" *Philosophy and Public Affairs* 33, no. 1 (2005), 4.
51. Ibid., 24.
52. Ibid., 14.
53. CIA, *KUBARK Counterintelligence Interrogation* (1963), 94.
54. Sussman, "What's Wrong with Torture?," 29.
55. Naomi Klein, *The Shock Doctrine: The Rise of Disaster Capitalism*, 1st ed. (New York: Metropolitan Books/Henry Holt, 2007); McCoy, *A Question of Torture.*
56. Amartya Sen, "Elements of a Theory of Human Rights,"*Philosophy and Public Affairs* 32, no. 4 (2004), 317–18.
57. Ibid., 321–22.
58. Ibid., 340; emphasis in original.
59. Peter A. Clark, "Medical Ethics at Guantanamo Bay and Abu Ghraib: The Problem of Dual Loyalty,"*Journal of Law, Medicine & Ethics* 34, no. 3 (2006), 576.
60. Ibid., 577.
61. Immanuel Kant, *Foundations of the Metaphysics of Morals*, trans. Lewis White Beck (Upper Saddle River, NJ: Prentice-Hall, Inc., 1997), 10.
62. Clark, "Medical Ethics at Guantanamo Bay and Abu Ghraib," 577.
63. Max Weber, "Politics as a Vocation," in *From Max Weber: Essays in Sociology*, ed. H. H. Gerth and C. Wright Mills (New York: Oxford University Press, 1946), 120.
64. Michael Walzer, "Political Action: The Problem of Dirty Hands," in *Torture: A Collection*, ed. Sanford Levinson (New York: Oxford University Press, 2004), 69, 71.
65. Ibid., 64–65.
66. Ibid., 73.
67. Ibid., 72.
68. Ibid., 73.
69. Elshtain, "Reflection on the Problem of 'Dirty Hands,'" 77–78. It might be noted that there is a solution to this problem that does not involve any torture: evacuate all the elementary schools in the city.
70. Ibid., 82.
71. Ibid., 83; emphasis in the original.
72. Michael Ignatieff, *The Lesser Evil: Political Ethics in an Age of Terror.* The Gifford Lectures. (Princeton: Princeton University Press, 2004), 8–9.
73. Ibid., 136.
74. Ibid., 8.
75. Ibid., 138.
76. Ibid., 144.
77. Sumner B. Twiss, "Torture, Justification, and Human Rights: Toward an Absolute Proscription," *Human Rights Quarterly* 29, no. 2 (2007), 246.
78. Ibid., 351.
79. Ibid., 355.
80. Ibid., 358.
81. Ibid., 359.
82. Ibid.; Ibid.
83. Ibid.
84. Ibid., 363; ibid. Twiss supports this contention with references to the "voluminous" literature on the subject available from human rights organizations such as Amnesty International and works such as John Conroy, *Unspeakable Acts, Ordinary People: The Dynamics*

of Torture (Berkeley: University of California Press, 2000), and Jennifer Harbury, *Truth, Torture, and the American Way: The History and Consequences of U.S. Involvement in Torture* (Boston, MA: Beacon, 2005).

85. Twiss, "Torture, Justification, and Human Rights," 363; Ibid.
86. Ibid.; ibid., 365.
87. Ibid., 366–67; ibid., 365.
88. Edward Feld, "Developing a Jewish Theology Regarding Torture," *Theology Today* 63, no. 3 (2006), 327.
89. Ibid., 326.
90. Ibid., 327.
91. William T. Cavanaugh, "Making Enemies: The Imagination of Torture in Chile and the United States," *Theology Today* 63, no. 3 (2006), 309.
92. Ibid.
93. Ibid., 311.
94. Ibid., 313.
95. Ibid.
96. Ibid., 314.
97. Scott Higham and Joe Stephens, "Punishment and Amusement: Documents Indicate 3 Photos Were Not Staged for Interrogation," *Washington Post*, May 22, 2004.
98. Cavanaugh, "Making Enemies," 315.
99. Ibid.
100. Ibid., 321.
101. I say "mistreatment" here, because no high-level member of the Bush administration has ever acknowledged that any of its practices, including any of the CIA's approved "enhanced interrogation techniques" constitute actual torture. This is not terribly surprising. The word "torture" invites such universal opprobrium today that no recent torture regime has ever officially described its treatment of prisoners as torture. That appellation is almost always bestowed by the regime's critics, whether internal or external.
102. Joby Warrick and Dave Eggen, "Waterboarding Recounted," *Washington Monthly*, December 10, 2007. http://www.washingtonpost.com/wp-dyn/content/article/2007/12/10/AR2007121002091.html?sid = ST2007121100844.
103. Both papers expect that torture would—and should—take place. The *Times* says, "We're not naïve enough to believe that if the C.I.A. nabs a Qaeda operative who knows where a ticking bomb is hidden, that terrorist will emerge unbruised from his interrogation."
104. Note the quotation marks on the word "torture." The *Journal* never uses this word in conjunction with U.S. treatment of prisoners unless it is flanked by those ironic punctuation marks.
105. A note about terminology: St. Thomas speaks of prudence as "wisdom about human affairs," and locates it only in the practical and not the speculative intellect. He distinguishes prudence from "wisdom absolutely," because it is concerned only with the "human good" and not with "the absolutely highest cause," which is the object of absolute wisdom. For St. Thomas, this is of course God. See Thomas Aquinas, *Summa Theologica*, trans. Fathers of the English Dominican Province (Ave Maria Press, 1981; reprint, 1981), II–II, Q.47, a.2. Wisdom about the absolutely highest cause belongs to the speculative intellect, which does not concern itself with practical matters.

It might be more precise therefore to speak of prudence as practical *reason* rather than as practical *wisdom*, but to do so risks falling into a different error, that is, confusing prudence with mere efficient instrumental thinking, akin to Machiavelli's *prudenzia*. "Prudence," says Machiavelli, "consists in knowing how to assess risk and in accepting the lesser evil as a good." See Niccolò Machiavelli and David Wootton, *The Prince* (Indianapolis: Hackett Pub. Co., 1995), 70.

When St. Thomas speaks of prudence, he has in mind Aristotle's Greek term *phronesis*, which is frequently rendered by translators into English as "practical wisdom," as for example in Aristotle and others, *The Nicomachean Ethics*, rev. ed. (London: Penguin Books, 2004), 312; Ibid. This may well be because the ordinary English use of the expression "practical wisdom" carries an ethical connotation not present in "practical reason." For these reasons I have chosen here to use the expressions "prudence" and "practical wisdom" interchangeably.

4

A Different Approach: Virtue Ethics

Every art and every inquiry, and similarly every action and pursuit,
is thought to aim at some good; and for this reason the good has
rightly been declared to be that at which all things aim.[1]

—Aristotle

The previous chapter concludes with the observation that something seems to be missing from both the academic and popular discussion about torture. That something, I suggested, is the willingness to come to grips with the actual, rather than the hypothetical, nature of institutionalized state torture. Limiting the ethical discussion to consequentialist and deontological arguments makes it possible to discuss torture primarily in imagined scenarios like the ticking-bomb problem. Many consequentialist arguments, especially those that focus on torture's immediate outcomes, divert attention from the realities of what can actually be "achieved" in a time-sensitive torture scenario. And even those deontological arguments that condemn torture because it treats the prisoner as a mere instrument rather than as a person fail to capture the continuing, institutional, socially embedded nature of torture.

Is there a better approach? This chapter explores one—an approach that allows us to understand how institutionalized state torture not only attacks individual and social bodies but also distorts the character of all those who make torture possible. This view is based on the contemporary virtue ethics of the philosopher Alasdair MacIntyre. In particular, it explores how his understanding of human *practices* illumines aspects of torture not addressed by consequentialist and deontological arguments alone. This new light allows for an ethical examination of torture that turns out to be even more concrete and "practical" than the most hard-nosed utilitarian arguments described in the previous chapter.

Readers who are primarily interested in the problem of torture rather than in philosophical ethics may be a bit startled by this excursion into the theories of one particular philosopher. I introduce MacIntyre here for two key reasons.

First, his work lies at the center of a revived interest in virtue ethics, an approach to the moral life that focuses as much on the kind of people humans may become across a lifetime of action as it does on the rightness or wrongness of particular, individual acts. Beginning in 1984 with *After Virtue*, MacIntyre set out to reclaim an ethical tradition whose roots lie in ancient Greece with branches spreading in the medieval Catholic church. This is a tradition that many Western philosophers considered (and still consider) to have been superseded by the consequentialist and deontological approaches explored in the previous chapter. If today's philosophers wish to think seriously about virtue, we cannot do so without recognizing MacIntyre's role in reopening the discussion.

A second reason for focusing on MacIntyre's particular approach to human practices is that it offers valuable theoretical purchase on the problem of institutionalized state torture. MacIntyre's technical concepts of *telos, practice, virtue,* and *tradition* help us to accurately characterize the thing and to consider how it affects the people involved at all levels. This includes the individual torturers, those who organize and oversee torture, and the larger society within which institutionalized torture is embedded. While it makes sense to say in a general way that such torture is a "practice," in the ordinary meaning of the word, it makes even more sense, I shall argue, to consider torture as a practice within the larger conceptual framework offered by MacIntyre.

Introducing MacIntyre's Virtue Ethics

Any discussion of this subject must necessarily begin with MacIntyre's best known work, *After Virtue*. This is an extended, dense, and closely argued defense of the superiority of Aristotle's approach to ethics, an approach that focuses less on the right or wrong of particular things people *do* than on what kind of people they become over the course of their lives. In this context, virtues are the good intellectual and moral habits that, enacted throughout a life, make up *eudaimonia,* happiness.

The gist of MacIntyre's appropriation of Aristotle's ethics is this: Any useful ethical method must begin with an understanding of what makes for a good life for human beings. For MacIntyre, a good human life is one that is dedicated to a "quest" for the good human life. In the course of this quest, human beings acquire the very moral and intellectual habits—the virtues—necessary to such a quest. They do this by participating in a variety of communal practices, which are themselves embedded in larger institutions and traditions.

After Virtue is also a profound indictment of the efforts of what MacIntyre calls the "Enlightenment project" to create a universalizable ethics, that is, a

form of ethics applicable in every time, place, and society. *After Virtue* specifically condemns that project's two main products (which we encountered in
the previous chapter): Kantian deontology and the various forms of consequentialism. What MacIntyre considers as the inevitable failure of this project
has, he says, bequeathed to its inheritors an ethics based entirely on personal
preference, an approach to moral philosophy that he calls "emotivism."[2]

MacIntyre opens *After Virtue* with the proposition that the discipline
of moral philosophy has suffered a calamity equivalent to the destruction
of scientific knowledge described in certain speculative novels set in post-
apocalyptic worlds.[3] That is, we still retain the vocabulary of an earlier moral
philosophy, and we can construct internally consistent manipulations of that
vocabulary, but the connection between that vocabulary and the real world
has become profoundly "disordered." One important result of this calamity is
that many contemporary moral arguments disintegrate into "shrill" screaming
matches, because although a particular position on an issue may be internally
consistent, it must ultimately appeal to valuations of some kind, which are not
themselves susceptible of rational proof. Moral disputants end up shouting at
each other about their first principles, which principles, says MacIntyre, although they look like axiomatic truths, are in fact only fancy wrapping paper
concealing their personal preferences and desires.[4]

But the problem of emotivism is more profound even than its role in rendering modern moral debates incapable of resolution. Emotivism elevates that
very incapacity to a position of epistemological privilege. MacIntyre continues:
"What I have suggested to be the case by and large about our own culture—that
in moral argument the apparent assertion of principles functions as a mask for
expressions of personal preference—is what emotivism takes to be universally
the case. . . . For what emotivism asserts is in central part that there are and
can be *no* valid rational justification for any claims that objective moral standards exist and hence that there are no such standards."[5] In other words, in the
modern view, ethics boils down to a matter of personal opinion.[6]

If MacIntyre is right that we have come to such a pass, this puts the person
who seeks to make a moral argument against the practice of torture in a most
difficult position. At best, it renders quixotic a quest for common ground for
such a discussion, because such discussion must take place within a culture
that denies the reality of any first principles; at worst, it reduces any moral
judgment that torture is wrong to a personal and idiosyncratic discomfort
with other people's pain.

What is MacIntyre's solution to this problem? It is a challenge to synthe-
size an argument that requires another 250 pages to develop, but in brief, it is
as follows: The Enlightenment project had to fail because it lost the concept
of *telos*—end or purpose—in relation to human life. To actually strive for a

meaningful *telos* in life would require the exercise of various *virtues*, which human beings develop largely through participation in a variety of *practices*, which themselves form parts of larger ongoing, dialectical *traditions*, whose internal unity, like the unity of an individual human life, has a narrative form. Although it is simplest to examine these concepts in a linear sequence, in MacIntyre's view they function together as a dynamic whole, and, as Theologian Brad J. Kallenberg points out, each can only be defined in relation to all the others.[7]

Telos: Why does the way that we define a good human life matter? One answer is that without some idea of what is good for human beings, it is difficult, if not impossible, to make ethical decisions. To judge whether an action (or an ongoing practice) is right, we need to ask, "right" in reference to what standard? Unless we have some idea of what counts as good for human beings, we cannot say whether some particular behavior contributes to or detracts from the goal of achieving that good.

What standard does MacIntyre propose? In any society, he argues, whether for individual persons—or for the communities, institutions, and traditions in which they are embedded—the good human life consists in a lifelong quest to understand what constitutes the good human life. This idea is not quite as circular as it sounds. It is an acknowledgement that even the most unexamined life involves a search—a quest—for whatever activities, experiences, and relationships will make that life a good one. In the course of this quest, MacIntyre believes, human beings can acquire the very moral and intellectual habits—the virtues—that will help and sustain them in such a quest. They do this in part by participating in a variety of communal *practices*, which are themselves embedded in larger *traditions*. Traditions are for MacIntyre ongoing arguments within an institution or an entire society about what is good for that institution or society.[8]

MacIntyre begins his discussion of *telos* with Aristotle. Most students of Aristotle can probably recite the first sentence of the *Nicomachean Ethics* by heart: "Every art and every inquiry, and similarly every action and pursuit, is thought to aim at some good; and for this reason the good has rightly been declared to be that at which all things aim."[9] Aristotle goes on to point out that different sorts of human activity have different *teloi* or goals. The purpose of medicine is health; of shipbuilding; a vessel, of military strategy, victory in war. All of these, however, are subsidiary to some overarching goal, something that is desirable for its own sake. That "something" is *eudaimonia* (variously translated as happiness, flourishing, fulfillment), which, for Aristotle, is the active process of living a long life, one that is blessed with a reasonable amount of good fortune and imbued with various kinds of excellence, or virtues.

Aristotle developed his ethics in a particular time and place, addressing his arguments about the purpose of human life to human beings of whom he (and they themselves) primarily conceived as citizens of the *polis*, the city-state. The good for the individual was in Aristotle's view inextricably bound to the good for the *polis,* just as the virtues were to be defined and developed within the context of one's life as a citizen. By contrast, the Enlightenment project of constructing universal ethics failed, according to MacIntyre, because it constructed an autonomous "universal" human being, abstracted from all social, political, and historical specificity, and cut off from any *telos* or purpose.[10] Kallenberg describes the problem this way: "Because the Enlightenment rejected the traditionally shared concept of what human life is for and started, as it were, from scratch, by inventing the idea of humans as 'autonomous individuals,' the concept of *telos,* so central to morality, was lost."[11]

Once the notion of human *telos* disappears from cultural discourse, it is no longer possible to make verifiable statements about morality. If human life has no purpose, then according to what scale are we to measure human lives and actions? Various "impostors," says MacIntyre, arose to fill this void of meaning. These include utilitarianism with its "ghostly substitute"—the idea of pursuing the greatest good for the greatest number—and the ethics of Kant and his followers, with its failed attempts to "provide 'rational' justification for statements deprived of their former teleological status."[12]

So for the first time we observe "the transformation of first-person expressions of desire themselves, without further qualification, into statements of a reason for action, into premises for practical reasoning." For the first time, the utterance, "I want it," becomes something other than a mere observation about one's personal desire; it has been transformed into a moral justification for one's own or others' actions. "And this transformation," MacIntyre continues, "is brought about by a restructuring of thought and action in a way which accords with the procedures of the public realms of the market and of liberal individualist politics."[13] It should not be surprising that in such a society ideas about the good and the right would be reduced to personal preferences because "in those realms the ultimate data are preferences."[14]

This reduction of ethics to preference has, in my view, a further corrupting effect. If we believe that all ethical claims are really nothing more than personal or group interests wrapped in fine language. any ethical claim that is *not* couched in instrumental terms becomes de facto illegitimate. Thus, the *Wall Street Journal* is perfectly justified in complaining that "we sure wish the moralizing critics would keep in mind that this is also a debate over how to protect the United States." The moralizers in this case are only expressing a preference (i.e., not to feel guilty, perhaps, or not to have their squeamishness confronted). The *Journal's* editorialists are expressing a preference, too, which they characterize as the protection of the United States.

Clearly then, what a person or a society takes as her or its *telos* will greatly influence the kinds of practices engendered, and the habits of character and mind developed, in the pursuit of that *telos*.

Practices: It is largely in the context of their ongoing, collaborative activities that human beings develop such habits of character and mind (which MacIntyre follows Aristotle and Aquinas in calling virtues). What, then, is a practice? It is, in MacIntyre's usage, a "coherent and complex form of socially established cooperative activity through which goods internal to that form of activity are realized in the course of trying to achieve those standards of excellence which are appropriate to, and partially definitive of, that form of activity."[15]

To qualify as a practice in MacIntyre's sense of the term, an area of human endeavor must thus satisfy three conditions:

1. It must be both coherent (i.e., directed toward some purpose in an organized way) and complex (chopping vegetables is not a practice; good cooking is).
2. It must be a cooperative activity, arising from and embedded in a larger social context (which MacIntyre calls a "tradition").
3. Its practitioners must share an understanding of the good things the practice seeks to achieve (the "goods internal" to it) and of the sorts of habits of excellence—or virtues—necessary to achieve those goods.

A practice in MacIntyre's sense has a history and standards of excellence developed in the course of that history. Its existence implies a community of practitioners who share the practice and initiate others into it. Such initiation involves learning and accepting the rules and standards of excellence and acknowledging the authority of those rules and standards (authority in the sense of legitimacy, not of domination) and the authority of one's elders in the practice. "To enter into a practice" is thus "to accept the authority of those standards and the inadequacy of my own performance as judged by them. It is to subject my own attitudes, choices, preferences and tastes to the standards which currently... define the practice."[16] Examples of practices include human activities as diverse as chess playing, farming, and the painting of portraits in the European tradition.[17]

Virtues: For MacIntyre, human beings develop virtues through involvement in such practices as they strive to recognize and pursue their *telos*. But what is a virtue? MacIntyre offers several definitions, each enlarging on the previous one. He acknowledges that different societies have not only produced different lists of virtues, they have also had differing understanding of the meaning and function of virtue itself. Nevertheless, he maintains there are certain commonalities, which he will seek to sift out.

He begins by defining virtues in terms of practices. *"A virtue,"* he says, *"is an acquired human quality the possession and exercise of which tends to enable us to achieve those goods which are internal to practices and the lack of which effectively prevents us from achieving any such goods."*[18] Beyond this, MacIntyre agrees with both Aristotle and Aquinas that virtues are *habits*. They are settled dispositions to act in certain ways in certain contexts. Human beings are born, not with virtues themselves, but with the capacity to acquire them, and this we do in the same way we acquire any habit—over time, with repetition, so that they become second nature.[19]

But this definition of virtue is not entirely satisfying, because it leads back to the question of how we are to adjudicate among competing practices and the virtues that they engender. How are we to measure the relative merits within a single life of, for example, devotion to art and devotion to family? In other words, how, except on the basis of personal preference, is one to order competing practices and the virtues they engender in their relative priority? Unless we can answer this question in some rational way, we have returned to the problem of emotivism with which MacIntyre began his inquiry. "Is it rationally justified," he asks, "to conceive of each human life as a unity, so that we may try to specify each such life as having its good and so that we may understand the virtues as having their function in enabling an individual to make of his or her life one kind of unity rather than another?"

He suggests that one of the modern philosophical barriers to recognizing the unity of a human life or of human life in general is "the tendency to think atomistically about human action and to analyze complex actions and transactions in terms of simple components." This failure to recognize the "unity" of human life, I think, is reflected in the deontological and utilitarian approaches to torture discussed in the previous chapter. Both ethical methods tend to view this complex behavior as a series of individual actions that are interruptible at any point, rather than as a practice that necessarily forms the characters of its practitioners and the society in which it is practiced.[20]

While MacIntyre may regret the separation of a life into its individual moments, others have celebrated it as the key to efficiency and profit. This view of human activity will be familiar to anyone who has encountered—in books or in the workplace—the ideas of scientific management.[21] Early in the twentieth century, Frederick Taylor introduced this method of organizing manufacturing processes by breaking the work down into its smallest, most meaningless components and separating physical from mental labor. When we think of human life as the stringing together of a series of "simple components," I believe that we reduce it to one long Taylorist time-motion study. It should not be surprising that in this context the only legitimate ethical arguments become instrumentalist ones.

MacIntyre believes that we are indeed "rationally justified" in conceiving of human life as having unity, so long as we understand this unity in terms of a *narrative*, a story with a beginning, a middle, and an end. This formulation is, in part, MacIntyre's answer to the problem of identifying what aspect of a particular person endures over time, such that we can reasonably speak of someone being "the same person" from one point in time to another. What ties the different points of a person's life into a "unity," he says, is the narrative, the story that connects one moment to the next. But the narrative of a life isn't just *any* story; it is a quest to discover one's *telos*—that which constitutes the good life for the one embarked on the quest.[22] This suggests to MacIntyre a further refinement of his definition of virtues:

> The virtues therefore are to be understood as those dispositions which will not only sustain practices and enable us to achieve the goods internal to practices, but which will also sustain us in the relevant kind of quest for the good, by enabling us to overcome the harms, dangers, temptations and distractions which we encounter, and which will furnish us with increasing self-knowledge and increasing knowledge of the good.[23]

So virtues are the enduring habits that we develop over time, through practices. They enable us to learn and to excel in our practices, and they sustain us throughout our lives in the quest to make sense of those lives and to make them good ones.

It might be useful to say a bit here about which particular dispositions of character MacIntyre takes to be virtues. Not every tendency to behave in a certain way necessarily assists in the pursuit of the goods internal to practices or of a good life in general. Nor is virtue for MacIntyre (or his predecessors Aristotle and Thomas Aquinas) an undifferentiated lump of goodness. So to what catalogue of virtues does MacIntyre refer?

This is not a simple question to answer because he mentions different virtues at different points in the trajectory of his work. The virtues considered in *After Virtue* are essentially those of Aristotle, a list that ranges widely, from courage in battle to wittiness at the dinner table.[24] In *Whose Justice? Which Rationality?* and in more recent work, however, MacIntyre has explicitly embraced Thomas Aquinas's Christian enlargement of Aristotle's virtue ethics. In this context, he follows Aquinas in replacing Aristotle's taxonomy of the virtues with the four classical virtues, which are courage, justice, temperance (or moderation), and (practical) wisdom.

The next chapter considers the relationship between these four virtues and the practice of torture. The first three are considered moral virtues; they are related to how well human beings behave in response to our emotions (e.g., fear, love, joy) and our desires to have or to avoid something. Practical wisdom (or practical reason), which Aristotle calls *phronesis* and Aquinas calls *prudentia*, is an intellectual virtue that is concerned with ethical action. It is a form of understanding that allows us to know what is the right thing to do and the best way to do it. It is *practical* wisdom in that, when it is in good order, it produces right and effective action. In addition to these four "pagan" virtues, Christian writers and theologians, including Aquinas and Dante, have also spoken of three "graces," or spiritual gifts, which are faith, hope, and love. The next chapter will also address these in relationship to torture.

Tradition: To say, as MacIntryre does, that the purpose of human life is the quest for the good human life would seem to entangle us in a meaningless circular search. And that would be true, he agrees, if each person, and indeed each society, had to begin the quest all over again. Fortunately, this is not the case. Individuals and societies live within larger historical streams MacIntyre calls *traditions.*

Rather than define a tradition in terms of a shared commitment to first principles, a reverence for founding individuals, or an attempt to preserve a particular way of life through time, MacIntyre thinks of traditions as ongoing "arguments." But arguments about what? A tradition, says MacIntyre, is "an argument precisely in part about the goods which constitute that tradition."[25] A tradition is an "historically extended" discussion about what constitutes the good life for members of that tradition. It builds on what has been learned in the past as it grapples with the important questions of the present moment.

This view has important consequences for individual human lives; we need traditions within which to quest for our own good, so we do not have to "start from scratch" as if no one had ever embarked on a similar quest before. "Hence," he says, "the individual's search for his or her good is generally and characteristically conducted within a context defined by those traditions of which the individual's life is a part."[26] Nor could we "start from scratch" if we wanted to. "I am born," says MacIntyre, "with a past; and to try to cut myself off from that past . . . is to deform my present relationships. The possession of an historical identity and the possession of a social identity coincide." As members of families, institutions, and states, we become part of the traditions of practices particular to those families, institutions, and states. We step into an ongoing stream of argument about goods sought by those practices and the general good for human beings.[27]

So, for example, in the United States there is a tradition that we might call "national defense" or "national security." This tradition involves the work of a variety of institutions, including the armed forces, intelligence agencies, local police forces, our federal and state governments, the various forms of mass media and the press, transportation systems, and schools and universities, among others. Each institution has its own history, its own practices, its own arguments about the good for that institution. Each contributes to the general argument about what exactly contributes to and what threatens U.S. national security. In recent years this argument has sometimes been framed (not entirely accurately, in my view) as an argument over what constitutes the right balance for Americans between freedom and security.

Within this ongoing tradition of national security, both the FBI and the CIA possess established practices that they call "interrogation." But they disagree about which agency's practice genuinely contributes to national security. They disagree first about which agency's methods (gradually securing the prisoner's trust in the case of the FBI, and "enhanced" techniques in the case of the CIA) are most effective. Equally important, they disagree about whether national security itself is being sustained at a price that threatens the integral values of the nation. This same argument—about the values and behavior that give the United States its specific national identity and the extent to which these may be threatened in the "war on terror"—animates many of the newspaper editorials discussed in the previous chapter.

Practices: An Example

Perhaps the relationship among practices, virtues, and traditions can be made clearer through an example taken from my own life, one that at first may appear quite trivial. I participate in the practice of knitting. Does knitting satisfy MacIntyre's three criteria for a practice? Does it require and engender virtues in the practitioner? What do we learn about knitting by considering it as a practice that we might otherwise not have understood about it?

MacIntyre's first criterion for a practice is that be a "coherent and complex" activity. Does knitting qualify? At first glance, the answer would appear to be "No." Knitting, after all, consists in creating connected loops in a long piece of string. Indeed, only two kinds of loop are involved, a knit stitch and a purl stitch, and even these two are simply opposite views of the same stitch. Every piece of knitting is composed of variations on these two stitches. Nonetheless, I maintain that knitting passes the "coherent and complex" test. The most extraordinary objects can be created by combining and arranging these stitches, ranging from serviceable garments to works of art, such as Debbie New's delicate floating coracle and Sarah-Marie bel Castro's three-dimensional illustrations of mathematical formulae.[28]

Complex, perhaps, but in what sense can we call knitting cooperative? Is it not a quintessentially solitary activity? I can knit alone for hours or days without appearing to "cooperate" with another human being. This is certainly true, but only in the sense that any form of art has its solitary moments—those times when the artist is focused entirely on his or her work. However, I would not be able to focus in this way in the first place were it not for the cooperation of many other knitters. I could not knit, for example, without a pattern to work from, and these are the results of the efforts of other knitters. Even if I work on a pattern of my own design, my understanding of the properties of different sorts of yarn, of the construction of a particular kind of garment, of the possibilities of combining colors and textures, even of the process of elaborating a new pattern—all this derives from the work of other knitters and designers.

It is also worth noting that while knitting can certainly be accomplished in solitude, like many of the domestic arts, it also lends itself to social interaction. Many knitters meet regularly in groups, where they work on their projects, ask and give advice, and discuss a wide range of subjects, often only tangentially connected to the knitting itself. In this sense, knitting is part of a larger set of textile traditions: the tradition found in many countries of women's cooperative domestic labor, the tradition in other places of men's or mixed-gender textile work, and the even larger tradition of human art and craft in general.

Such cooperation among knitters, as in other arts, stretches across the boundaries of time and geography. Through oral and written transmission, new knitters have available the accumulated wisdom of past generations. As new materials and techniques are invented, these are incorporated into a shared body of knowledge, from which other knitters can draw. In recent years, this process has experienced exponential amplification through the Internet. Today, knitters have available not only the knowledge of centuries but also of the distinctive technical and aesthetic styles of many different cultures. Knitting has also developed its own literature, one that often combines investigations of skill and technique with interrogations of the place of art, creativity, and the production of practically useful objects in a whole human life. In this sense, for many practitioners, the practice of knitting opens the participant to serious discussions of his or her own—and the human—*telos*. Similarly it contributes to the ongoing discussions and arguments within the *tradition* of human art-making about questions such as, what constitutes "real" art, and how we recognize "good" art.

Knitting is thus complex and cooperative, perhaps, but what are the "goods internal" to the practice of knitting? These are surprisingly numerous and various. To begin, there is the obvious good of the well-made product, whose creation requires mastery of particular techniques together with, as in any of the arts, the capacity to imagine and bring into the world something that does not yet exist. Many knitters also find that the process itself is one of the goods of knitting, the tactile experience of yarn, the rhythmic, often meditative work of repetitive stitches, the sensory pleasures of color and texture. In addition, there is the good of learning new things and of improving one's skills. Then there is the good of human connection, created when knitting an object for a specific other, or when creating an object that will appeal to the sensory inter-est of many other people.

Knitting has a variety of *teloi,* of purposes internal to the practice. But what sort of virtues, if any, might a knitter possibly expect to develop? What "harms, dangers, temptations and distractions" as MacIntyre puts it, must a knitter overcome in the development of such virtues?[29] It is true that the harms and dangers of knitting are relatively minor (although anyone who has accidentally impaled herself with a size 0 metal sock needle might beg to differ!). Of temp-tations and distractions, however, there are many. The greatest temptations is perhaps that of leaving errors that one knows ought to be corrected. There is the opposing temptation of demanding of the work a level of perfection that is not available to human skill. Like Aristotle's virtues, that of truthfully evaluat-ing one's work is an average, a mean—and the mean relative to the particular knitter. This truthfulness about one's knitting is a kind of *justice*, a rendering to the work what it is due: an accurate and fair description of its quality, in view of one's own level of development as a knitter.

A good knitter needs the fortitude or *courage* necessary to an honest evalu-ation of the work and the determination to complete a project, even through long stretches of boring repetition. Courage also carries the knitter through the frustration of needing more than once to rip out and rework an unsuccess-ful or mistaken portion of work. It also takes courage to begin a challenging project, one that may exceed the knitter's skills.

A knitter also needs the virtue of *temperance,* the ability to judge for example when that nagging pain in the wrist must be accepted as a warning of potential injury. No matter how strong the urge to complete just one more row, temper-ance requires resisting desire that is proving harmful. Many knitters say that the forbearance thus acquired has proved invaluable in other aspects of their lives, when, for example, caring for a difficult child or an ailing parent.

Finally, knitting requires and engenders a most practical sort of wisdom— the ability not only to judge and evaluate one's work but also to place that work within the confines of a whole life. Attentive knitting engenders understanding and appreciation of others' work, of the interconnectedness of human beings as social animals, of the economic and ethical implications of daily decisions and actions. Knitters, for example, were among the most ardent proponents of 2009 as the United Nations International Year of Natural Fibres, organized to support and expand the natural fiber traditions and enterprises of many developing countries.[30] As with any practice, each practitioner achieves these goods and virtues to a different degree at different stages of his or her own development within the practice.

Challenges to MacIntyre's Ethics

Relativism

Virtue ethics is not without its critics, however. One common criticism is that MacIntyre's virtue ethics are hopelessly relativistic.[31] If virtues arise out of practices that in turn are rooted in culturally and historically specific traditions, how can anyone standing outside that tradition make an ethical judgment of it? If, the argument goes, leaving infants born with disabilities outdoors to die is acceptable in your culture, it is meaningless for someone from outside your culture to accuse you of murder. What you are doing is not, by your definition, murder; by another definition, it is. You and your accuser are at an ethical impasse. This problem must be faced squarely if one hopes to make an ethical claim about torture, or indeed about any human activity, that can hold across the boundaries of different societies.

MacIntyre makes a lengthy response to the charge of relativism, both in the afterword of the second edition of *After Virtue* and in the later *Whose Justice? Which Rationality?* Rather than rehearse that defense (which is probably mostly of interest to philosophers and is not directly relevant to a discussion of torture), I am going to propose a somewhat different one, developed by the philosopher Martha Nussbaum.[32]

Like MacIntyre and his critics, Nussbaum is concerned about the problem of making ethical judgments across cultures.[33] This is not just an academic issue. The ability to make ethical judgments about events in other societies has practical consequences when, for example, the countries that have joined the International Criminal Court seek to try a former head of state for war crimes. Or, closer to our own inquiry, when the members of the United Nations sign a covenant against torture.

Nussbaum does not believe that all societies are or ought to be the same, or that they do or should share identical ethics. What she does believe, however, is that different ethical systems can be compared. It is certainly true, for example, that societies differ about what counts as courage (as opposed to cowardice or recklessness). Every society, however, shares the common human experience of confronting the risk of injury or death; hence, every society has a corresponding virtue of something like what English speakers call "courage."[34]

Elsewhere Nussbaum has continued this line of thought, arguing that there are certain experiences so basic to the nature of the human species that they form the parameters within which all cultures develop. Among them she includes "mortality," "the human body," "cognitive capability" (including "perceiving, imagining, thinking"), "early infant development," "practical reason" (including planning and organizing one's life), "affiliation with other human beings," "relatedness to other species and to nature," "humor and play," and varying degrees of "separateness."[35] These universal human experiences, she argues, correspond to a set of shared human *capabilities,* recognition of which should inform cross-cultural discussions of, for example, economic and social development policies. She offers what she calls a "vague, thick" list of these capabilities, among them:

1. Being able to live out a complete human life as far as is possible; not dying prematurely or before one's life is so reduced as to be not worth living;
2. Being able to have good health, adequate nourishment, adequate shelter, opportunities for sexual satisfaction; being able to move from place to place;
3. Being able to avoid unnecessary and nonbeneficial pain and to have pleasurable experiences;
4. Being able to use the five senses; being able to imagine, think, and reason; and
5. Being able to have attachments to things and persons outside ourselves; to love those who love and care for us, to grieve at their absence; in general, to love, to grieve, to feel longing and gratitude.[36]

Nussbaum completes her argument in the article where this list appears by calling for an "essentialist" public policy—one that considers the opportunity to develop these capabilities (or some similar list) as essential to any description of a good human life. "Without an account of the good—however vague—that we take to be *shared*," she says, "we have . . . no adequate way of justifying the claim that any deeply embedded tradition we encounter is unjust."[37] This is true, I believe, whether we are discussing the practice of women's education or the practice of torture.

The "Unity of the Virtues"

Is it possible to be courageous without being just? Can one who is not practically wise be temperate, having good control of his or her appetites and desires? In general, is it possible to possess some of the key virtues without possessing all of them to some degree or other? Those who answer these questions in the negative defend the "unity of the virtues," the idea that, unlike a set of technical skills, virtue is an interlocking system in which all of the various parts are necessary for the whole to function.

Indeed, critics of virtue ethics have long considered the separability of the virtues to be one of its key faults. Immanuel Kant makes this critique at the beginning of the *Foundation of the Metaphysics of Morals*. In an argument directed against Aristotle's ethics, Kant maintains that, absent a good will, neither the intellectual nor the moral virtues are good at all. In fact, such dispositions of mind and character can "become extremely bad, and the coolness of a villain makes him not only far more dangerous but also more directly abominable in our eyes than he would have seemed without it."[38]

MacIntyre makes a similar point in *After Virtue*. Like Kant, who condemns the courageous "coolness of a villain," MacIntyre posits the existence of such a villain, in this case, "a devoted and intelligent Nazi," who possesses the virtue of courage. He says that someone committed to believing that having one key virtue requires having them all would have a problem with this Nazi: Either the Nazi is not really courageous, or courage is not really a virtue. Neither answer seemed satisfactory to MacIntyre.[39]

In his preface to *Whose Justice? Which Rationality?* MacIntyre indicates that he has changed his mind on this point, however. "I now," he writes, "think that my earlier criticism of Aquinas' theses on the unity of the virtues was simply mistaken."[40] What is the mistake MacIntyre believes that he made? Theologian Christopher Stephen Lutz argues that when in his earlier work MacIntyre divided up the virtues, and particularly when separating the moral virtues of courage, temperance and justice from the intellectual virtue of prudence (practical wisdom), he robbed the moral virtues of their content and reduced prudence to knowledge that has no practical effect on action.

Consider courage, for example. "Courage," says Lutz, "is a moral virtue, not an intellectual one. It is concerned with the subjection of desires to reason. Yet it clearly demands certain intellectual judgments in order to function."[41] Without the intellectual judgments made possible by prudence, which Aquinas, following Aristotle, calls right reason applied to action, how are we to know what is the right response to danger?[42] "What is to count as cowardice?" asks Lutz. "What is to count as rashness? What is the purpose to which my courageous acts are to be directed?" He continues, "These are intellectual judgments that demand practical wisdom." In other words, if we are to understand courage as the virtue that allows reason to control and direct into proper action our feelings of fear, the part of our reason responsible for making such decisions must be in good working order.[43]

Similarly, MacIntyre argues in *Whose Justice?*, if we have prudence, or practical wisdom, without the moral habits that permit us to control our passions, we may *know* what the right thing is to do, but we will be unable to do it. Indeed, as Aquinas observes, when those moral virtues are missing, practical wisdom devolves into "those simulacra of the virtue of prudence—worldly good sense, caution, and cunning.”[44] Moreover, if we are lacking the virtue of justice, of giving to each what is owed or due, our practical reason is likely to be distorted by greed, distaste, or even an excessive and ill-placed tenderness for those we care about.

In an article called “Social Structures and Their Threats to Moral Agency,” MacIntyre addresses a particular failure of prudence, one I call “culpable ignorance.”[45] The article asks whether we are justified in holding someone morally responsible for his or her actions when the social structures surrounding the individual prevent him or her from forming the moral and intellectual virtues that are necessary for right action in the first place. MacIntyre posits as his primary example an individual named “J” who in his role as a train operator, which he discharged admirably over a period of years, learned early on that performing well meant not asking questions about the nature of the trains’ cargo. “Hence he acquired the habit of taking no notice of what his trains carried, a habit that endured through a later period, when the freight consisted in munitions and the passengers were Jews on their way to the concentration camps.” MacIntyre stipulates that J genuinely did not know what his trains were carrying. Was he then morally responsible for his actions?[46]

While many people will respond, “Yes! Of course,” MacIntyre wants us to think the question through more carefully. We can hold moral agents responsible, he says, in at least three ways: for their intentional actions, for “incidental aspects of those actions of which they should have been aware,” and for “at least some of the reasonably predictable effects of their actions.” The problem in making such judgments arises when we ask whether there are “or might be types of social structure that would prevent those who inhabited them from understanding themselves as moral agents” or at least make it very difficult to do so.[47]

MacIntyre imagines such a society, one in which, as people move from role to role—acting now as parent, now as a corporate CEO—they are required to adopt a different stance toward various virtues, such as truthfulness. In this society, the standards of truth that govern scientific inquiry, for example, are inappropriate in the realm of advertising. To succeed within the terms defined by such a society requires a certain flexibility, a quality that MacIntyre considers the antithesis of the virtue of integrity, which he defines as “the refusal to be, to have educated oneself so that one is no longer able to be, one kind of person in one social context, while quite another in other contexts.”[48] This is an example of a social structure in which it is indeed difficult for a person to conceive of him- or herself as an integrated moral agent.

But MacIntyre believes that the person who has allowed him- or herself to become divided in such a way must have cooperated intentionally (if not

consciously) in the process. He argues that the acquisition of this sort of flexibility, the division of the self into different roles with different moral systems,
requires some active participation on the part of that self. Even in a fully com-
partmentalized society, where there are few spaces in which people act as undi-
vided selves, human beings must still apply their practical reason if only to play
their roles as well as possible. At some level, however inarticulate, they must
ask how their role can best be played; by what standard their performance is
to be judged. "It is the inescapability on occasion of such questions," he says, "
that suggests that the practical reasoning that is adequate for doing whatever
a particular role requires will itself generate reasons for acting beyond those
requirements and even sometimes against those requirements." To do otherwise involves a conscious effort—an effort that when practiced often enough
becomes a habit:

> To resist asking such questions, to insist upon terminating one's prac-
> tical reasoning whenever it directs one beyond one's role requires a
> peculiar kind of self-discipline. To be able to restrict one's practical
> reasoning to what will enable one to discharge the responsibilities
> of one's socially approved roles is to have imposed on one's timing a
> set of artificial restrictions. It is to have arbitrarily closed one's mind
> to certain possibilities of action. And, although others may provide
> one with motives for effecting such a closure, it is only with one's own
> active cooperation that the habits of mind can be developed which
> make such closure possible.[49]

MacIntyre argues that "to learn to focus one's attention in this way . . . requires
active cooperation."[50] If his argument holds, and I believe it does, then it follows that people in the United States can fairly be held responsible for having
formed "habits of mind" that allow us to ignore, for example, the incoherence
between a nation's self-definition as champion of human rights and its institutionalized practice of torture. "We didn't know" is not a sufficient defense. As
in the case of MacIntyre's J, refusing to know is indeed culpable.

Evil Practices?

I have argued in previous chapters that one of the key failings of most contemporary ethical approaches to torture is that they treat it as an isolated incident, rather than as an ongoing, socially embedded practice. I have suggested
that understanding torture as a practice, in the sense intended by MacIntyre,
might reveal its otherwise invisible and unacknowledged aspects, including
the goods pursued by those who practice it and the habitual qualities of mind

and character engendered in that pursuit. However, one serious obstacle remains to treating torture as a practice in the sense described in this chapter. It would seem that an "evil practice" is a contradiction in terms. MacIntyre anchors his definition of a practice in the larger context of an individual and societal quest for the good life for human beings and a description of the virtues such a quest requires. How can we suppose that that an inherently evil practice and the qualities engendered by its pursuit could contribute to identifying or living the good life for human beings?

The answer is that we cannot. An "evil practice" really is a contradiction in terms. However, I believe that a complex, collaborative, but evil activity is very *like* a practice, with the important caveat that what it requires and produces in its practitioners is not virtue but vice. It makes good sense to call this sort of activity, of which institutionalized state torture is an example, in Christopher Lutz's words, a "false practice."

Lutz argues that the "apparent goods internal to wicked practices cannot be real goods." In fact, he says that one aspect of a real virtue is that it allows us to tell the difference between what is genuinely good and imposters. *"A virtue,"* he says, *"is an acquired human quality the possession and exercise of which may effectively prevent us from achieving the apparent goods internal to wicked practices and the lack of which tends to enable us to achieve such goods."*[51]

Here is an example of someone whose habits of courage and practical wisdom prevented him or her from being able to accept cruelty as a good thing, even when that cruelty was dressed up as courage and loyalty. It is found in MacIntyre's own account of an actual Nazi physician who, in great shame wrote to his superiors that he was "too gentle" for the work of murdering Germany's mentally disabled children. What this doctor perceived in himself—and in this he was confirmed by the other practitioners of Nazi eugenics—as vicious cowardice, Lutz counts as virtue: "While the Nazis may have regarded his inability to act on his 'convictions' about the euthanasia policy as cowardly squeamishness, we may recognize instead a conscience that barred him from killing innocent children, and demanded that he take the risk of stepping down from his position instead."[52]

I am reminded by this example of another, found not in the historical record but in Mark Twain's novel *The Adventures of Huckleberry Finn*. In the climactic moments of the novel, Huck has written a letter to the woman from whom his friend Jim, a slave, has run away, telling her where she can find her "property." Huck is convinced that only his own wickedness stands between him and doing the right thing, turning Jim in. And yet, what he describes as his wickedness will not allow him to do it. The virtues formed through the practice of friendship will not permit him to do what his whole social order—political, philosophical, and theological—tells him would be just. Huck says:

I felt good and all washed clean of sin for the first time I had ever felt so in my life, and I knowed I could pray now. But I didn't do it straight off, but laid the paper down and set there thinking—thinking how good it was all this happened so, and how near I come to being lost and going to hell. And went on thinking. And got to thinking over our trip down the river; and I see Jim before me, all the time; in the day, and in the night-time, sometimes moonlight, sometimes storms, and we a floating along, talking, and singing, and laughing. But somehow I couldn't seem to strike no places to harden me against him, but only the other kind. I'd see him standing my watch on top of his'n, stead of calling me, so I could go on sleeping; and see how glad he was when I come back out of the fog; and when I come to him agin in the swamp, up there where the feud was; and such-like times; and would always call me honey, and pet me, and do everything he could think of for me, and how good he always was; and at last I struck the time I saved him by telling the men we had smallpox aboard, and he was so grateful, and said I was the best friend old Jim ever had in the world, and the only one he's got now; and then I happened to look around, and see that paper.

It was a close place. I took it up, and held it in my hand. I was a trembling, because I'd got to decide, forever, betwixt two things, and I knowed it. I studied a minute, sort of holding my breath, and then says to myself:

"All right, then, I'll go to hell"—and tore it up.[53]

At first glance this example may seem closely analogous to those offered by Elshtain and Walzer, described in the previous chapter. How is Huck Finn different from the good politician with dirty hands, the one who is willing to bear the guilt of ordering the torture of a suspected terrorist? MacIntyre has given us, I think, a good answer. Huck's practice of friendship has formed him in justice and courage, even courage in the face of the demon God of his imagination. His practical wisdom allows him to recognize the particularities of his situation, of what is due to a person who has stood watch so one can sleep, who has cared tenderly for one. Compare Huck's practice of friendship to Walzer's Machiavellian *realpolitik*. The virtues are not empty shells; their particular content matters. There is a difference between choosing to know the real nature of slavery and risking everything by rejecting it and choosing not to know the real nature of torture and risking nothing by permitting it.

I am perfectly comfortable, then, with characterizing torture as a "false practice." This description maintains the recognition that like other practices, torture is a complex, collaborative, socially and historically embedded human activity that is also a locus of the formation of habits of character and mind. To call torture a *false* practice, indicates that it does not tend to produce in its practitioners the virtues of courage, justice, temperance, and practical wisdom but rather, as I shall argue in the following chapter, their opposites.

Notes

1. Aristotle, *Nicomachean Ethics*, trans. David Ross (New York: Oxford University Press, 1998), 1.
2. My discussion of MacIntyre's work on virtue ethics is partly informed by Brad J. Kallenberg's essay, "The Master Argument of Alasdair MacIntyre's *After Virtue*" in *Virtues and Practices in the Christian Tradition: Christian Ethics after Macintyre*, ed. Nancey C. Murphy, Brad J. Kallenberg, and Mark Nation (Harrisburg, PA: Trinity Press International, 1997), S64.
3. Although MacIntyre speaks of "novels" I suspect that he is thinking here particularly of Walter J. Miller Jr.'s haunting 1959 novel, *A Canticle for Leibowitz*, in which engineering texts on nuclear physics have come to serve as the basis of religious ritual. See Walter M. Miller, *A Canticle for Leibowitz* (New York: Bantam Books, 1961).
4. Alasdair MacIntyre, *After Virtue*, 2d ed. (Notre Dame, IN: Notre Dame University Press, 1984), 19.
5. Ibid.; emphasis in the original.
6. I see the evidence for MacIntyre's contention in the hundreds of students who have passed through my university ethics classes. With depressing regularity they conclude that, "ethics are different for each person" and "in the end ethics just comes down to what you personally believe."
7. Murphy, Kallenberg, and Nation, *Virtues and Practices in the Christian Tradition*, 20–21.
8. MacIntyre, *After Virtue*, 222.
9. Aristotle, *Nicomachean Ethics*, 1 (1094a).
10. MacIntyre, *After Virtue*, 58–59; ibid.
11. Murphy, Kallenberg, and Nation, *Virtues and Practices in the Christian Tradition*, 13.
12. Ibid.
13. MacIntyre is using the word "liberal" as it is understood in political philosophy: a model of human beings and society that privileges individuality, equality among individuals, and liberty of individual action. In the liberal view, the individual, rather than, for example, the family or the social group is the fundamental unit of society.
14. Alasdair MacIntyre, *Whose Justice? Which Rationality?* (Notre Dame, IN: University of Notre Dame Press, 1988), 338–39.
15. MacIntyre, *After Virtue*, 187.
16. Ibid., 190.
17. Ibid., 188–89.
18. Ibid., 187; emphasis in original.
19. Aristotle, *Nicomachean Ethics*, 1103a11.
20. MacIntyre, *After Virtue*, 203.
21. Frederick Winslow Taylor, *The Principles of Scientific Management*, The Norton Library (New York: Norton, 1967).
22. MacIntyre, *After Virtue*, 219.
23. Ibid.
24. Aristotle, *Nicomachean Ethics*, 1107a25–08b12.
25. MacIntyre, *After Virtue*, 222.
26. Ibid.
27. Ibid., 222–23.

28. Debbie New, *Unexpected Knitting* (Cary Bluff-Pittsville, WI: Schoolhouse). For information on mathematical knitting, see mathematician Sarah-Marie Belcastro's website, http://www.toroidalsnark.net/mathknit.html.
29. MacIntyre, *After Virtue*, 219.
30. See http://www.naturalfibres2009.org/
31. It is odd, indeed, that MacIntyre, who seeks to recapture an ancient Athenian ethics should find himself accused of being, in effect, too postmodern.
32. Nussbaum shares credit for the development of capabilities theory with the philosopher and economist Amartya Sen.
33. Note that Nussbaum and MacIntyre are far from being in perfect agreement about what sort of society best contributes to human flourishing. See, for example, her review of MacIntyre's *Whose Justice? Which Rationality?* (Martha C. Nussbaum, "Recoiling from Reason,"*New York Review of Books*, December 7, 1989.)
34. Martha C. Nussbaum, "Non-Relative Virtues: An Aristotelian Approach," *Midwest Studies In Philosophy* 13 (1988).
35. Martha C. Nussbaum, "Social Justice and Universalism: In Defense of an Aristotelian Account of Human Functioning," *Modern Philology* 90 suppl. (1993), S55–S57.
36. Ibid., S58–S59. In recent years Nussbaum and Sen have each made different use of the capabilities apporach, which also find echoes in the definition of justice found in Iris Marion Young's *Justice and the Politics of Difference* (Princeton, NJ: Princeton University Press, 1990). Young defines social justice as the existence of structures which allow for "developing and exercising one's capacities and expressing one's experience" and "participating in determining one's action and the conditions of one's action" (37).
37. Nussbaum, "Social Justice and Universalism: In Defense of an Aristotelian Account of Human Functioning"; emphasis in original.
38. Immanuel Kant, *Foundations of the Metaphysics of Morals*, trans. Lewis White Beck (Upper Saddle River, NJ: Prentice-Hall, Inc., 1997), 10.
39. MacIntyre, *After Virtue*, 180.
40. MacIntyre, *Whose Justice? Which Rationality?*, x.
41. Christopher Stephen Lutz, *Tradition in the Ethics of Alasdair Macintyre: Relativism, Thomism, and Philosophy* (Lanham, MD: Lexington Books, 2004), 101.
42. Thomas Aquinas, *Summa Theologica*, trans. Fathers of the English Dominican Province (Notre Dame, IN: Ave Maria, 1981; reprint, 1981), II–II, Q.47, a.4.
43. Lutz, *Tradition in the Ethics of Alasdair Macintyre*, 101.
44. MacIntyre, *Whose Justice? Which Rationality?*, 197.
45. Alasdair MacIntyre, "Social Structures and Their Threat to Moral Agency," in *Ethics and Politics: Selected Essays*, ed. Alasdair MacIntyre (New York: Cambridge University Press, 2006).
46. Ibid., 186–87.
47. Ibid., 189.
48. Ibid., 192.
49. Ibid., 201.
50. Ibid.
51. Lutz, *Tradition in the Ethics of Alasdair Macintyre*, 103; emphasis in the original.
52. Ibid.
53. Mark Twain, *Adventures of Huckleberry Finn* (New York: Penguin, 1953), 330–31.

5

Considering Torture as a (False) Practice

> If the choice of technique is entirely arbitrary and random, one
> would not expect to find national styles of torture. But since they
> do exist, they need to be explained. My explanation for these per-
> sisting styles takes seriously the notion that torture is a craft, not a
> science.... When explaining why regional craftsmen differ in the
> way they make clothes, one might consider habit and training (this
> is how we do it here) ...[1]
>
> —Darius Rejali, *Torture and Democracy*

Is institutionalized state torture a "false practice," in the sense described in the
previous chapter? Is it a complex, collaborative activity with its own internal
goods? Does it engender moral habits in its practitioners? Is it embedded in
a larger tradition or traditions? If so, how does this understanding of torture
enlarge our ethical view of it, beyond what is illumined by the consequentialist
and deontological approaches discussed earlier?

One important issue must be addressed directly first. Even if we accept the
argument that torture is a practice and therefore contributes to the moral formation of torturers, to what extent are we justified in extending those effects
beyond the walls of the actual torture sites? Is it legitimate to claim that allowing institutionalized torture to continue affects anyone besides (most obviously) its victims, the torturers, and perhaps their immediate superiors? I will
argue that it is.

If institutionalized state torture is a practice, then like any practice it must
be embedded in institutions. In the case of the United States, these include institutions such as the various armed forces, the CIA, the Justice Department,
and the presidency. A practice also resides within one or more traditions. There
are different levels of involvement in torture, including those who do it, those
who order it, and those who are, to use a Latin American expression, its "intellectual authors." Responsibility extends outward, taking in Congress and the
judiciary, the press, academics, civic organizations, religious organizations,
political parties, and finally citizens in general. All of these are involved in the

ongoing arguments about the nature of the United States of America, arguments that MacIntyre would call "traditions." These include centuries-old debates about what constitute "American values" and an equally long argument
about what makes for "national security." The latter stretches back at least as far
as the preamble of the U.S. Constitution, which names among the document's
purposes the need "to provide for the common defense."

These traditions involve, whether consciously or not, almost everyone who
lives in this country. They are invoked whenever a president or an editorial
writer talks about the contradiction between torture and "American values"—
and when an audience responds to that invocation. We participate in an ongoing argument about the meaning of national security when we mutter (or
choose not to mutter) to fellow passengers about submitting to a full body scan
before boarding an airplane. We ourselves may not be torturers, but we are
all part, whether we choose to be or not, of the ongoing argument about what
practices we will permit to continue, as long as we believe they will keep us
secure. Over time, the part we play in that argument can, I believe, become a
habit.

That the practice of torture can affect the character of a society is attested
to by many scholars, among them the psychologist Ervin Staub,[2] whose argument John Conroy summarizes as the view that "a society can be an incubator
for human rights abuse, that nations can march gradually along a continuum
of destruction until the employment of torturers is no radical step and the men
and women hired for the job merely reflect the attitudes of the larger society."
The process begins during periods of instability—in which a society's leaders identify a group (Marxists, Jews, Arabs, Muslims) as the source of danger
and uncertainty. "The scapegoated group is humiliated, ridiculed, dehuman-
ized, and eventually finds itself beyond the compassion of the public at large."
Indeed, the very fact that they have been imprisoned and tortured can create
contempt for the sufferers.[3] "Torture, kidnapping, and execution follow," adds
Conroy. "In Staub's analysis, the whole society learns by doing, and the torturer is part of the process."[4]

Torture as Practice

It makes sense to speak of torture as a practice. (For the sake of simplicity, I
am abandoning the qualifier "false," but the reader should keep in mind that
insofar as we conclude it is wicked per se, torture can only ever constitute a
false practice in MacIntyre's understanding of practice.) People often call torture a practice in ordinary conversation. Indeed, the expression "the practice
of torture" has a familiar ring to the ear of an English speaker, while "an act of

torture" sounds a bit odd. Casual speakers seem to assume that torture represents a form of human behavior that at the very least is too extended in time to be called an act. A student in one of my college-level ethics classes provides a good example of this view. "Torture is a process," he writes. "Unlike murder it is not a spontaneous thing. You can't just torture someone in a short fit of rage. Torture is something that is ongoing over a period of time. This period of time gives a person more than ample opportunity to realize that what they are doing is wrong."[5] This brief observation expresses two important aspects of torture that make it something other than an isolated act or acts: its repetitive extension in time and the fact that torture is not a spontaneous action; it must be planned and organized.

In fact, it appears that it is mainly ethicists and lawyers who have rejected such common-sense understandings and opted to parse "something that is ongoing over a period of time" into individual, isolated actions. For example, in a series of memos written to the CIA in May 2005 at its request, Steven G. Bradbury of the Justice Department's Office of Legal Counsel (OLC) examines thirteen specific interrogation "techniques." These include "dietary manipulation, nudity, the attention grasp, walling, the facial hold, the facial or insult slap, the abdominal slap, cramped confinement, wall standing, stress positions, water dousing, extended sleep deprivation, and the 'waterboard.'" (This list later came to be known as the CIA's "enhanced interrogation techniques," sometimes abbreviated as EITs.) Two of these memos assess each technique in isolation to determine whether its use would constitute torture as defined either by the UN Convention against Torture or by the sections of U.S. law enacted to implement the Convention. Bradbury concludes that no one of these activities, taken by itself, does in fact violate either the Convention or the U.S. law.[6]

One OLC memo, for example, subjects such terms as "severe," "suffering," and "harm" to careful interrogation by way of examining their dictionary definitions and their interpretations in past legal decisions. The memo then examines each technique in turn, considering whether the technique might violate Section §2340 of the federal legal code (the text of which is found in Chapter 1). One such technique is a maneuver called "walling." According to the memo, walling

> involves the use of a flexible, false wall. The individual is placed with his heels touching the flexible wall. The interrogator pulls the individual forward and then quickly and firmly pushes the individual into the wall. It is the individual's shoulder blades that hit the wall. During this motion, the head and neck are supported with a rolled hood or towel that provides a C-collar effect to help prevent whiplash.[7]

This procedure, Bradbury concludes, cannot be legally construed as torture because, "although the walling technique involves the use of considerable force to push the detainee against the wall and may involve a large number of repetitions in certain cases, we understand that the false wall that is used is flexible and that this technique is not designed to, and does not, cause severe physical pain to the detainee." Bradbury is further reassured by his "understand[ing] that medical and psychological personnel are present or observing during the use of this technique (as with all techniques involving physical contact with a detainee), and that any member of the team or the medical staff may intercede to stop the use of the technique if it is being used improperly or if it appears that it may cause injury to the detainee."[8]

It would have been worrisome enough had this technique been implemented in the way described in the OLC memo. However, a report about the CIA's treatment of fourteen "high-value detainees" compiled by the International Committee of the Red Cross (ICRC) suggests that in actual practice, walling is even less benign than the memo's description of it. The ICRC report characterizes walling as "beating by use of a collar" and observes that six of the detainees "alleged that an improvised thick collar or neck roll was placed around their necks and used by their interrogators to slam them against the walls." Abu Zubaydah told the Red Cross that "when the collar was first used on him in his third place of detention, he was slammed directly against a hard concrete wall." He then spent several hours in a narrow upright box (the "cramped confinement" described in the memo). "After he was taken out of the box," the Red Cross report continues, "he noticed that a sheet of plywood had been placed against the wall. The collar was then used to slam him against the plywood sheet." Presumably, the plywood was there to supply the "flexibility" mentioned in the OLC memos.[9]

The Bradbury memo also considers whether sleep deprivation might violate Section §2340. It concludes that the main method of ensuring a detainee's remaining awake—forcing him to remain standing for days by shackling his arms over his head—was unlikely to cause severe physical pain or suffering. "Although edema, or swelling, of the lower legs may sometimes develop as a result of the long periods of standing associated with sleep deprivation," Bradbury writes, "we understand from OMS [the CIA's Office of Medical Services] that such edema is not painful and will dissipate once the subject is removed from the standing position."[10]

The experience of Walid Bin Attash, one of the high-value detainees discussed in the memos, appears to be at variance with this sanguine view that sleep deprivation achieved by enforced standing causes no pain. Bin Attash told the ICRC:

On arrival at the place of detention in Afghanistan I was stripped naked. I remained naked for the next two weeks. I was put in a cell measuring approximately 1m x 2m. I was kept in a standing position, feet flat on the floor, but with my arms above my head and fixed with handcuffs and a chain to a metal bar running across the width of the cell. The cell was dark with no light, artificial or natural. . . . After some time of being held in this position my stump began to hurt so I removed my artificial leg to relieve the pain. Of course my one good leg then began to ache and soon started to give way so that I was left hanging with all my weight on my wrists. I shouted for help but at first nobody came. Finally, after about one hour a guard came and my artificial leg was given back to me and I was again placed in the standing position with my hands above my head. After that the interrogators sometimes deliberately removed my artificial leg in order to add extra stress to the position.[11]

Bradbury's May 10, 2005 memo then considers other possible physical effects of this treatment, taking comfort from the fact that the CIA's "OMS personnel have informed us that the shackling of detainees is not designed to and does not result in significant physical pain. A detainee subject to sleep deprivation would not be allowed to hang by his wrists, and we understand that no detainee subjected to sleep deprivation to date has been allowed to hang by his wrists or has otherwise suffered injury." Taking all this into consideration and "particularly given the imprecision in the statutory standard and the lack of guidance from the courts" and not withstanding the circumstance that "some individuals would eventually feel weak physically [after standing for several days] and may experience unpleasant physical sensations from prolonged fatigue, including such symptoms as impairment to coordinated body movement, difficulty with speech, nausea, and blurred vision" the memo concludes that "extended sleep deprivation, subject to the limitations and conditions described herein, would not be expected to cause 'severe physical suffering.'"[12]

Bradbury then considers the psychological effects of sleep deprivation, asking whether these might conceivably risk violation of the statute. He acknowledges that "it may be questioned whether sleep deprivation could be characterized as a procedure 'calculated to disrupt profoundly the senses or the personality' within the meaning of section 2340(2)(B)" but concludes that it does not, for two reasons. First, even if a sleep-deprived detainee were to experience hallucinations, such apparent disruption of the senses would not be sufficiently "profound" to be prohibited under the law.

Second, and perhaps more important, "even assuming, however, that the extended use of sleep deprivation may result in hallucinations that could fairly be characterized as a 'profound' disruption of the subject's senses," it would not violate the law, because such hallucinations are merely a byproduct of sleep deprivation, not its "calculated" purpose. Thus, writes Bradbury, "We do not believe it tenable to conclude that in such circumstances the use of sleep deprivation could be said to be 'calculated' to cause such profound disruption to the senses, as required by the statute," which prohibits "procedures calculated to disrupt profoundly the senses or personality."[13] Bradbury then consults Webster's *Third New International Dictionary,* discovering there that "the term 'calculated' denotes something that is planned or thought out beforehand." Because producing hallucinations is not the *goal* of sleep deprivation, he concludes that "any hallucination on the part of a detainee undergoing sleep deprivation is not something that would be a 'calculated' result of the use of this technique."[14]

Punctilious attempts like these to justify torture might be amusing, if the subject were not so serious. I have discussed these examples at some length (although not nearly the length covered by more than one hundred pages of memos) to illustrate the pitfalls of treating a complex activity like torture as if it were simply a series of isolated actions. By breaking torture down into smaller and smaller constitutive "acts," Bradbury and his fellows at the OLC attempt to make it disappear altogether.

But intuition alone cannot prove that torture is a practice nor that it qualifies as the sort of "false" practice described in the previous chapter. What are the criteria for such a practice? Here again is Alasdair MacIntyre's description: A practice is a "coherent and complex form of socially established cooperative activity through which goods internal to that form of activity are realized in the course of trying to achieve those standards of excellence which are appropriate to, and partially definitive of, that form of activity."[15] A practice in MacIntyre's sense has a history and standards of excellence developed through that history. Its existence implies a community of practitioners who share the practice and initiate others into it. A practice arises in the context of, and in turn contributes to the development of, a tradition—an ongoing argument about what is good for those who share the tradition.

"A Coherent and Complex Form of Socially Established Cooperative Activity"

Coherent and Complex

Is institutionalized state torture a "coherent and complex form of socially established cooperative activity?" It is certainly coherent and cooperative, in the sense that it focuses the theoretical acumen and practical skills of diverse individuals on a single goal—the fragmentation of individual psyches and social bodies. It is complex in that this goal is achieved via multiple and various means. It is socially established, in that it resides within the purview of one or more government institutions and is often organized with a bureaucratic efficiency.

Indeed, while torture is generally conducted in secret, meticulous record keeping is a hallmark of many torture regimes. This was certainly the case under military rule in Brazil, for example. Lawrence Weschler describes a conversation with Jaime Wright, a Brazilian Presbyterian minister who oversaw a five-year clandestine project to photocopy thousands of accounts of torture by the Brazilian police: "The Brazilian generals," he told Weschler, "were technocrats. . . . They were obsessed with keeping complete records as they went along."[16] The generals, said Wright, never thought they would be prosecuted for what they were doing. As another informant told Weschler, "They imagined that they were laying the groundwork for a civilization that would last a thousand years—that, far from having to justify themselves for occasional lapses, they would be celebrated by all posterity for the breadth of their achievement."[17]

Members of the Bush administration appear to have been less complacent about their place in history and their safety from prosecution, as is evidenced by the cocoon of legal opinions with which they sought to surround themselves. Nonetheless, it appears that the various U.S. agencies involved in torture have also kept records, although the majority of these remain classified. Records that are publicly available include one interrogation log from Guantánamo (that of Mohammad al-Qahtani, the so-called 20th hijacker);[18] the informal photographs and videos taken by the military police at Abu Ghraib;[19] and at least two thousand photographs and other records of interrogations in Afghanistan and Iraq kept by the U.S. military.

These last were the subject of a Freedom of Information Act suit by the American Civil Liberties Union and were scheduled to be released by the end of May 2009, but the Obama administration prevented their publication. ACLU lawyer Amit Singh contends that "These photographs provide visual proof that prisoner abuse by US personnel was not aberrational but widespread, reaching far beyond the walls of Abu Ghraib."[20] The matter was still being discussed in Congress in April 2011, but to date the photos have not been released.

One of Steven Bradbury's 2005 memos to John Rizzo, then-Acting General Counsel of the CIA, notes that that agency also recorded its work assiduously. Bradbury wrote that according to information his office had received from the CIA, "Careful records are kept of each interrogation." This procedure, he continues, "ensures accountability and allows for *ongoing evaluation of the efficacy of each technique* and its potential for any unintended or inappropriate results."[21] In other words, records were kept, at least in part, as data in an ongoing experiment in the effectiveness of particular kinds of treatment. This suggestion accords with what one of the CIA's subjects told the ICRC: "It felt like they were experimenting and trying out techniques to be used later on other people."[22]

Waterboarding sessions, in particular, were closely observed and recorded. A May 2004 CIA *Special Review of Counterterrorism Detention and Interrogation Activities* describes these records as necessary "to best inform future medical judgments and recommendations." Whatever reason, the level of detail required is impressive:

> It is important that every application of the waterboard be thoroughly documented: how long each application (and the entire procedure) lasted, how much water was used in the process (realizing that much splashes off), how exactly the water was applied, if a seal was achieved, if the naso- or oropharynx was filled, what sort of volume was expelled, how long was the break between applications, and how the subject looked between each treatment.[23]

It also became known that the CIA videotaped at least some of the 266 waterboarding sessions referred to in the May 2005 Bradbury memos, when the *New York Times* reported in 2007 that some of the tapes had been destroyed.[24]

"Socially Established"

A practice does not arise through the efforts of an individual; rather, practices are established by and embedded within larger social groups and institutions. To speak of a human activity as "socially established" also implies that it has an established place within the society where it occurs. To suggest that state torture is a socially established activity has implications for the society in which it takes place. For an activity to be socially established—to occupy an enduring place within a society—requires that it be recognized as valuable by at least some members of the society and accorded some measure of social and material resources.

Can we say that state torture enacted by the United States is a socially established practice? I believe we can. U.S. involvement with torture did not begin in the panicked days following the attacks of September 11, 2001. Scholars and journalists have documented a long history of U.S. research into psychological and physical tortures, stretching back at least as far as the end of World War II.[25] This history also includes the training and technical assistance provided to torture regimes in Latin America, Europe, and Asia, including the

Philippines.[26] Indeed, the revelations of CIA waterboarding were reminders that more than a century ago, U.S. soldiers subjected Filipinos to what was then called the "water cure" during this country's fight to subdue the Philippines at the end of the Spanish-American war.[27]

Torture as Foreign Aid

> Through the 1980's, the United States Army trained Latin American police and military officers in techniques that the Pentagon now acknowledges were "clearly objectionable and possibly illegal": torture, extortion, censorship, false arrest, execution and the "neutralizing" of enemies.
>
> —*New York Times*, October 1996[28]

An examination of historical U.S. involvement in torture suggests that, rather than representing episodic aberrations, the practice of torture has long been established within a variety of U.S. institutions. The list of foreign torture regimes that have received direct financial and logistical assistance from the United States is a long one, including such diverse states as Greece, Turkey, Nicaragua, Honduras, El Salvador, Brazil, Argentina, Chile, Indonesia, Iran, South Vietnam, the Philippines, apartheid South Africa, and, many would argue, Israel.

The Other September 11: The case of Chile provides a good example of such U.S. assistance. For almost three decades prior to 2001, people around the world had gathered every year on September 11 to remember the victims and to mourn the disappeared. The date now seared in our memories as numerical shorthand—9/11—was also the date on the day in 1973 when the Chilean military overthrew Salvador Allende's elected socialist government in a bloody coup. The Nixon administration gave the military the go-ahead, and the CIA provided advice and financing in the period immediately before and during Allende's overthrow.[29] Within the first few days of the coup, 40,000 people were imprisoned at the National Stadium in Santiago. Many were tortured and murdered. The great Chilean folksinger Victor Jara was among a smaller group held at the nearby Estadio Chile. Like many of these detainees, Jara was tortured and murdered.

In the days immediately following the coup, 110 men and women were also imprisoned and tortured aboard the tall sailing ship the *Esmeralda*. As the Baltimore *Sun* reported years later, one prisoner, the former mayor of the city of Valparaiso, "described being tied to one of the ship's masts and subjected repeatedly to electric shock. 'I couldn't sleep for six days because they woke me up every six minutes, night and day,' he told Amnesty International. 'We could hear how the others were tortured right where we were.' "[30]

During the following seventeen years, the government, now headed by General Augusto Pinochet, routinely used torture and "disappearances" to neutralize its organized opposition. Amnesty International and the UN Human Rights Commission report that as many as 250,000 people were detained during this period.[31] Under a general rubric of anti-communism, the United States government publicly embraced the Pinochet government, providing hundreds of millions of dollars in economic support. In 1979, six years after the coup, Congress cut off military funds to Chile. Nevertheless, other support continued throughout the years of dictatorship, whose demise began with a plebiscite in 1988 and the election in 1989 of the civilian president Patricio Aylwin.

One ongoing form of support for the Pinochet regime, and others in Latin America, was the training that U.S. governments provided for their military and police. If there is one preeminent symbol of U.S. support for torture in other countries, it is surely the institution known as the School of the Americas, originally housed in Panama and now located at Fort Benning, Georgia. This is the place where, for half a century, more than 60,000 members of Latin American military and police forces studied the techniques of counter-insurgency and torture. Graduates have included many of the most feared men in countries like Nicaragua, Honduras, Chile, Argentina, Peru, Brazil, and El Salvador. This is where the operatives of Somoza's National Guard in Nicaragua and Pinochet's DINA in Chile, along with the military dictatorships of Argentina and Brazil, learned their crafts. The Chilean torturer Osvaldo Roma, whom we met in Chapter 1, told journalists in 1995 that he had received his counter-insurgency training at the School of the Americas in Panama.[32] In 1996 the New York *Times* published excerpts from some of the (now officially discontinued) training manuals that were used until 1991 at the School of the Americas. The manuals covered subjects like "torture, extortion, censorship, false arrest, execution and the 'neutralizing' of enemies."[33] In January 2001, under intense pressure from national and international campaigns, the Department of Defense made a cosmetic change, renaming the school the Western Hemisphere Institute for Security Cooperation.

Central American Echoes: There is direct historical and social connection between U.S. torture training in Latin America and in the "war on terror," found in the person of at least one individual who has participated in both. Colonel James Steele, a veteran of the wars in Central America, helped set up detention centers for the Iraqi Special Police Commandos and trained them in "interrogation." Steele, a Special Forces veteran, reported directly to then-Secretary of Defense Donald Rumsfeld. During the 1980s he had headed a team of U.S. advisors to the Salvadoran military at the height of that country's torture regime.[34] Together with a collaborator, retired Colonel

James H. Coffman, Steele had access to "millions of dollars of U.S. money" to spend in Iraq setting up Special Police Commandos detention centers, which became sites of routine torture. Iraqi General Muntadher al-Samari, who worked with Steele and Coffman for a year, told the U.K. *Guardian*, "They knew everything that was going on there . . . the torture, the most horrible kinds of torture." Samari described the teams that the Americans organized and their work:

> Each one was made up of an intelligence officer and eight interrogators. This committee will use all means of torture to make the detainee confess like using electricity or hanging him upside down, pulling out their nails, and beating them on sensitive parts.[35]

Torture Within the United States

> The Christian in me says it's wrong, but the corrections officer in me says, "I love to make a grown man piss himself."
> —Spec. Charles A. Graner, Jr., Abu Ghraib prison guard[36]

The use of torture also has a long, if unrecognized, history within the United States. The majority of its sufferers have been people of color, beginning with the tortures used in the context of slavery and the genocide of native peoples, continuing with those associated with organized lynching campaigns in the nineteenth and twentieth centuries[37] and extending to our contemporary prison institutions.

This last is a rarely recognized locus of routine torture that is hidden in plain sight within U.S. borders. When *Newsweek* columnist Jonathan Alter first suggested in October of 2001 that the September 11 attacks might require the United States to torture someone, he could be sure that his readers would recognize the techniques to which he was referring. "In this autumn of anger," Alter wrote, "even a liberal can find his thoughts turning to . . . torture. OK, not cattle prods or rubber hoses, at least not here in the United States." It is disconcerting that Jonathan Alter should mention cattle prods and rubber hoses as items that ought not to be used "here in the United States." It is precisely their well-known, if unexamined, history of use in U.S. police stations and prisons that makes these instruments familiar to the U.S. imagination. When a columnist makes reference to them, we know exactly what he is talking about.[38]

Occasionally, a respected public figure will draw attention to the generally unacknowledged practice of torture in U.S. prisons. In 1992 Supreme Court Justice Harry A. Blackmun did just that, observing,

Various kinds of state-sponsored torture and abuse—of the kind ingeniously designed to cause pain but without a telltale 'significant injury'—lashing prisoners with leather straps, *whipping them with rubber hoses*, beating them with naked fists, *shocking them with electric currents, asphyxiating them short of death, intentionally exposing them to undue heat or cold,* or forcibly injecting them with psychosis-inducing drugs-techniques, commonly thought to be practiced outside this nation's borders, are hardly unknown within this nation's prisons.[39]

One locus of psychological torture in U.S. prisons is those special facilities variously known as "Security Housing Units," "control units," or "supermax facilities." Here, as Amnesty International reports, "Prisoners . . . may be confined for nearly 24 hours a day in sometimes windowless cells with solid doors, with no work, training or other programs." Prisoners live in almost complete isolation in permanently-lit, eight-by-ten-foot rooms under constant video surveillance; they encounter no other human beings. Doors are opened and shut by remote control; meals appear through slots in cell doors. "The length of time inmates are assigned to such units varies, but some prisoners spend years, or even their whole sentence, in isolation."[40]

Attorneys for Guantánamo prisoners report that their clients have been placed for months and in at least one case more than a year in isolation cells that might well have been modeled on these supermax facilities. Jumah Bin Muhammad Al-Dossari, for example, described his ordeal of isolation in a newly constructed, computerized prison block. "There was an order to move me to Camp 5 for me to finish off the rest of my days in solitary isolation there," he said, in a hand-written journal he slipped to his civilian lawyers in 2005. The journal continues:

> All the cells in Camp 5 were isolation cells and the whole building was made entirely of pre-cast concrete. . . . Camp 5 has harsh rules that are the harshest rules of all the camps in Cuba, such as Camp Delta and Camp Echo. Everything here is computerised, even the doors, lighting, cameras; everything is computer-operated. . . . Here in Camp 5 . . . the cells have no windows except for a small hole covered with glass that no one can see anything from in spite of it being small. The light here inside the cells is permanent and very strong. On the doors, there are small windows covered from the outside. If a soldier wants to look inside, he can lift the cover and look in. The glass on it is like mirror glass which, from the inside, no one can look out.[41]

The effects of such isolation develop rapidly and endure for years. Psychiatrist Stuart Grassian, who has interviewed hundreds of prisoners held in isolation, reports that "about a third developed acute psychosis with hallucinations."[42] Grassian outlines six routinely observed psychiatric effects of solitary confinement: hypersensitivity to external stimuli; panic attacks; perceptual distortions including hallucinations; cognitive difficulties, including problems with thinking, concentration, and memory; "intrusive obsessional thoughts" including unwanted fantasies of violence and revenge; full-blown paranoia; and inability to control impulses, such as an urge to slit one's wrists.[43]

At least 25,000 U.S. prisoners are presently isolated in federal or state supermax facilities, according to physician and researcher Atul Gawande. "An additional fifty to eighty thousand," he reports, "are kept in restrictive segregation units, many of them in isolation, too, although the government does not release these figures." Such widespread use of isolation is relatively recent, says Gawande. It is, "almost exclusively, a phenomenon of the past twenty years." Federal courts have come close to declaring solitary confinement unconstitutionally cruel, as long ago as 1893 and as recently as 1995. In the latter case,

> a federal court reviewing California's first supermax admitted that the conditions "hover on the edge of what is humanly tolerable for those with normal resilience." But it did not rule them to be unconstitutionally cruel or unusual, except in cases of mental illness. The prison's supermax conditions, the court stated, did not pose "a sufficiently high risk to all inmates of incurring a serious mental illness." In other words, there could be no legal objection to its routine use, given that the isolation didn't make everyone crazy.[44]

Who is held in the U.S. supermax facilities? A very small number are people like the Black Panther supporter Silvia Baraldini (now repatriated to Italy) and the Puerto Rican *independista* Alejandrina Torres, who have been convicted of politically motivated crimes. But the vast majority are either ordinary convicts or people who have been identified as gang members. The latter remain in isolation sometimes for years—until they agree to "debrief," that is, to inform on other gang members. It is said that there are only three ways a prisoner ever leaves a Security Housing Unit: parole, debriefing, or death.

It is distressing to note that in the spring of 2013, as prisoners in Guantánamo continued their hunger strike, inmates at California's Pelican Bay Secure Housing Unit prepared to renew their own—in continued protest against indefinite detention in solitary confinement. California prison officials have responded by adding sleep deprivation to the routine experience of Security Housing Unit inmates. "Both guards and prisoners complained to lawyers conducting legal visits last week," reports a prisoner advocacy organization, "about a new policy requiring prison guards to conduct 'welfare checks' every thirty minutes on prisoners isolated in the prison's Security Housing Units (SHU)." In other words, prisoners in solidary confinement at Pelican Bay are now awakened every thirty minutes, depriving them of sleep, in an effort disguised as concern for their welfare.[45]

A September 2012 Amnesty International report details the extent of solitary confinement in California alone. "More than 3,000 prisoners in California are held in high security isolation units known as Security Housing Units, where . . . they are confined for at least 22 and a half hours a day in single or double cells, with no work or meaningful rehabilitation programs or group activities of any kind," says Amnesty. "Over 1,000 are held in the SHU at Pelican Bay State Prison, a remote facility where most prisoners are confined alone in cells which have no windows to the outside or direct access to natural light." Many prisoners have endured these conditions for more than a decade. "According to figures provided by the California Department of Corrections and Rehabilitation in 2011," the report's authors found, "more than 500 prisoners have spent ten or more years in isolation, more than 200 had spent over 15 years and 78 in excess of 20 years."[46]

Violent rape of both female and male prisoners is another form of torture so common in U.S. prisons that it is almost never remarked upon except in reports issued by international human rights agencies—or when treated as a routine threat issued by characters in television police dramas attempting to extract a confession before a suspect "lawyers up." Male prisoners are most often raped by other prisoners. This makes it possible to argue that despite its frequency, prison rape is an aberration, rather than a part of the structure of the prison experience. In practice, however, a system of violent sexual dominance of some prisoners by others is recognized and even encouraged by prison authorities. It is used as a form of discipline and punishment; guards frequently place vulnerable prisoners in cells where they know rape will occur. Human Rights Watch confirms this. In their 2001 report, *No Escape: Male Rape in U.S. Prisons,* they write, "It must be emphasized that rape and other sexual abuses occur in prison because correctional officials, to a surprising extent, do little to stop them from occurring." Furthermore, those who are being raped repeatedly have little recourse. "An absolutely central problem with regard to sexual abuse in prison, emphasized by inmate after inmate," reports Human Rights Watch, "is the inadequate—and, in many instances, callous and irresponsible—response of correctional staff to complaints of rape."[47]

When women prisoners are raped, it is most often guards who are responsible, rather than fellow prisoners. In fact, 70 percent of those who guard the 190,000 women in U.S. prisons are male. Amnesty International reports that sexual violence "is a harsh reality faced by many women who are incarcerated in the U.S., regardless of their sentence. Women are subjected to sexually offensive language, male staff touching their breasts and genitals when conducting searches, male staff watching while they are naked, and sexual assault. Furthermore, says Amnesty, "The Department of Justice's Bureau of Justice Statistics reports that, in 2004, allegations of staff sexual misconduct were made in all but one state prison and in 41% of local and private jails and prisons."[48]

One direct connection between U.S. prison torture and the torture of prisoners taken in the "war on terror" is the deployment of an estimated five to nine thousand civilian prison guards in the military reserves and National Guard. In fact, several reservist and National Guard companies, chosen because so many of their members have prison jobs in civilian life, have made up the majority of those working as military prison guards in Guantánamo, Iraq, and Afghanistan. Very few active-duty soldiers are trained for prison work, and most of those are stationed at military prisons inside the United States. So as the number of prisoners in the "war on terror" increased, the particular experience of civilian prison guards was pressed into service.[49]

According to Lieutenant Colonel Mark Inch, Corrections and Internment Branch chief in the office of the Provost Marshal General, prison guard reservists are crucial to the U.S. ability to detain and control the large number of people seized in the "war on terror":

> Under the current organization, the military personnel who are more likely to perform enemy prisoner of war and detention operations during war reside almost exclusively in the Army Reserve and Army National Guard. Therefore, the synergy between the reservist's civilian employment in the corrections field and his or her duty to confine enemy combatants in Afghanistan and Guantanamo Bay, Cuba, and enemy prisoners of war and civilian detainees in Iraq . . . could not be more evident and essential to mission success.[50]

The military has also drawn on the expertise of civilian-life corrections officers for help designing U.S. detention centers abroad. For example, the majority of the 300th Military Police Brigade, which designed Camp Delta at Guantánamo, are prison guards in civilian life. In 2006, sociologist Avery F. Gordon reported similar assignments in other overseas detention centers. "Members of the 327th Military Police Battalion, many of whom are Chicago area prison guards and police, currently guard those imprisoned in Afghanistan and run detention operations there," says Gordon. "The most well known army reserve and National Guard unit, the 800th Military Police Brigade was put in charge of 're-establishing Iraq's jail and prison system' as well as staffing and managing the army's prisons for enemy combatants and prisoners of war" in

Iraq. "Captain Michael Mcintyre and Master Sgt Don Bowen, 'designers of the emerging Iraqi prison system,' both work at the US penitentiary at Terre Haute, Indiana; they are joined by reservists normally employed by other state prison systems and by the US Federal Bureau of Prisons."[51]

At Abu Ghraib, officials also relied on soldiers who worked as prison guards in civilian life. Major General Taguba, who investigated the abuses there, reported, "I find that without adequate training for a civilian internee detention mission, Brigade personnel relied heavily on individuals within the Brigade who had civilian corrections experience, including many who worked as prison guards or corrections officials in their civilian jobs."[52]

There is nothing unreasonable in and of itself about deploying people with corrections experience to work in overseas military detention centers. The problem lies with the habits that accompany that deployment. Civilian prison guards are no strangers to abusive, dehumanizing practices, and they bring those practices with them on deployments around the world. Referencing the "annexes" to Major General Taguba's report on Abu Ghraib, Gordon argues that to the reservists on duty there, many of whom were prison guards in civilian life, the abuse that outraged the world was perfectly ordinary:

> None of what the Abu Ghraib personnel saw—prisoners handcuffed to the wall with nylon bags over their heads being deprived of sleep; "retraining" of detainees spread-eagled on the floor, yelling and flailing; naked prisoners kept prone on wet floors; men ordered to strip and then placed in isolation; use of electric shock; police guards repeatedly kicking prisoners in the stomach; threats to harm family members; burning; branding—none of this "rose to the level of mistreatment" in the minds of observers because these were, to quote the respondents in the report, "no different from . . . procedures we observed used by guards in US jails."[53]

Race and Torture

> You just sort of try to block out the fact that they're human beings and see them as enemies. You call them hajis, you know? You do all the things that make it easier to deal with killing them and mistreating them.
> —Carlos Mejía, *soldier who was jailed for refusing to serve a second tour in Iraq*[54]

That the race of prisoners plays a role in their abuse is also "nothing unfamiliar" to observers of U.S. prisons. It is well-known that the racial distribution of the U.S. prison population does not correspond to that of the country's population. My own analysis, based on figures supplied by the U.S. Census and the U.S. Justice Department's Bureau of Justice Statistics, shows that in 2008, while African Americans constituted about 13 percent of total U.S. population, they represented 40 percent of U.S. prisoners. Seventy-two percent of the U.S. population is white, compared to only 35 percent of the prison population. The discrepancy is smaller but still significant for Latinos, who represent 20 percent of the prison population, but only 15 percent of the general U.S. population. Incarceration rates also vary by race. While less than one-half of one percent of all whites living in the United States were incarcerated in 2008, the figure for African Americans was over two percent, and for Latinos just under one percent. (See note for graphic representations of this data.)[55]

The reasons for disproportional rates of imprisonment are many and varied—and are not the subject of this book. However, this disproportion is relevant in a setting like prison, where abuse is often routine and where people of color make up 60 percent of prisoners, while almost three-fourths of prison guards are white. When prison guards move from a civilian setting where the difference between themselves and prisoners is marked by race, to guard duty at places like Guantánamo or Bagram, it is not surprising that they should interpret the "otherness" of their prisoners at least partly in racial terms.[56]

There is another group of persons who have been convicted of no crime, but who yet are held for weeks and months in solitary confinement in this country—immigrants suspected of being in the United States illegally. "On any given day," the *New York Times* reported in March 2013, "about 300 immigrants are held in solitary confinement at the 50 largest detention facilities . . . overseen by Immigration and Customs Enforcement officials." These prisoners are kept confined alone for all but one or two hours of each day. Some have attempted suicide. Almost half are kept isolated for at least 15 days, "the point at which psychiatric experts say they are at risk for severe mental harm," says the *Times*, while others spend more than 75 days in solitary confinement.[57]

The reasons given for the isolation vary from rule infraction, to "talking back to guards" to being identified as gay. The *Times* found the use of solitary confinement in Immigration and Customs Enforcement detention centers "startling" because, whatever the justifications, the detainees are held because they are suspected of civil, not criminal, violations. As suggested above, there is substantial empirical evidence that solitary confinement causes severe mental suffering, of the sort described in the UN Convention against Torture. Like many others who fall into the class of those who may properly be tortured, immigrants to the United States are often perceived as being other than white. This brings us to a consideration of the historical relationship between race and torture in the United States.

A common feature of societies with institutionalized torture is the designation of specific groups as legitimate torture targets. While among the ancient Greeks torture was reserved for slaves,[58] under a modern Greek dictatorship, it was reserved for the junta's political enemies, human beings redescribed by their torturers as "beasts" or "worms." Very often, the differentiation between those who may and may not be tortured has a racial character. "The victim is portrayed as belonging to a fundamentally different class or inferior ethnic group than the one on whose behalf the torturer is acting," says Mika Haritos-Fatouros, who has studied torturers in Greece and Brazil. Not only are members of groups vulnerable to torture "regarded as clearly inferior," but their very membership in such groups renders them "less than human" in the eyes of their tormentors and "a threat to the most central values of the torturer's class and ethnic identity."[59]

It should not be surprising that the United States has a long history of treating as "torturable" those who at any particular political moment are classified as outside the boundaries of whiteness. Slaves—almost exclusively persons of African descent—are treated as literally "less" than human in Article 1 of the U.S. Constitution; for purposes of apportioning representatives to Congress to the various states, a slave was to count as three-fifths of a person. "Indians not taxed" did not count as persons at all. Members of both groups fell into categories of persons who might be tortured with impunity.

It should hardly be necessary to repeat here the litany of institutionalized abuses that were ordinary practice among slaveholders: whipping, shackling, and branding and other mutilations were common. Nor did state-sanctioned torture of African Americans end with slavery. The practice of lynching, which continued well into the twentieth century with a resurgence during the civil rights movement of the 1960s, in addition to its culminating murder by hanging or burning, often involved whippings and castration of male victims prior to death. Lynching served the usual purpose of institutionalized state torture (i.e., the establishment and maintenance of the power of white authorities over Black populations). That the practice was indeed institutionalized is attested to by the fact that lynchings were treated as popular entertainment and were not only permitted but encouraged by local officials, who may themselves have participated. Lynching developed a collateral form of popular art: photographs of lynchings decorated many postcards printed in the early part of the twentieth century. One such example is a postcard bearing a photo of a man identified as Dennis or Bennie Simmons, who on June 13, 1913 was soaked in oil and burned alive, while hanging from a tree in Oklahoma.[60]

Disproportionate punishment of Black bodies also extends to the U.S. public schools. While the number of states that permit corporal punishment in public schools is declining, twenty states still permit beating children in school, generally with a wooden paddle or stick. Extensive use of corporal punishment is greatest in southern states, with Mississippi, where 7.5 percent of students were beaten in 2008, leading the way. Projections from the U.S. Department of Education indicate that African American children, expected to compose seventeen percent of public school children in 2009, would account for 37 percent of those beaten in school.[61] I am not claiming that the beatings endured by public school children are torture, but they are certainly examples of institutionalized state cruelty disproportionately visited on young people of color.

It is hard to avoid recognizing the racialized nature of U.S. torture in the post-September 11 period. Some observers of the abuse at Abu Ghraib have remarked on the similarity between the photos taken by the torturers and those early-twentieth-century postcards of cheerful white picnickers attending lynchings in the southern United States.[62] The symbolic emasculation of Iraqi men enacted by covering their heads with women's underwear or forcing them into sexual acts with other men is perhaps an echo of the castration of Black men practiced in decades past.[63] I am struck as well by the now-famous image of an Iraqi prisoner in dark hood and poncho standing with arms outstretched on a small wooden box. He looks for all the world like the photographic negative of a white-hooded, white-sheet Ku Klux Klansman. His tormenters have turned him into an ironic symbol of racial hatred.

Certainly there is a long history of racializing U.S. enemies—as "Japs" during World War II, as "gooks" and "slants" during the Korean and Vietnam War, and as "towel heads," "rag heads," and "sand niggers" in Afghanistan and Iraq. Here the objection might be raised that the primary category of those who are marked for torture in the "war on terror" is not so much racial as political or religious. U.S. torturers do sometimes think of their targets in terms that may appear to reside outside of racial categories, terms such as "terrorists" and "insurgents" or "Muslims" (i.e., as adherents of a strange and barbaric religion). I would suggest, however, that in U.S. usage these categories also carry racial connotations. The image of a "terrorist" in the minds of most Americans is not that of Timothy McVeigh, the white man who blew up the Oklahoma City Federal Building. It is not that of another white man, Eric Robert Rudolph, who bombed Atlanta's Centennial Park during the 1996 Summer Olympics, followed by attacks on several abortion clinics and a lesbian bar. In the American imagination, even before September 11, 2001, a "terrorist" was almost by definition a dark-skinned person.[64]

"Muslim" is a confusing category to many non-Muslim Americans. For some, like Lt. General William Boykin, Muslim inferiority derives from acceptance of an inferior religion. In 2003 Boykin described a military encounter with a Somalian warlord. Boykin, then a deputy undersecretary of Defense for intelligence, explained why he hadn't been afraid. "I knew my God was bigger than his," he told a Christian audience in Oregon. "I knew that my God was a real God and his was an idol."[65] For others, however, the negative associations with Muslims have a racial or ethnic content. For them, Muslims are by definition Arabs, Africans, or other dark-skinned people. Of course adherents of Islam are not the only group for whom religion and race have historically been conflated in European and American imaginations. Both Jews and gentiles have long debated whether what makes Jews "different" is religion, race, culture, or some combination of the these. There is no question, however, that those who murdered millions in the Holocaust saw Jews as members of a biologically and morally inferior race.[66]

U.S. support for state torture in other countries, its training of foreign torturers, and the use of torture in its own prisons demonstrate that the practice of torture is indeed "socially established" within the United States. In each of these arenas, policies of systematic, structural support for the use of torture are visible to those who wish to see. However, in none of these situations had U.S. government officials—or, in the case of state prisons, officials of the various states—publicly embraced torture as a legitimate implement of state policy, until the post-September 11 period. In the days and years following the April 2009 release of the Bybee and Bradbury memos, former high officials of Bush administration have come forward with an explicit utilitarian argument that the contributions of torture to national security in the "war on terror" justify its use. "One of the things that I find a little bit disturbing about this recent disclosure," former Vice President Cheney told Fox Television, "is they put out the legal memos, the memos that the CIA got from the Office of Legal Counsel, but they didn't put out the memos that showed the success of the effort."[67] The socially established practice of torture continues to reside within the larger "national security" tradition, an ongoing argument about the meanings and values of nation and security in U.S. society.

A "Cooperative Activity"

Institutionalized state torture satisfies another term in MacIntyre's definition of a practice. Torture is a "cooperative" activity. It is true that the drama of interrogation which William Cavanaugh and Elaine Scarry have described as the basic dynamic of modern state torture very often involves only two or three players—the torturers and their target.[68] But the systematic application of torture at the level of a state requires the organized and concerted work of many people: jailers and torturers, record keepers, architects who design the spaces whose only purpose is the infliction of pain, psychologists who advise interrogators, and physicians who keep prisoners alive and conscious for further torture.

Social psychologist and ethicist Jean Maria Arrigo has written about the level of interpersonal and institutional cooperation necessary to establish and maintain a state torture program. In this context, as noted in Chapter 3, she makes a consequentialist argument against torture, on the grounds that its use deforms a variety of social and governmental organizations. "Many agencies must coordinate in a counterterrorist operation," says Arrigo. "Reliability and accountability are therefore essential. . . . The torturers have to be well trained and professional." Such training and professionalism require the organized efforts of many people.[69]

The cooperative nature of torture is also explicated in the work of the esteemed British lawyer Philippe Sands. In his book, *Torture Team: Rumsfeld's Memo and the Betrayal of American Values*, Sands recounts the efforts of officials at Guantánamo and in the U.S. Defense Department in Washington, DC, to devise a set of eighteen "enhanced interrogation techniques" to apply to their prisoners. These included techniques such as isolation, sensory deprivation, and sleep derivation as well as sexual humiliation and the use of dogs—methods that General Geoffrey Miller would eventually carry from Guantánamo to detention centers in Iraq, including Abu Ghraib. Sands describes the multiple brainstorming meetings held by representatives of several government branches at Guantánamo to devise ways to respond to pressure from Washington for more vigorous interrogations of the prisoners held there. Attendees included members of the Defense Intelligence Agency, several CIA psychologists, and executive branch attorneys including David Addington, then-Vice President Cheney's attorney, and Alberto Gonzalez, then-White House Legal Counsel. John Rizzo, to whom Steven Bradbury would later address his memos guaranteeing the legality of CIA interrogation methods, was also present for some discussions, in his capacity as a counter-terrorism lawyer for the CIA.[70]

Despite the high-power expertise in the room, and the CIA's decades-long history of researching and teaching torture techniques, the picture that emerges from Sands's interviews of people who attended these sessions is a portrait of a cooperative, if oddly amateur "Gang That Couldn't Torture Straight." The sources of the new techniques that they developed were "unconventional to say the least" and included inspiration from the military's Survival, Evasion, Resistance, and Escape (SERE) program, as well as from season two of the Fox Network television program *24*, whose hero Jack Bauer uses torture to save the city of Los Angeles from a nuclear explosion.[71]

Nothing in the description of state torture as socially embedded and cooperative suggests that all those who work together need be directly employed by the state itself. Perhaps as an instance of the Bush administration's dedication to privatizing government functions, the United States has to a large degree privatized torture, contracting with corporations such as the Virginia- and London-based CACI to assist in interrogations in Iraq.[72] Another Virginia-based company, Anteon, has provided training in interrogation methods at the U.S. Army's training facility at Fort Huachuca in Arizona.[73]

Furthermore, as then-CIA Director Mike Hayden told the Senate Select Intelligence Committee in 2008, private contractors did not merely participate in CIA interrogations; often, they led them. "At our facilities during this," Hayden told Senator Dianne Feinstein, "we have a mix of both government employees and contractors. Everything is done under, as we've talked before, ma'am, under my authority and the authority of the agency. But the people at the locations are frequently a mix of both—we call them blue badgers and green badgers." The term "green badgers" refers to private contractors who presumably wear green badges and who may be either corporate employees or private individuals.[74] United States torture has also been "outsourced" through the well-documented practice of "extraordinary rendition," in which people detained by the United States are transferred to other countries for torture. See for example the cases of Maher Arar and Binyam Mohammed al-Habashi, described in Chapter 1.

Taking into account the complex, cooperative, and socially established nature of institutionalized state torture, it seems reasonable to conclude that it is indeed a practice, rather than a string of isolated episodes.

An Empirical Challenge: Milgram and Zimbardo

No consideration of torture as a practice would be complete without addressing the empirical research of Stanley Milgram[75] and Philip Zimbardo. Milgram's experiments in obedience to authority in the 1960s and Zimbardo's 1971 Stanford Prison Experiment would seem to contradict the view that torture is an ongoing practice, with its own internal goods and standards of excellence, into which people are initiated through a period of training and formation. The research of these psychologists appears to show that, on the contrary, given the right conditions, most people can very quickly be made into torturers. If this is true, then the Milgram and Zimbardo results present a significant challenge to the assertion that torture is a practice, a "coherent and complex form of socially established cooperative activity."

Subjects in Milgram's famous experiment were told they were participating in a study of memory. Each subject was asked to teach a "learner" a list of paired words ("blue/box, nice/day, wild/duck, etc."). The subject would then read the first word of each pair, to which the "learner" was to respond with the second word. Every time the "learner" made an error, the subject was to administer an electric shock, gradually increasing the shock level each time along a scale from 15 to 450 volts. The "learner," who was actually an actor employed by the experimenters, would exhibit greater and greater distress as the shock setting went higher. The white-coated experimenter would encourage reluctant subjects with a series of four "prods" ("Please continue, or Please go on; The experiment requires that you continue; It is absolutely essential that you continue; You have no other choice you *must* go on").[76]

And go on they did. One experiment required the subjects to physically press the palm of a resisting "learner" onto what they believed was a shock plate.[77] Subjects complied. Another version required subjects to continue administering shocks despite screaming and banging on the wall, followed by deathly silence. Subjects complied.[78]

Milgram conducted his experiments in the shadow of Nazi fascism and at the start of a Cold War conceived in this country as an epic battle between freedom and totalitarianism. He framed his results as measures of his subjects' obedience to authority. Many of his subjects proved obedient, even to authorities who ordered them to violate the fundamental "moral requirement of refraining from action against a helpless victim."[79] He observed that, contrary to their own stated moral views, in the proper setting people were willing (if not happy and not without painful internal conflict) to violate those values. "Values," Milgram concluded, "are not the only forces at work in an actual, ongoing situation. They are but one narrow band of causes in the total spectrum of forces impinging on a person. Many people" among the thousands who eventually participated, "were unable to realize their values in action and found themselves continuing in the experiment even though they disagreed with what they were doing."[80] Those other "forces" included what Milgram called "binding factors" such as politeness, desire to keep the promises implicit in agreeing to participate in (and be paid for) an experiment, and the potential awkwardness and embarrassment of withdrawing. Gradual "adjustments in the subject's thinking" allow the subject to "maintain his relationship with the experimenter," for example, by focusing exclusively on the task while ignoring its consequences, and by displacing responsibility for one's own actions onto the experimenter's shoulders.[81]

In the 1971 Stanford Prison Experiment, Philip Zimbardo constructed a life-like prison in a basement at Stanford University and peopled it with experimental subjects who were Stanford undergraduates. Volunteers were randomly assigned roles of "prisoner" and "guard." Soon after the experiment began, Zimbardo's guards were abusing their prisoners both psychologically and physically.[82] Within a day or two, they were marching prisoners to and from the bathroom in paper bag hoods, keeping them naked, stepping on their backs while they did push-ups, and sexually humiliating them.[83] The experiment ended early when Zimbardo asked his then-girlfriend (and later wife)

Christina Maslach to come take a look, and her horrified response convinced him to call a halt.[84]

Zimbardo agrees with Milgram that human behaviors spring from something more and other than personal volition. Unlike Milgram, however, he does not take obedience to authority as his explanatory frame for the actions of the "guards" in his experiment, or for the real guards at Abu Ghraib and Guantánamo, about whom he has also written. He proposes instead a three-part hierarchy of influences, which he calls PSS—Person, Situation, and System:

> The Person is an actor on the stage of life whose behavioral freedom is informed by his or her makeup—genetic, biological, physical, and psychological. The Situation is the behavioral context that has the power, through its reward and normative functions, to give meaning and identity to the actor's roles and status. The System consists of the agents and agencies whose ideology, values, and power create situations and dictate the roles and expectations for approved behaviors of actors within its spheres of influence.[85]

Zimbardo also invokes the psychologist Lee Ross's expression "fundamental attribution error" to criticize any descriptive or normative view of the human person that "locates the inner qualities of people as the main source of their actions."[86] In other words, he denies that people's moral habits, if these indeed exist, have much effect on their actions.

It has been suggested by other social scientists and by some ethicists that experiments such as Milgram's and Zimbardo's invalidate a practice- and virtue-based approach to ethics.[87] Social psychologists Sabini and Silver give the name "situationism" to this contention that it is situation, and not stable dispositions of character such as virtues or vices, that most influences human behavior.[88] "Situationism is the idea that we are pushed around by 'subtle situational forces,' but," they argue, "that way of putting things is, to our minds, vague and misleading." It is not sufficient to invoke the "metaphor" of subtle forces; we must try to understand what those forces are and how they work. Although experiments like Milgram's clearly show that people are influenced by their situations, such influence does not invalidate virtue or virtue ethics; it rather demonstrates how difficult it is for people to behave what one might call "in character" when faced with very particular kinds of circumstances.[89]

Sabini and Silver point out that in experiments like Milgram's (and others that illustrate the power of a cohesive group to influence moral and even sensory perceptions), people generally *want* to do the right thing but find themselves too weak to do so. Such research "has revealed just how weak, morally weak, we are when confronted with a resolute authority or a unanimous group of other seemingly normal people who seem to see the social, moral, and even physical world differently from the way we do." Sabini and Silver also observe (with less emphasis) that this "weakness is partly cognitive—people tend to lose their moral compass." They also point out the extraordinary power of potential embarrassment; this moral weakness is "partly a matter of people's being unable or unwilling to expose themselves, to disrupt social situations, by exposing their different perceptions of the world."[90]

To say that our characters are vulnerable in particular situations is not to say that we do not possess characters at all. Sabini and Silver conclude their article by suggesting that it is a waste of time to warn people who do not wish to become torturers to stay away from "subtle situational forces"—a warning that they consider as useless as a color change in the terrorist threat level. Our warning should be rather more specific, that is, that "people should stay away from slippery slopes, that they should be very wary when their moral perceptions seem to clash with others', and that they should understand both that it is hard and that it is possible to confront other people who are doing wrong."

Despite his emphasis on Situation and System, Zimbardo concludes his recent reevaluation of the Stanford Prison Experiment with a chapter on how we might encourage people to develop what I would call the traditional virtues of justice, courage, temperance, and wisdom and which he names "heroism." He offers a "Ten-Step Program to Resist Unwanted Influence" through which people might become more heroic. His ten steps are phrased as first-person declarative sentences: "I am mindful;" "I am responsible;" "I respect just authority but rebel against unjust authority;" "I am Me, the best I can be." Each affirmation is followed by an explanatory paragraph. Oddly, for all Zimbardo's emphasis on social and political systems that place people in a position to torture, his "program" strikes me as naïvely voluntarist. He imagines a purely personal solution to a problem that he has described as being for the most part socially constructed.

Virtue ethicists offer a more nuanced understanding than does Zimbardo of the dialectic between individual and society, agency and contingency. In the *Nicomachean Ethics,* for example, Aristotle describes ethics as belonging to a larger discipline (i.e., political science) that "master art" whose *telos* (purpose) is bringing about "the good for man." In his view, the purpose of the state is the ethical formation of good citizens. Good laws tell us "what we are to do and what we are to refrain" from doing, in order to form human beings in those habitual moral excellences that will lead us to our proper end, which is *eudaimonia,* or human flourishing. Thus Aristotle's *Nicomachean Ethics,* which one commentator has suggested might better be entitled "Matters to Do with Character," is designed to give his young students, the future citizen lawmakers of Athens, an understanding of the virtues their laws ought to engender.[91]

Similarly, in the *Politics,* Aristotle argues that "a state's purpose is not merely to provide a living but to make a life that is good." He goes on to argue that "that which is genuinely and not just nominally called a state must concern itself with virtue. Otherwise the association is a mere military alliance." Thus he deplores the sophist's understanding of the state as merely "a mutual guarantor of justice" (i.e., a guarantor of the right to monetary recompense for wrongs done) that is "quite unable to make citizens good and just."[92]

Having demonstrated that institutionalized state torture satisfies MacIntyre's multipart definition of a practice, it is time to consider what are the internal goods of that practice and what moral habits it generates in its practitioners. That is the subject of the following chapter.

Notes

1. Darius M. Rejali, *Torture and Democracy* (Princeton: Princeton University Press, 2007), 20.
2. Ervin Staub, *The Roots of Evil: The Origins of Genocide and Other Group Violence* (New York: Cambridge University Press, 1989).
3. For some people in the United States, Guantánamo detainees fell lower even than beasts; they became vegetables. In a reference to their orange jumpsuits, one author called them "carrots." In *The Carrot Patch,* an amateur online video popular at one time among Guantánamo guards, stick figure soldiers gleefully shoot, kick, and beat their hapless orange charges until they spurt satisfying quantities of animated blood. Rob Lewis, "The Carrot Patch," 2002. http://web.archive.org/web/20110623031705/http://www.stickdeath.com/qcamup.html.
4. John Conroy, *Unspeakable Acts, Ordinary People: The Dynamics of Torture* (Berkeley: University of California Press, 2000), 110. It is worth noting that Conroy's *Unspeakable Acts, Ordinary People* is a study of torture in three countries generally considered to be democracies—United Kingdom, Israel, and the United States.
5. George Seto, 2006, personal communication with author.
6. See, for example, the May 2005 memos produced for the CIA by the Office of Legal Counsel (e.g., Steven G. Bradbury, *Memorandum for John A. Rizzo, Senior Deputy General Counsel, Central Intelligence Agency, May 30, 2005. Re: Application of United States Obligations under Article 16 of the Convention against Torture to Certain Techniques That May Be Used in the Interrogation of High Value Al Qaeda Detainees,* May 30, 2005). In this series of memos, the author examines a series of "techniques," including forced standing, "cramped confinement," "walling," in which the target's shoulders are methodically slammed into a wall, and use of "the waterboard." Each technique is examined separately to determine whether it falls under any of the prohibitions contained in the Convention against Torture or—in other memos—the enabling U.S. legislation.
7. Steven G. Bradbury, *Memorandum for John A. Rizzo, Senior Deputy General Counsel, Central Intelligence Agency, May 10, 2005. Re: Application of §§ 2340–2340a to Certain Techniques That May Be Used in the Interrogation of a High Value Al Qaeda Detainee,* May 10, 2005, 8.
8. Ibid., 32.
9. International Committee of the Red Cross, *ICRC Report on the Treatment of Fourteen "High Value Detainees" in CIA Custody* (Washington, DC: International Committee of the Red Cross, 2007), 14.
10. Bradbury, *Memorandum for John A. Rizzo, Senior Deputy General Counsel, Central Intelligence Agency, May 10, 2005,* 37.

We should not, perhaps, accept without question the view of the CIA's Office of Medical Services that the edema caused by prolonged standing is not painful. See, for example, Conroy, *Unspeakable Acts, Ordinary People*. Conroy describes the ordeal of Jim Auld, who was tortured for nine days by the British military in 1971, using several of the techniques described in the Bradbury memo, including sleep deprivation and the innocuous-sounding "wall-standing," which actually places tremendous strain on the legs, wrists, and hands. After nine days, Auld recalled, "My feet were all swollen up, my hands were all swollen up; I was in agony with them, I couldn't do anything" (9).

11. International Committee of the Red Cross, *ICRC Report on the Treatment of Fourteen "High Value Detainees" in CIA Custody*, 31–32.

12. Bradbury, *Memorandum for John A. Rizzo, Senior Deputy General Counsel, Central Intelligence Agency, May 10*, 2005, 37.

13. Ibid., 1.

14. Ibid., 39. Such attempts to slice torture into a series of individually justifiable actions is reminiscent of the first legal defense presented on behalf of the four Los Angeles police officers who beat an African-American man named Rodney King half to death in 1991. Millions of people had seen an amateur video of the beating, which split the skin on King's face from chin to ear and left him with permanent short-term memory damage. In court however, an expert witness for the defense, Sergeant Charles L. Duke Jr. of the Los Angeles Police Department, examined the video frame-by-frame, justifying each blow and each kick as falling within the dictates of Los Angeles Police Department policy. See "Expert Testifies Officers' Beating of Motorist Complied with Policy," *New York Times*, March 20, 1993.

15. Alasdair MacIntyre, *After Virtue*, 2d ed. (Notre Dame: Notre Dame University Press, 1984), 187.

16. Lawrence Weschler, *A Miracle, a Universe: Settling Accounts with Torturers* (New York: Penguin, 1990), 15.

17. Ibid., 48.

18. Interrogation Log: Detainee 063," 2002–2003. Available from *Time Magazine* at http://content.time.com/time/2006/log/log.pdf.

19. See "The Abu Ghraib Files," *Salon*, March 14, 2006. http://www.salon.com/news/abu_ghraib/2006/03/14/introduction/.

20. Tony Harnden, "Barack Obama to Release up to 2,000 Photographs of Prisoner Abuse," *Telegraph*, April 24, 2009.

21. Bradbury, *Memorandum for John A. Rizzo, Senior Deputy General Counsel, Central Intelligence Agency, May 30*, 2005, 8; emphasis added.

22. International Committee of the Red Cross, *ICRC Report on the Treatment of Fourteen "High Value Detainees" in CIA Custody*, 32.

23. CIA Office of Inspector General, *Special Review of Counterterrorism Detention and Interrogation Activities*, 2004, Appendix F.

24. Mark Mazetti, "C.I.A. Destroyed 2 Tapes Showing Interrogations " *New York Times*, December 7, 2007.

25. See, for example, Chalmers A. Johnson, *Nemesis: The Last Days of the American Republic*, 1st ed. (New York: Metropolitan Books, 2006); Naomi Klein, *The Shock Doctrine: The Rise of Disaster Capitalism*, 1st ed. (New York: Metropolitan Books/Henry Holt, 2007); Alfred W. McCoy, *A Question of Torture: C.I.A. Interrogation, from the Cold War to the War on Terror*, 1st ed. The American Empire Project. (New York: Metropolitan Books/Henry Holt, 2006).

26. For details on U.S. support of the dictatorship of Ferdinand Marcos in the Philippines, see Alfred W. McCoy, *Closer Than Brothers: Manhood at the Philippine Military Academy* (New Haven, CT: Yale University Press, 1999).

27. Klein, *The Shock Doctrine: The Rise of Disaster Capitalism*; Paul Kramer, "The Water Cure: Debating Torture and Counterinsurgency—A Century Ago," *New Yorker*, February 25, 2008.

28. Steven Lee Meyers, "Be All That You Can Be: Your Future as an Extortionist," *New York Times*, October 6, 1996.

29. Seymour M. Hersh, *The Price of Power: Kissinger in the Nixon White House*, 1st ed. (New York: Summit Books, 1983), 277ff. See also documents obtained by the National Security Archive, under the Freedom of Information Act, such as a situation report sent by a naval attaché in the days following the September 11, 1973 coup, which he calls "our D-Day." Patrick Ryan, *Situation Report #2*, Valpaiso, Chile, 2973.

30. Stacie Jonas and Sarah Anderson, "This Tall Ship Has a Bloody, Brutal History," *Baltimore Sun*, June 18, 2000.

31. "Pinochet's Chile," *Washington Post*, 2000. http://www.washingtonpost.com/wp-srv/inatl/longterm/pinochet/overview.htm.

32. Nancy Guzmán Jasmen, *Romo, Confesiones de un torturador*, 1st ed. (Santiago, Chile: Editorial Planeta Chilena, 2000), 39, 70, 194.

33. Meyers, "Be All That You Can Be."

34. Mona Mahmood, Maggie O'Kane, Chavala Madlena, and Teresa Smith, "Revealed: Pentagon's Link to Iraqi Torture Centres," *The Guardian*, March 6, 2013. http://www.guardian.co.uk/world/2013/mar/06/pentagon-iraqi-torture-centres-link.

35. Ibid.

36. Scott Higham and Joe Stephens, "Punishment and Amusement: Documents Indicate 3 Photos Were Not Staged for Interrogation,"*Washington Post*, May 22, 2004.

37. Philip Dray, *At the Hands of Persons Unknown: The Lynching of Black America*, 1st ed. (New York: Random House, 2002), 4.

38. Jonathan Alter, "Time to Think About Torture,"*Newsweek*, November 5, 2001.

39. *Hudson v. Mcmillan*, 503 U.S. (1992); emphasis added.

40. Amnesty International, *"Not Part of My Sentence": Violations of the Human Rights of Women in Custody* (New York: Amnesty International, 1999); ibid.

41. Amnesty International, "Days of Adverse Hardship in US Detention Camps—Testimony of Guantánamo Detainee Jumah Al–Dossari," December 16, 2005. http://www.amnesty.org/en/library/asset/AMR51/107/2005/en/98c38595-d477-11dd-8743-d305bea2b2c7/amr511072005en.html. For more discussion of isolation and its effects on prisoners held at Guantánamo, see Laurel E. Fletcher and others, *Guantánamo and Its Aftermath: U.S. Detention and Interrogation Practices and Their Impact on Former Detainees* (Berkeley: University of California at Berkeley, 2008).

42. Atul Gawande, "Hellhole," *New Yorker*, March 30, 2009.

43. M. D. Grassian, Stuart, "Psychiatric Effects of Solitary Confinement," *Journal of Law & Policy* 22, no. (2006), 335–36.

44. Gawande, "Hellhole."

45. Prison Hunger Strike Solidarity, "Sleep Deprivation Intensifies Torture Conditions for Prisoners in Advance of Hunger Strikes and Work Actions," June 10, 2013. http://prisonerhungerstrikesolidarity.wordpress.com/2013/06/10/sleep-deprivation-intensifies-torture-conditions-for-prisoners-in-advance-of-hunger-strikes-and-work-actions/#more-2431.

46. Amnesty International, *USA: The Edge of Endurance; Prison Conditions in California's Security Housing Units* (London: Amnesty International, 2012), 5.

47. Human Rights Watch, *No Escape: Male Rape in U.S. Prisons*, 2001. http://www.hrw.org/reports/2001/prison/; ibid.

48. Amnesty International, "Women in Custody" May 24, 2006. http://www.amnestyusa.org/pdf/custodyissues.pdf

49. Avery F. Gordon, "Abu Ghraib: Imprisonment and the War on Terror," *Race & Class* 48, no. 1 (2006): 46–47.

50. Ibid., 46.

51. Ibid., 47.

52. Maj. Gen. Antonio M.Taguba, *Article 15–6 Investigation of the 800th Military Police Brigade* (U.S. Department of Defense, 2004), 37.

53. Avery F. Gordon, "Abu Ghraib: Imprisonment and the War on Terror," 49.

54. Bob Herbert, "'Gooks' to 'Hajis,'"*New York Times*, May 21, 2004.

55. Data from www.census.gov and Heather C. West and William J. Sabol, *Prison Inmates at Midyear 2008—Statistical Tables*. NCJ225619 (Washington, DC: U.S. Department of Justice, 2009), 24. Note that the Bureau of Prisons data disaggregate Latino inmates, whereas

U.S. Census data treat "Hispanic" as an *ethnicity* that is co-extensive with a variety of *racial* identities. The Census does, however, provide a breakdown between white and non-white Latinos, the latter being a very small group. For purposes of this comparison, I have treated Census Bureau figures for "white Hispanic" as Latino, subtracting that number from the total white population. This is admittedly less than ideal, but this and the longitudinal changes in Census Bureau racial categories are problems well known to anyone working with Census data.

On the other hand, the Bureau of Prisons treats all inmates who are not African American or Latino (including Asian Americans, Pacific Islanders, American Indians, Alaskan and Hawaiian natives, and persons claiming more than one racial identity) as white. The Census disaggregates these groups from whites. For purposes of comparison with Bureau of Justice data, I have restated the Census data, combining all non-African Americans and non-Latinos into the "white" category. This does not represent a huge distortion, however, because the numbers involved are small compared to the total U.S. population. Here are two charts of the relevant data.

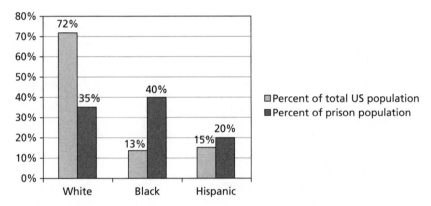

Figure 5.1 Comparison by Race: Prison Population to Total U.S. Population.

Note that prison population percentages do not total to one hundred. This reflects the figures supplied by the Bureau of Justice.

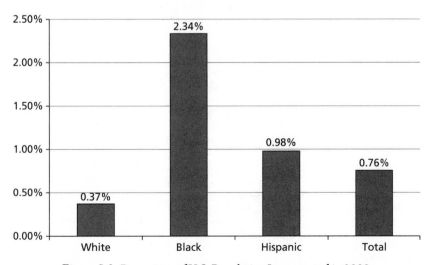

Figure 5.2 Percentage of U.S. Population Incarcerated in 2008.

Data table:

Table 5.1 **Data on U.S. Prison and Total Populations, 2008**

	White	*Black*	*Hispanic*	*Total*
U.S. prison population, 2008	807,000	913,800	460,400	2,311,200
U.S. total population, 2008	218,057,277	39,058,834	46,943,613	304,059,724
% of total U.S. population	72	13	15	100
% of prison population	35	40	20	95
% of population incarcerated	0.37	2.34	0.98	0.76

56. Division of Labor Force Statistics Office of Employment and Unemployment Statistics, *Labor Force Characteristics by Race and Ethnicity, 2007* (Washington, DC: U.S. Bureau of Labor Statistics, 2008), 1005, 15.
57. Ian Urbina and Catherine Rentz, "Immigrants Held in Solitary Cells, Often for Weeks," *New York Times*, March 22, 2013. http://www.nytimes.com/2013/03/24/us/immigrants-held-in-solitary-cells-often-for-weeks.html.
58. Hannah Arendt, *The Human Condition* (Chicago: University of Chicago Press, 1958), 129.
59. Mika Haritos-Fatouros, *The Psychological Origins of Institutional Torture*, ed. W. Peter Robinson, Routledge Research International Series in Social Psychology (New York: Routledge, 2003), 176–77.
60. See the harrowing collection of photos and other material at James Allen, "Without Sanctuary," 2000–2005. http://www.withoutsanctuary.org/main.html.
61. U.S. Department of Education, "2009 Civil Rights Data Collection: 2009–10 National and State Estimations," http://ocrdata.ed.gov/Projections_2009_10.aspx?v=1
62. Bob Wing, "The Color of Abu Ghraib," *War Times/Tiempo de Guerras*, June 2004. Reprinted in *Community Alliance*, June 2004. http://fresnoalliance.com/home/magazine/2004/June2004.pdf.
63. I do not mean to imply that participation in consensual sex with another man does in fact "unman" a person, except in the minds of those who equate male homosexuality with effeminacy, and effeminacy with degradation. There is a great deal of work yet to be done on the role of gender identity in torture and ways that torture may reproduce a society's depreciation of women in general. But that is a subject for a different, although necessary, study.
64. In my college-level ethics courses I often observe that some of my American students cannot bring themselves to apply the label "terrorist" to Timothy McVeigh. Certainly they abhor his crime, but they are unwilling to call it "terrorism," nor can they say why. I suspect it is because of the cognitive dissonance created by the conjunction of whiteness and terrorism. The two appear to be mutually exclusive categories for these students.
65. Richart T. Cooper, "General Casts War in Religious Terms," *Los Angeles Times*, October 16, 2003.
66. This confusion between religion and ethnicity had an odd effect on the shelving practices at a feminist bookstore where I once worked. Books about women in India were shelved in the "Arab Women" section. An Indian woman asked me about this one day, pointing out that India is indisputably in Asia and that books about her compatriots ought to be found in the "Asian Women" section. Not having devised the shelving scheme myself, all I could imagine was that whoever was responsible had associated Indian women (not Pakistani women, mind you) with Muslims, and Muslims with Arabs, and stuck the Indians in with the Arabs as being somehow the same.

67. Fox News, "Cheney Calls for Release of Memos Showing Results of Interrogation Efforts," April 20, 2009. http://www.foxnews.com/politics/2009/04/20/cheney-calls-release-memos-showing-results-interrogation-efforts/. It might be pointed out here that the most complete record of any such "successes" is contained in the comprehensive report on the CIA's interrogation efforts prepared for the U.S. Senate. At this writing, that 6,000-page report has yet to be released.

68. William T. Cavanaugh, *Torture and Eucharist: Theology, Politics, and the Body of Christ* (Malden, MA: Blackwell, 1998); Elaine Scarry, *The Body in Pain: The Making and Unmaking of the World* (New York: Oxford University Press, 1985).

69. Jean Maria Arrigo, "A Consequentialist Argument against Torture Interrogation of Terrorists," paper presented at Joint Services Conference on Professional Ethics. (Springfield, VA, January 30–31, 2003).

70. Philippe Sands, *Torture Team: Rumsfeld's Memo and the Betrayal of American Values*, 1st ed. (New York: Palgrave MacMillan, 2008), 63–64.

71. Ibid., 62.

72. Seymour M. Hersh, *Chain of Command: The Road from 9/11 to Abu Ghraib* (New York: HarperCollins, 2004), 32–33.

73. Pratap Chatterjee, "Intelligence, Inc.: Military Interrogation Training Gets Privatized," March 7, 2003. http://www.corpwatch.org/article.php?id=11940.

74. Noah Schactman, "Hayden Admits: Contractors Lead 'Enhanced Interrogations' at CIA Black Sites," *Wired*, February 7, 2008. http://blog.wired.com/defense/2008/02/in-testimony-be.html.

75. Historian Alfred McCoy has suggested that "the famed Yale obedience experiments by a young psychologist, Stanley Milgram, seem a likely candidate" to be among the 185 research programs funded under the CIA's MKULTRA program, its post-World War II research on torture. Because the CIA has never released the names of those who received its funding, it is impossible to be say this with any certainty. McCoy suggests that "the timing, at the peak of the agency's academic involvement, and the topic, torture, raise the possibility that Milgram's work may well have been a part of its larger mind–control project." McCoy, *A Question of Torture*, 47.

76. Stanley Milgram, *Obedience to Authority: An Experimental View* (New York: Harper & Row, 1974); Philip Zimbardo, *The Lucifer Effect: Understanding How Good People Turn Evil* (New York: Random House, 2007); Philip G. Zimbardo, "Stanford Prison Experiment," 1999–2013. http://www.prisonexp.org/; emphasis in the original.

77. Milgram, *Obedience to Authority*, 20.

78. Ibid., 45. I was actually a subject in an undergraduate imitation of the Milgram experiment, in the days before institutional review boards would have prohibited such research. The student experimenters considered me a very peculiar outlier, because I never turned up the juice beyond the original forty-five-volt sample shock they'd given me. To my shame, I did give those shocks, but at the final round I refused, on the grounds that if this were the last time through the list of words, there was no reason to use shocks to teach the "learner" anything more. The reward I'd been offered if my "student" learned well was to be considered a very good teacher and of interest therefore for further study. This was something that appealed greatly to my fragile undergraduate ego, and I was very sad to conclude that in fact I was a dismal teacher, as my "student" seemed incapable of learning. Why wouldn't I turn up the juice? Perhaps I was not as impressed as I should have been by the authority of college seniors only a few years older than I. Or perhaps I had been brought up in habits of action and thought that prevented me from inflicting pain on a harmless fellow student for no very good reason.

79. Ibid., 32.

80. Ibid., 6.

81. Ibid.

82. Ibid., 7.

83. Philip G. Zimbardo, "Preface," in *The Psychological Origins of Institutional Torture*, ed. Mika Haritos-Fatouros. Routledge Research International Series in Social Psychology (New York: Routledge, 2003), xvii.

84. Zimbardo, *Lucifer Effect*, 20. Maslach recalls that Zimbardo asked her what she thought of it. "I think he expected some sort of great intellectual discussion about what was going on. Instead, I started to have this incredible emotional outburst. I started to scream, I started to yell, 'I think it is terrible what you are doing to those boys!' I cried. We had a fight you wouldn't believe, and I was beginning to think, wait a minute, I don't know this guy. I really don't, and I'm getting involved with him?"

85. Kathleen O'Toole, "The Stanford Prison Experiment: Still Powerful after All These Years," *Stanford University News Service*, January 8, 1997. http://news.stanford.edu/pr/97/970108prisonexp.html.

86. Zimbardo, *Lucifer Effect*, 445.

87. Ibid. In this article Sabini and Silver refer to the work of situationists such as Lee Ross and particularly to John Doris, *Lack of Character* (Cambridge, U.K.: Cambridge University Press, 2002).

88. John Sabini and Maury Silver, "Lack of Character? Situationism Critiqued," *Ethics* 115, no. 3 (2005).

89. Ibid., 537.

90. Ibid., 560.

91. Aristotle, *Nicomachean Ethics*, trans. David Ross (New York: Oxford University Press, 1998), 1094b1–10.

92. Jonathan Barnes, "Introduction," in *The Nicomachean Ethics*, by Aristotle (London: Penguin Books, 2004), xxv. The idea that people should look to government to shape citizens' characters deeply contradicts, of course, liberal and Enlightenment ideas about the freedom and autonomy of the individual and the proper relationship between citizen and state. To be fair to virtue ethicists such as Aristotle and MacIntyre, neither would desire to place the formation of character in the hands of a modern nation-state such as the contemporary United States of America.

‖ 6 ‖

Goods and Virtues

Could the generation who came of age since the towers fell have a different notion of what's acceptable in a time of war? "Over the past 10 years, they've been exposed to many new conflicts," says Isabelle Daoust, who heads [the American Red Cross's] humanitarian law unit. "But they haven't been exposed to the rules." "For young people, to put themselves in place of a soldier is a level of empathy that most people simply don't have anymore."

—Daniel Stone, *from "Red Cross Study Finds 60 Percent of Young People Support Torture"*[1]

The "Goods" of Torture

When MacIntyre speaks of the "goods internal" to a practice, he distinguishes these from the external goods, such as fame or wealth, that may accrue to successful participants of a particular practice. Of internal goods, there are two kinds: the good things that a practice produces (whether concrete goods, such as a portrait, or more abstract ones, such as a way of using portraiture to reveal the model's character) and "the good of a certain kind of life," the kind that is achievable through participation in a particular practice.[2] So, to use an example from Chapter 4, one of the first type of goods internal to the practice of knitting is the production of a wide variety of well-knitted objects—from the sturdiest of garments to three-dimensional depictions of mathematical theorems.[3] Another good produced by knitting is the ability to imagine how various materials might be transformed into entirely different ones through manipulation of yarn in space. This is an ability gradually acquired over many years of practice. The second type of good internal to the practice of knitting is the sort of life a good knitter can lead, one involving certain kinds of connection to the geographically and culturally diverse history of knitting and one that requires the acquisition of certain kinds of skills and virtues.

What then are the "goods"[4] that are internal to the practice of torture, that are sought by those who do it and by those who direct and order it? Of the first type, torture's practitioners recognize and value two in particular. I call these

155

the production of truth and the production of enemies. Another kind of good, one related to torture as part of a "certain kind of life" is the production and reproduction of torturers themselves.

There is, however, a potential objection to describing these things as goods "internal" to torture. Are not the internal "goods" of torture named above merely instruments for achieving another purpose, that is, establishing and maintaining state power? In what sense are they "internal" to the practice of torture? In the understanding of practice laid out in the previous chapter, a practice's internal goods are so specific that they can only be achieved by that practice or one very similar to it.[5] I think this is true of torture. Only torture can produce the particular relationships between people and truth described below. Only torture can produce more torturers.

The production of truth: Chapter 1 makes the argument that a primary purpose of the practice of torture is the establishment and maintenance of the power of a political regime. This is achieved in part by cementing the relationship between torture and the production of truth in the minds of the regime, the torturers, their targets, and the general public. Contemporary regimes that practice torture, whether openly or covertly, justify the practice in terms of the information, the "actionable intelligence" that it produces.

As more of the official record of the United States' use of torture since 9/11 becomes public, former and present administration officials seek to justify it on the grounds that the use of torture has either directly prevented further attacks or has provided information about the structure of al Qaeda and the identities of its upper echelon or the location of Osama bin Laden. Each of the ethical arguments supporting torture canvassed in Chapter 2 also rests on the assumption that, to the extent torture is justifiable, it is because it can at least sometimes elicit true and life-saving information from unwilling persons.

The connection between torture and truth would seem to be self-evident: People are tortured so they will divulge information that would otherwise be unavailable to those doing the torture. That it is sometimes the case that the tortured cannot reveal the required information, because they do not possess it, does not invalidate this claim. Torturers, like anyone else, can make mistakes, can select the wrong target. But as long as torture can be demonstrated to "work" on some occasions, the conceptual link between torture and eliciting of truth is maintained. However, to speak of torture as eliciting the truth from a prisoner is not the whole story. In torture, truth is as much *created and established* as it is brought out. The internal good that relates torture and truth is primarily that of establishing as true whatever reality is recognized or desired by the torture regime. This work of establishing truth occurs at two sites: in the relationship between torturer and victim and between the torture regime and the larger society.

What truths can be established through torture? First, there is the truth of the nature of relationship between the torturer and the tortured, between the regime and the prisoner. Elaine Scarry describes the dynamic of torture as one through which the victim's pain establishes the absolute reality of the torturer's power. Through complete control of the victim's sensory, personal, and social worlds, the torturer defines the real and the true. Scarry writes:

> Some of pain's attributes—its incontestable reality, its totality, its ability to eclipse all else, its power of dramatic alteration and world dissolution—can be lifted away from their source, can be separated from the sufferer and referred to power, broken off from the body and attached instead to the regime. Now, at least for the duration of this obscene and pathetic drama, it is not pain but the regime that is incontestably real.[6]

The English writer John Collier captured this dynamic in an odd little story called "Thus I Refute Beelzy,"[7] written over sixty years ago. In a few deft pages, Collier sketches the story of an interrogation in the form of a family tea party. The father, Mr. Carter, explains the difference between reality and fantasy to his six-year-old son, whom he calls "Small Simon." His son is supposed to call him "Big Simon" in turn, as an illustration of how modern and friendly their relationship is.

> "Small Simon, are you sorry to see me at tea with you?"
>   "No, Daddy."
>   "No, what?"
>   "No, Big Simon."
>   "That's right. Big Simon and Small Simon. That sounds more like friends, doesn't it? At one time, little boys had to call their father 'sir.' If they forgot—a good spanking. On the bottom, Small Simon! On the bottom!" said Mr. Carter, washing his hands once more with his invisible soap and water.
>   The little boy turned crimson with shame or rage.
>   "But now, you see,' said [a visitor called] Betty, to help, "you can call your father whatever you like."

Only of course, Small Simon cannot call his father whatever he likes. He cannot for instance call him "Daddy." His father goes on to quiz him about what he has been doing. It appears that Small Simon has been playing in the garden with his not-always-visible friend Beelzy. His father becomes angrier and angrier as Simon refuses to admit that Beelzy is imaginary.

"I am explaining that Mr. Beelzy is a fantasy of yours. Do you hear? Do you understand?"

"Yes, Daddy."

"He is a game. He is a let's-pretend.'"

The little boy looked down at his plate, smiling resignedly.

His father tells Simon what he must do to end the interrogation:

"All you have to do is to say, 'I have been playing a game of let's-pretend. With someone I make up, called Mr. Beelzy.' Then no one will say you tell lies, and you will know the difference between dreams and reality. Mr. Beelzy is a daydream."

Simon says nothing, so his father shows him the difference between dreams and reality with a domineering physical gesture.

"You can't touch him. You can touch me. I can touch you." Mr. Carter stretched out his big, white dentist's hand, and took his little son by the nape of the neck. He stopped speaking for a moment and tightened his hand. The little boy sank his head still lower.

"'Now you know the difference," said Mr. Carter, "between a pretend and a real thing. You and I are one thing; he is another."

The interrogation continues:

"Which is the pretend? Come on. Answer me. Which is the pretend?"

"'Big Simon and Small Simon,'" said the little boy.

Thus the boy unmasks the father's lie that the two of them are friends. Faced with this intransigence, with his little boy's refusal to acknowledge reality as his father defines it, Mr. Carter grows furious. He sends his son off to his room to await a spanking.

"You'll learn how real he is!" shouted his father after him. "If you can't learn it at one end, you shall learn it at the other. I'll have your breeches down."

In Collier's story, however, unlike much of real-life torture, reality has the last laugh. Simon's "imaginary" friend Beelzebub makes short work of Big Simon. His mother and the visitor discover that Beelzy has truly gobbled Big Simon up, leaving behind only "the shoe, with the man's foot still in it, much like that last morsel of a mouse, which sometimes falls unnoticed from the side of the jaws of the cat."[8]

Torture produces relationships of power in life and fiction. The Irishman Jim Auld told John Conroy how he felt about the member of the British Special Branch whom he first saw when, after a week of torture, Auld's hood was finally removed. "And he brought me something to eat. . . . And because I couldn't hold it—my hands were useless—he fed me. He gave me a Mars bar, he gave me a Coke. . . . And at that stage, I thought he was God. I thought he was the nicest human being alive. He was my friend and mentor."[9]

Binyam Mohammed Al-Habashi, whom the United State sent to Morocco to be tortured, later recorded in a diary what it was his torturers wanted. "One time I asked a guard," he says, "What's the point of this? I've got nothing I can say to them. I've told them everything I possibly could." "'As far as I know,' the guard told him, "it's just to degrade you. So when you leave here, you'll have these scars and you'll never forget. So you'll always fear doing anything but what the U.S. wants.'"[10] The point was to establish in Binyam Mohammed's mind the truth that he lived or died at the mercy of the U.S. government.

Then there is the second kind of truth produced by torture, that which affects the relationship between a government and its people: the establishment of specific desired bits of "actionable intelligence." This was something else Binyam Mohammed discovered his tormentors in Morocco wanted from him. "About once a week or even once every two weeks I would be taken for interrogation, where they would tell me what to say. They said if you say this story as we read it, you will just go to court as a witness and all this torture will stop. I eventually repeated what was read out to me." Mohammed continues:

> When I got to Morocco they said some big people in al-Qaida were talking about me. They talked about Jose Padilla and they said I was going to testify against him and big people. They named Khalid Sheikh Mohamed, Abu Zubaidah and Ibn Sheikh al-Libi [all senior al-Qaida leaders who are now in U.S. custody]. It was hard to pin down the exact story because what they wanted changed from Morocco to when later I was in the Dark Prison (a detention centre in Kabul with windowless cells and American staff), to Bagram and again in Guantánamo Bay.[11]

But whatever story was wanted, Mohammed told it. Nor was he the only torture victim to provide specific "intelligence" demanded by the Bush administration. It has been clear at least since 2005 that the Bush administration used torture to establish its case for a U.S. war against Iraq. In 2002, a Libyan, Ibn al-Shaykh al-Libi, who does seem to have been an Al Qaeda trainer, was captured and sent to Egypt for interrogation. There, to escape further torture, he said what the interrogators wanted to hear: that Iraq had trained Al Qaeda, as President Bush put it in October 2002, "in bomb-making and poisons and deadly gases," a claim repeated by then-Secretary of State Colin Powell in his speech at the United Nations.[12] Al-Libi later recanted this claim, and in March 2004, with the war well under way, "intelligence based on his remarks was withdrawn by the C.I.A."[13]

Lawrence Wilkerson, former Secretary of State Colin Powell's then-chief of staff, corroborates Al-Libi's recantation:

> As the administration authorized harsh interrogation in April and May of 2002—well before the Justice Department had rendered any legal opinion—its principal priority for intelligence was not aimed at pre-empting another terrorist attack on the U.S. but discovering a smoking gun linking Iraq and al-Qa'ida.
>
> So furious was this effort that on one particular detainee, even when the interrogation team had reported to Cheney's office that their detainee "was compliant" (meaning the team recommended no more torture), the VP's office ordered them to continue the enhanced methods. The detainee had not revealed any al-Qa'ida-Baghdad contacts yet. This ceased only after Ibn al-Shaykh al-Libi, under waterboarding in Egypt, "revealed" such contacts. Of course later we learned that al-Libi revealed these contacts only to get the torture to stop.
>
> There in fact were no such contacts.[14]

It appears that the need to establish a link between Iraq and Al-Qaeda also drove the introduction of torture at Guantánamo. Major Charles Burney, a former U.S. Army psychiatrist told the Senate Armed Services Committee, that since no such link existed, this proved difficult to do. "A a large part of the time we were focused on trying to establish a link between Al Qaeda and Iraq," he told the Army Inspector General, "and we were not being successful in establishing a link between Al Qaeda and Iraq. The more frustrated people got in not being able to establish that link," said Burney, "there was more and more pressure to resort to measures that might produce more immediate results."[15]

Why would a government bother to use torture to establish the truth of something it knew was probably not the case, such as a nonexistent link between Al Qaeda and Saddam Hussein? Would it not be simpler just to lie? It might be simpler, if the only need were to convince a regime's prisoners and its external audience (a national populace, the United Nations) that what the regime says is true. But it is also possible that torture regimes must sometimes convince *themselves* that the world they are constructing is real. They need the "facts" established through torture to confirm their own beliefs. Having constructed a world of absolute friends and absolute enemies, in which the United States and its allies squared off against "the really bad guys," the Bush administration needed "evidence" to reinforce its own view of the world.

Elaine Scarry describes this process: "The torturer's questions—asked, shouted, insisted upon, pleaded for—objectify the fact that he has a world, announce in their feigned urgency the critical importance of that world, a world whose asserted magnitude is confirmed by the cruelty." Only the continuation of such an important, heroically conceived world could justify the torture. But it is in part the torture itself that confirms the reality of the torturer's world. "It is only," says Scarry, "the prisoner's steadily shrinking ground that wins for the torturer his swelling sense of territory. The question and the answer are a prolonged comparative display, an unfurling of world maps."[16] The process of verifying the torturer's world through the prisoner's pain need not—indeed cannot—occur entirely at the level of conscious thought. That would require the regime to admit to doubts about its own construal of reality, something it cannot allow. Perhaps this is why, as Scarry says, the structure of torture—inherent in the relationship between pain and power—"may be in part premeditated" but also "seems for the most part unconscious."[17]

Another sort of truth produced by torture is the confession. Scarry calls torture the "inversion" of a trial, "a reversal of cause and effect. While the one," she says, "studies evidence that may lead to punishment, the other uses punishment to generate evidence." Torture victims are always already guilty; the proof is that they have been tortured. "The question of whether or not they are guilty never arises," says Harvard ethicist Herbert Kelman. "The whole torture apparatus operates on the assumption that those who are brought in for torture are guerillas, insurgents, or terrorists who have committed and/or were about to commit dangerous crimes against the state."[18]

In the United States, civilian courts are not permitted to accept confessions produced under torture. Indeed it is in part to prevent torture that the Constitution's fifth amendment prohibits a defendant's being "compelled to be a witness against himself." This is why the legal scholar Alan Dershowitz acknowledges that although the torture warrants he proposes would produce evidence true enough to save a city, such evidence would not be true enough to be admissible in court.

In contemporary English the word "confession" generally signifies an admission of guilt. But "confession" has an older meaning as well, one buried in the Latin roots of the word. A confession is a statement of faith, of belief. Tortured confessions—even the multitude of contra-factual confessions that torture produces—are often true statements of belief. Those who make them do, at least in the moment of confession, believe what they are saying. So Saddam

Saleh Aboud believed he was telling the truth when, after three weeks of torture, he told his captors at Abu Ghraib that he was Osama bin Laden in disguise.[19]

George Orwell gives this phenomenon its classic fictional rendition in the novel *1984*. As Winston Smith's torturer O'Brien coolly turns a dial to increase Smith's pain, Smith struggles to experience the truth the Party wants him to acknowledge—in this case, the simple "fact" that two plus two makes five. In the end O'Brien extracts the necessary confession, by applying the kind of electroshock one might characterize as a procedure "calculated to disrupt profoundly the senses or the personality."

> O'Brien held up the fingers of his left hand, with the thumb concealed.
> "There are five fingers there. Do you see five fingers?"
> "Yes."
> And he did see them, for a fleeting instant, before the scenery of his mind changed. He saw five fingers, and there was no deformity.[20]

The production of truth through torture extends beyond the immediate relationship between torturer and prisoner. The external audience is just as important. Michel Foucault has argued that modern societies have replaced the "sovereign power" enforced through the public spectacle of torture of the few with a "disciplinary power" that controls and normalizes everyone's bodily experiences.[21] Anthropologist Talal Asad takes up this argument. "In premodern societies of the kind Foucault called Classical," he argues, "'torture' was carried out unapologetically and in public. It was the object not of exposure but of display." In the transition to modernity, says Asad, "a liberal sensibility regarding pain" has developed, one which does not approve of the cruelty involved in inflicting "unnecessary" pain. This is why the "the public discourse on inflicting pain on a prisoner in the two cases (modern and premodern) is quite different" and why "modern or modernizing" governments that use torture must obscure that use with a rhetoric of denial.[22]

The Bush administration produced a paradigmatic example of this rhetoric of denial: the claims that any torture that happens is the unauthorized work of "a few bad apples" and the redefinition of torture as "enhanced interrogation techniques." But the rhetoric that conceals modern torture is less like a thick blanket than a diaphanous veil. The illusion of secrecy—the undisclosed locations, the hidden identities of the torturers, the sly hints at things too terrible ever to be revealed—what William Cavanaugh has called the "striptease of power"—this illusion enhances torture's effects.[23] The knowledge that the government of a liberal democracy has been driven to do such terrible things reminds the U.S. populace of the terrible danger in which we live—a danger from which only our nation's secret apparatus can protect us.

We become the audience in a "theater of fear." "Fear is constantly stoked," says Cavanaugh, but in contrast to the way authoritarian regimes use torture, "it is not the fear of the state but of the enemies of the state against whom the state protects us. The tragedy of 9/11 is incessantly invoked, not so that history will not be repeated but so that—to the contrary—it will continually recur in our imagination."[24]

That the mask occasionally slips and reveals the face of cruelty underneath may be a miscue, but it is one that can be turned to advantage. Indeed, the Bush administration appears almost instinctively to have known how to use unplanned exposures of torture to emphasize the enormity of the danger from which they were protecting us. The smartest people in the administration may well have realized that sooner or later some of what was happening would leak out. They prepared the public with suggestions and feints. Vice President Dick Cheney began as early as September 16, 2001, when speaking with NBC's *Meet the Press*. "We also have to work, though, sort of the dark side, if you will," he said. "A lot of what needs to be done here will have to be done quietly, without any discussion, using *sources and methods that are available to our intelligence agencies*, if we're going to be successful." The United States was entering "the world these folks operate in," he explained, "and so it's going to be vital for us to use *any means at our disposal*, basically, to achieve our objective."[25] It was classic striptease; displaying just enough to keep the show interesting.

In September 2002, CIA counter-terrorism expert Cofer Black added more hints when testifying to Congress about what he considered the agency's "operational flexibility," its ability to detain or kill potential enemies. "This is a highly classified area," he said. "All I want to say is that there was 'before' 9/11 and 'after' 9/11. After 9/11 the gloves come off." Black continued saying, "Nearly three thousand al-Qa'ida terrorists and their supporters have been detained," It was left to Congress and the public to imagine what might happen to those nearly three thousand, now that the gloves were off.

Along with the tragedies, this theater of fear has its comedies, too. If you travel by ferry to the island of Martha's Vineyard off Cape Cod, you will—at apparently random times—find Coast Guard boats flanking your vessel on either side. Each has a fifty-millimeter machine gun mounted on its bow. Your escort will accompany the ferry from the harbor, just until you reach deeper water, and then abandon you—right at the point in the journey when your boat is actually vulnerable to an attack. The first time I attended this one-act play, I burst out laughing. Our little vessel made a pretty unlikely terrorist target, and the machine guns an unlikely deterrent to a bomb on board. A middle-aged white man heard me laughing. He looked annoyed. "Well," he said, "it makes me feel more secure, just knowing they're there to protect us." This observation brings us to the next "good" internal to torture—the effective production of enemies, real and imagined, from whom the state protects us.[26]

The production of enemies: If the United States had enemies before the launch of the "war on terror," it certainly has more now. British Journalist Patrick Cockburn is one of many who have called U.S. torture al Qaeda's best recruiting tool. Cockburn writes that U.S. Army Major Alexander Maxwell (a pseudonym assumed for security reasons) told him, "The reason why foreign fighters joined al-Qa'ida in Iraq was overwhelmingly because of abuses at Guantanamo and Abu Ghraib and not Islamic ideology."[27] Maxwell is the veteran of more than three hundred interrogations in Iraq, and the author of *How to Break a Terrorist,* in which he argues that torture is worse than ineffective; it is counterproductive.[28]

And indeed it *would* be counterproductive, if institutionalized state torture were primarily a means of extracting information from prisoners. However, as Chapter 1 argues, such torture's main purpose is the establishment and maintenance of the power of the regime that employs it. Critics of this view such as Talal Asad have argued that it is a mistake to say that gathering information is not the true goal of torture or, indeed, to identify any one outcome as torture's goal, because the motives and purposes of those who torture are both various and unknowable.[29] Whatever its intent, the not-unwelcome *effect* of the practice of state torture is to maintain the power of the state, and one way that torture achieves this effect is through the creation of enemies.

Some of the enemies thus created have proven difficult to dispose of, once they are no longer useful. The bounties that the United States paid for captives in Afghanistan and Pakistan netted some odd fish, including twenty-two Uyghur men, members of a Central Asian ethnic group living in parts of China. Uyghurs, who are generally Muslims, speak a Turkic language. By 2003, most of the Uyghurs held at Guantánamo had received the official designation "NLEC"—No Longer Enemy Combatants. Yet twenty months later they remained in prison, some of them still shackled to iron rings in the floors of their tiny cells. A strong separatist current among Chinese Uyghurs has produced a repressive response from the Beijing government; for this reason, they could not be repatriated to China, where they would likely face serious reprisals.[30] Five of them ended up in Albania in 2006, and in 2009 four went to Bermuda. Later that year the tiny Pacific island nation of Palau granted asylum to twelve of them.[31]

Human Rights Watch reports that these are not the only prisoners "stuck in a U.S.-created limbo": As of March 2009 Letta Taylor of Human Rights Watch reports that almost one hundred Yemeni prisoners were "entering their eighth year without charge at Guantánamo."[32] The current U.S. proposal seems to be repatriation and imprisonment in Yemen, until the Yemeni government deems they have been "rehabilitated." If these men were not enemies before, they are now, after seven years in Guantánamo. One Yemeni who was repatriated in 2004 told Human Rights Watch, "They [the Yemeni authorities] beat me with shoes. There were insults, bad words and threats. I told them, 'If you're going to torture me, it won't be anything new. The Americans already put me through torture.'"[33]

It could be argued that even if it had not tortured many detainees, the U.S. government would still face difficulties adjudicating their cases, because of their irregular legal status as "unlawful enemy combatants." However, it is worth remembering that the Bush administration conceived of this status precisely to deny detainees held in the "war on terror" the protections afforded to prisoners of war under the Geneva Conventions. Absent the desire to use interrogation methods prohibited by the Conventions, there was no reason not to treat these captives as prisoners of war. Absent the use of torture to produce evidence against them, any who were suspected of war crimes might have been tried in open court, rather than in secret military commissions.

Some of the most important and powerful enemies torture creates live primarily in the imagination of the people living in a country that tortures. William Cavanaugh argues that "one of torture's primary purposes is the fostering of a certain kind of social imagination of who our enemies are." Just as the Chilean dictatorship claimed to defend its people from Marxist humanoids, "terrorists are our humanoids."[34] Without many dangerous and far-flung enemies, the "war on terror" loses its justification. One might think that torturing prisoners would evoke public sympathy for the prisoners, but the opposite seems to be the case. This is why to have its effect, torture cannot remain a complete secret.

This dynamic operates in two ways. First, images like the ones taken at Abu Ghraib present the prisoner as simultaneously dangerous and cowardly, a superhuman threat embodied in a subhuman being. Cavanaugh writes:

> The detainees in the photos are made to play the role of deviant, of the filth that the terrorist is in the morality play that we call the war on terror. Hooded, contorted, stacked naked, chained to cages, cowering before snarling dogs, covered with excrement, dragged around on leashes, made to masturbate and howl in pain, the prisoners become what terrorists are in our imagination: depraved subhumans.[35]

Stanley Milgram observed a similar phenomenon in his obedience experiments, discussed earlier. "Of considerable interest . . . ," he writes, "is the fact that many subjects harshly devalue the victim *as a consequence* of acting against him." Milgram continues:

Such comments as "He was so stupid and stubborn he deserved to get shocked," were common. Once having acted against the victim, these subjects found it necessary to view him as an unworthy individual, whose punishment was made inevitable by his own deficiencies of intellect and character.[36]

Second, the vileness of torture reinforces the vileness of the prisoner in the minds of the public. A "good" government could only be driven to such extremes by a terrible enemy. And only people of "the highest moral seriousness" would be willing to sacrifice themselves in such awful service to their country.[37] This brings us to the third internal good of torture, the making of torturers.

The production and reproduction of torturers: New torturers are incorporated into the practice in particular ways. To put it bluntly, torturers are not born; they are made. They are "a professional force with a significant role in protecting the state," as Harvard ethicist Herbert C. Kelman puts it. "A central component" of the mobilization of a state "torture apparatus" is "the recruitment of a cadre of torture practitioners through the development of what is in effect an organized profession."[38]

Studies of torturers around the world confirm a surprisingly similar training process consisting of brutal and brutalizing initiation, desensitization to their victims' humanity, and confirmation as members of an elite group. Initiation into the practice of torture begins with specialized training, whose central element is the endurance of weeks or months of ritualized physical, psychological, and emotional abuse. Often recruits are repeatedly beaten, tormented, insulted, spit upon, and made to follow pointless and capriciously changing rules. They are taught to take pride in surviving these ordeals, which are the route to "a special job that represents a significant service to the state and that often carries with it membership in an elite corps."[39] For example, recruits for interrogation training under Greece's military junta "were terrorized by kicking, flogging, punching, and cursing. Initiation took place in isolated sites in which moral displacement could occur without interference." Later in training, the abuse continued, "including being restricted from drinking water and from urinating or moving their bowels. Extreme fear led some to retain urine up to 4 days and feces up to 15 days during training."[40]

Alfred McCoy describes a similar pattern of brutal initiation undergone by the military officers who trained to torture their fellow Filipinos during the Marcos dictatorship. The violence of their treatment at the hands of upperclassmen, says McCoy, "would serve as a gateway to their use of torture when martial law placed civilians under their control."[41] The effects of such abuse are often worn as badges of pride. Chilean torturer Osvaldo Romo bragged to his interviewer about the burn scars on one of his legs ("*Claro, ésas son quemaduras de corriente* [Sure, those are burns from electric current]"), which he claimed to have received as part of a U.S. interrogation training program in Panama.[42]

A series of interviews with Brazilian torturers who had served in the Militarized Police reveals similar procedures, called *trote* in Portuguese (which the authors translate as hazing). Training culminated in a "Hell Week," during which trainees "were cursed, humiliated and hit; their faces were pushed into dirt as they did endless push-ups; and they were subjected to anything else that the officers could think of as an appropriate test of their resolve." This included rolling through a trench filled with used motor oil, in a "baptism-like ritual performed by a training officer at a makeshift altar." Like Christian catechumens, the trainees "were required to 'receive the Eucharist,' which involved drinking blood, urine, or some other equally dangerous and noxious liquid from the trainer's ceremonial cup." The authors add that "'Receiving the Eucharist' was also the euphemism for a notoriously violent form of military and police torture, involving a strong electric shock being administered to a victim's mouth or genitals by a live wire."[43]

My own personal experience also confirms the view that the process of making torturers includes psychological and physical brutality. In 1984 I worked in Nicaragua's war zones for six months, during the time when the Reagan administration was illegally funding the counter-revolutionary force known as the *contras*. Most of the *contras* operating in the northern part of the country were former members of the deposed dictator Anastazio Somoza's National Guard. Their military strategy was primarily one of attacks on civilians and public employees such as teachers and telephone and health-care workers. Such attacks very often involved rape, torture, and mutilations of victims' bodies and were intended to terrify the rural population of the country. Often as well, the men who were not killed were kidnapped and pressed into service in the *contra* army. I once interviewed a *contra* escapee, who described his *contra* training. This involved a combination of anti-communist indoctrination and torture, including lengthy immersions in frigid water.

While in Nicaragua, I often was told that it had been the habit of the National Guard to kidnap young boys and train them as torturers. I heard this, for example, from Felipe Barreda, the mayor of town called Ocotal, whose own parents were tortured to death by the *contra* in 1983. One of their tormentors was a thirteen-year-old girl. Barreda said that children were better at torture "than adults, it seems, because they hadn't developed so many inhibitions." But before they became torturers, the children were themselves tortured.[44]

I was never sure that this story—which I heard also from other Nicaraguans— was anything more than a Central American urban legend, until I came across a Canadian psychiatrist's report of interviews with former members of Somoza's

National Guard. In an earlier study he had interviewed forty-one "young ado-
lescent" soldiers and "concluded that the training was characterised by extreme
discipline very often including physical violence to the recruits, that it was conducted in a moral climate which had the most basic disregard for the rights of
civilians, and that the children themselves showed evidence of limited moral understanding and development."[45]

Another important part of the initiation period involves learning to think
of those whom they will torment as less than fully human. Mika Haritos-
Fatouros reports that the Greek torturers whom she interviewed were taught
to consider their prisoners "beasts" or "worms."[46] As torture proceeds, the
debasement and humiliation of the victim only serve to reinforce the original
impression that he or she is less than human. The best-known example of this
dehumanizing process at Abu Ghraib is the now-famous photograph of PFC
Lynndie England holding a naked Iraqi man on a leash like a dog.

Torture victims are sometimes reduced below the status even of pets. They
become laboratory animals. A Brazilian judge at the trial of a twenty-three-
year-old student observed that "tortures are an institution," in which victims
are reduced to living audiovisual aids. He described the defendant as "an instrument for the practical demonstration of this system, in a class in which
more than 100 sergeants participated and whose teacher was an officer of the
Army Police, called Lt. Ayton.... In this room, while slides about torture were
being shown, practical demonstrations were given using the defendant ... and
other prisoners in the Army police unit as guinea pigs."[47]

Through the training process, initiates are formed in, and taught to value,
certain qualities such as a simulacrum of courage—ruthlessness—and
loyalty to fellow corps members and country. As the Greek torturer Major
Nikolaos Hajizisis put it, "This training was not intended to annihilate their
human personalities but to steel their characters." Canadian criminologist
Ronald D. Crelimsten observes, "The phrase 'steel their characters' is interesting here, as it shows the ideology of toughness, of being a man, of remaining impervious to the temptations or corruptions of the outside world, the
subversives, the Communists, the enemy."[48] As in any practice, torture has
standards of performance, by which new torturers are measured and their
improvement noted and encouraged. Torture "is a job that involves hard
work, that can lead to promotion and other rewards, that may offer opportunities to demonstrate innovativeness and that one can excel and become
expert in."[49]

Not all torture regimes treat this initiation period as frankly as those of
Latin America, the Philippines, or Greece. Often such indoctrination is pre-
sented as training in *resisting* torture. For example, many members of U.S. and
British military intelligence deployed to Iraq participated in a program called

R2I (Resistance to Interrogation). The course is designed to teach resistance to a number of methods of interrogation, including the kind of sexual humiliation employed by the guards at Abu Ghraib.[50]

Another likely locus of such training for U.S. personnel is the Survival, Evasion, Resistance, and Escape (SERE) courses required for elite Special Forces troops. SERE training was ostensibly developed to train U.S. personnel to resist the kinds of torture encountered by U.S. prisoners of war captured during the Korean War. In 2002, a CNN camera crew gained permission to film at a SERE course held at Ft. Bragg, North Carolina. The most difficult part of these courses is a period spent in a mock POW camp, during which, as CNN reports, "the 'prisoners' are hooded and roped together. After their capture, the school instructors attempt to strip soldiers of their identities." The details of the methods—physical and psychological—by which this is accomplished said the report, are classified, but the camera crew noted the "flood of emotion" experienced by those who complete the course.[51]

In the years since CNN reported on SERE training, some of those classified details have emerged. It appears that SERE personnel assisted both the CIA and the commanders at Guantánamo in developing "enhanced" interrogation techniques. According to the 2005 Bradbury memos from the White House Office of Legal Counsel, these include all the methods approved for use by the CIA, such as "walling" and waterboarding. Indeed, Bradbury repeatedly justifies the use of such techniques on the grounds that "each of the specific enhanced techniques has been adapted from SERE training, where similar techniques have been used, in some form, for years on United States military personnel."[52]

Ordinary basic training for U.S. soldiers may differ from the training of torturers in degree more than in kind. Janice Gibson refers to the work of Gwynn Dwyer when she observes that "military training the world over makes use of many of the same techniques used to train military interrogator-torturers. Military training, after all, is designed to create soldiers obedient to all orders," she says, "even when those orders require them to commit acts that they were taught throughout their lives to be repugnant."[53] Yet most U.S. soldiers do not torture; indeed opposition to torture from within the U.S. armed services was a source of conflict with senior civilian Bush administration officials such as Defense Secretary Donald Rumsfeld.

Huggins et al. suggest that another element is necessary if ritual brutality is to successfully initiate new torturers. The trainees must emerge from their training not as individuals who have survived an ordeal but as members of an elite group who have been formed together. Speaking of the Brazilian experience they write, "Hazing shapes Militarized Police trainees into atrocity *teams* by modeling violence, creating blind obedience to authority, bringing about group bonding for reflexively meting out violence, and nurturing the moral disengagement that disguises and justifies such violence."[54]

These, then, are my candidates for the "goods internal to" the practice of torture: the production of truth, the production of enemies, and the production and reproduction of torturers themselves.

The "Virtues" of Torture

> However monstrous the deeds were, the doer was neither monstrous
> nor demonic, and the only specific characteristic one could detect ...
> was something entirely negative: it was not stupidity but a curious,
> quite authentic inability to think.
>
> —Hannah Arendt[55]

This section examines the relationship between torture and the four cardinal virtues described in Chapter 4: courage, temperance, justice, and prudence. Three of these Aristotle and Thomas Aquinas called "moral virtues"; that is, their absence or presence in a person has ethical implications. They arise in response to human emotion; in Thomas's taxonomy each completes, or perfects, a human desire or appetite.

The name of the fourth cardinal virtue, "prudence," has a strange ring to contemporary ears. We generally associate "prudence" either with a kind of caution or with a lack of appreciation for life's pleasures, as in the appellation "prude." A better term might be "practical wisdom," an expression often used to translate Aristotle's notion of *phronesis*. Practical wisdom is an intellectual virtue; in this sense it is similar to other intellectual virtues such as wit, cleverness, or scientific understanding. But it differs from these in its subject matter. Practical wisdom is "right reason applied to action."[56] It is the intellectual ability to think clearly about moral matters and to judge rightly how one ought to act in particular situations.[57]

In addition to these four virtuous qualities, this chapter looks at another three: faith, hope, and love. In Christian theology, these are sometimes called "graces" and are sometimes considered to be divine gifts, rather than habits people acquire through practice. I think, however, that these are important human qualities, of interest to people of many religions and to those whose ethics are purely secular.

The pages that follow are an effort to show that the practice of torture engenders its own version of each of these virtues, but that in each case, the virtue represents a twisted—"tortured"—version, a *per*version, of that virtue when it is healthy. I also suggest ways that the presence of the practice of institutionalized state torture within a society affects not only those directly engaged in the practice but also the society in which the practice is embedded. What are the effects on the moral habits of a society that accepts torture, whether tacitly or explicitly, if that is what it takes to keep it safe? The more the people of the United States know (or refuse to know) about the details— the photos and videos, the lists of "enhanced interrogation techniques," the personal testimonies of victims—the more deeply and directly, I believe, we ourselves become implicated in the practice.

Before examining the "virtues" engendered by torture, it may be helpful to have a reminder of how this book has defined virtue. A virtue is an acquired moral habit, a stable tendency to behave a certain way in certain circumstances. For Alasdair MacIntyre, moreover, virtues are qualities that people form through their practices and that allow them to pursue the goods that are internal to those practices.[58]

But I have suggested that torture is actually a *false* practice and that the moral habits that it engenders are shadow versions of the real things. The real things, as theologian Christopher Lutz suggests, help us avoid the attractions of the false goods that torture offers.[59] For each of these four virtues then, we will be examining both the "false" virtue that informs the practice of torture and makes its "goods" available to us and the "true" virtue that prevents us from seeking or achieving those "goods."

Courage

I have already alluded to some of the kinds of courage, or fortitude, that torture requires. First, there is the physical and emotional stamina necessary to endure the process of initiation. Whether it is the regimen required of recruits to the interrogation units of Brazil's Militarized Police or Chile's DINA or the U.S. military's basic training and elite SERE courses, successful completion requires great strength of body and of purpose.

There is also that particular kind of courage, a resistance to the power of squeamishness, which allows a person to withstand the distress involved in causing or even merely observing the pain of others. That distress is real enough, and resistance to it must be learned. (Recent neurobiological discoveries even suggest a physical locus for this unpleasant experience of others' pain in so-called mirror neurons, which fire in our own brains when we are exposed to the pain of others.[60])

This ability to withstand others' misery can form a genuine aspect of the virtue of courage, as when for example an orthopedist must set a bone in a conscious patient. Speaking from personal experience, I can guarantee that the patient in question will scream. A doctor who stops the procedure at that point because of his or her own distress does the patient no good at all. The difference between medicine and torture of course is that the doctor bears the patient's pain for the ultimate *good* of the patient; in the case of torture, the prisoner's pain does the prisoner only harm.

The Chilean novelist Ariel Dorfman argues that this perverse courage in the face of others' torment affects not only the torturer but also everyone who knows torture is happening. Torture demands this capacity "of the torturer, placing the victim outside and beyond any form of compassion or empathy, but also demands of everyone else the same distancing, the same numbness, on the part of those who know and close their eyes, those who do not want to know and close their eyes, those who close their eyes and ears and hearts."[61]

Torturers are capable, then, of a perverse courage in the face of their own or others' pain. I would argue, however, that the practice of torture does not engender the *primary* kind of courage, the kind that is necessary to face a threat to one's own continued existence. Far from it; the torturer is an existential threat to the prisoner, to his or her personhood, to his or her world, to his or her very life. Torture reverses this reality, presenting the victim as the threat. The "Marxist," the "humanoid," the "Islamofascist terrorist"—all these are presented both to the torturer and to the public at large as threats to the very existence of the nation, as matters of life and death.

The virtue of courage is often most necessary when human beings face the threat of death. In the practice of torture, courage is defined not as willingness to risk losing one's life, but the willingness to do anything necessary to another human being to avoid that risk. This is the "courage" that the Bush administration asked of the American people: the "courage" to accept any cruelty done in our name, if it is even only possible that such cruelty might spare the United States another terrorist attack.

This response to danger—that anything is permitted, if it will only make us safer—is also encouraged by media supporters of torture. "Torture," wrote *Washington Post* columnist Charles Krauthammer in 2009, "is an impermissible evil. Except under two circumstances." The first of these is of course the ticking-bomb scenario, but the second turns out to be any time the country thinks it is in danger and torture is "likely to save lives."

> The second exception to the no-torture rule is the extraction of information from a high-value enemy in possession of high-value information likely to save lives. This case lacks the black-and-white clarity of the ticking time bomb scenario. We know less about the length of the fuse or the nature of the next attack. But we do know the danger is great.[62]

This call to cowardice has been repeatedly amplified by members of the Bush administration and its supporters in the press. Nor did the call cease with the election of Barack Obama. Former Bush administration figures continue to speak out in favor of using torture to increase our security. Michael Hayden, for example, a former head of the CIA, told Fox News in April 2009, "The use of these techniques against these terrorists really did make us safer, it really did work."[63] Using torture may possibly (although probably not) make us "safer," but it certainly does not make us braver.

Temperance

If courage is the virtue that allows people to react appropriately to threats and dangers, temperance, or moderation, is the one that allows us to respond rightly to the things that delight and attract us, which form part of what Thomas Aquinas calls the "concupiscible" faculty. It is tempting to suggest that in torture, that which ought to repel the practitioner—causing harm to a helpless fellow person—instead attracts the torturer, that is, to argue that torturers love what they do. But most studies of torturers suggest that the "good" ones do not especially enjoy their work; they are not sadists, but professionals.

Huggins et al. report that the torturers whom they interviewed made a clear distinction between "good" police torturers and "bad" ones: "'Good' police torturers were described by accounts that justified their violence: trained and 'rational' police who had tortured acceptably had a clear knowledge of their limits." By contrast, "'bad' police torturers had illegitimately used violence for pleasure—they were deliberately sadistic, permanently lacked self-control, or had tortured under the temporary influence of drugs or alcohol."[64]

Once again, I would argue that this sort of moderation is an inversion of the real thing. Real temperance is the habit of moderate response to the real joys of one's *own* embodied life—the pleasures of everything from music to food to sex, so that one is the master and not the slave of those pleasures. The torturer's temperance is instead a measured response to the mental and physical torments suffered by *another* embodied life, a measured response to the deprivation and overwhelming of the senses, the sexual humiliations, the self-inflicted pain prescribed by the CIA's KUBARK manual and the "enhanced interrogation techniques" approved for use at Guantánamo, Abu Ghraib, and in the CIA's secret detention centers.

In the public's mind the torturer's "moderation" has been associated with the actions of fictional heroes like *24*'s Jack Bauer, who tortures more in sorrow than in anger, or of Michael Walzer's honest revolutionary leader who keeps his "dirty hands" at least partially clean by merely "ordering" the torture of a member of a possible bomb plot, rather than doing it himself. We are encouraged to think of torturers as secular ascetics who sacrifice their own desire for clean consciences for our benefit. We are encouraged to think of ourselves in the same way.

Justice

Justice is perhaps the trickiest of the moral virtues to define. Aristotle embraced the traditional Greek view that justice consists in giving to each what he or she is due, and he illustrated this approach with metaphors from the world of mathematics.[65] MacIntyre adopted this view of justice in *After Virtue*. In recent years, however, he has amended this model of justice to include the concept of "just generosity," which arises in response to the radical dependence on other people that characterizes all human lives. More than merely giving to others what they have earned, just generosity is the "appropriate response" to the deprivations that others suffer. These are, he says, "characteristically not only deprivations of physical care and intellectual instruction but also and most of all deprivations of attention and affectionate regard for the other."[66]

One obvious inversion of justice in torture is its use to demonstrate guilt. In institutionalized state torture, by definition, only the guilty are tortured. Torture, as practiced in the "war on terror," subverts the usual temporal order of justice, in which trial precedes penalty. In torture the victim is punished before—and often instead of—receiving a trial. William Cavanaugh suggests that those who learn that people have been tortured assign torture a sort of justice when they "think darkly [about the victims] 'they must have done something to deserve it.'"[67] In other words, by torturing someone, we prove that person's guilt, prove that because the person is being tortured, he or she deserves to be tortured.

A very particular subversion of justice undergirded the Bush administration's justifications of torture. This is the explicit attempt to shield U.S. torturers and their superiors from being brought to the bar of criminal justice. We have seen some of the highest legal officials in the United States distort the law and the meanings of ordinary words like "severe pain or suffering" or "calculated to cause" until they mean nothing like what was quite plainly intended by those who composed the UN Convention against Torture or its enabling U.S. legislation. Such impunity serves both to deny justice to the victims of torture and to validate the justice of torture in the public mind.

Torture twists the idea of justice as giving people what they are due in yet another way. It conflates justice with vengeance. It was in an "autumn of anger" that *Newsweek* columnist Jonathan Alter wrote that he found his "thoughts turning to . . . torture." He was concerned not so much with future safety as with "jumpstarting" a "stalled investigation of the greatest crime in American history." In November 2001, Alter believed that the FBI had in its custody "four key hijacking suspects" who "aren't talking at all." (It is not clear who these four were, or whether—if they existed at all—they were in FBI custody. It is likely Alter was referring to some of the hundreds of Muslim men arrested immediately after September 11, none of whom were ever shown to be connected to the attacks.) In any case, he was prepared, and encouraged the rest of us to be prepared, to torture people in pursuit of the "investigation" not of some future danger but of a crime that had already been committed.[68]

Warfare conducted by unpiloted aircraft ("drones") provides a different example of the ways that practice associated with war can corrupt the habit of justice. Brandon Bryant, a young man who worked for some years controlling drones flying over Pakistan and Afghanistan, describes how his experience changed over time. He still remembers one of the first missions, in which three Afghan men died. He watched one, whose leg had been blown off, bleed to death. "'The guy that was running forward, he's missing his right leg,' he recalled. 'And I watch this guy bleed out and, I mean, the blood is hot.' As the man died his body grew cold, said Bryant, and his thermal image changed until he became the same color as the ground." He never was sure exactly whom he'd killed that day. Were they Taliban insurgents, or "just men with guns in a country where many people carry guns?" After participating in the deaths of more than 1,600 people, however, Bryant says he stopped even wondering whether this killing was just—whether he was truly giving to people what was due to them. He "lost respect for life" he says, "and began to feel like a sociopath."[69] In fact, Bryant is not a sociopath. He left the drone program, unable to overcome his habit of moral self-examination, which is sometimes called prudence.

Prudence

Prudence, or practical wisdom, is the virtue that brings the other three out of the realm of theory and into the world of activity. It is practical wisdom that shows us how to act in accord with courage, temperance, and justice. In Thomistic language, prudence is "right reason about things to be done."[70] It is the use of reason to identify what is the right thing to do in any particular situation and to understand the best way to do that right thing. And it is this virtue, I would argue, whose nature is most perverted in the practice of torture.

This section opens with a quotation from Hannah Arendt. In commenting on perpetrators of great evil, including torturers, she observed that the one thing they appeared to have in common was "something entirely negative: it was not stupidity but a curious, quite authentic inability to think."[71] Elsewhere she writes, "Without taking into account the almost universal breakdown, not of personal responsibility, but of personal *judgment* in the early stages of the Nazi regime, it is impossible to understand what happened."[72] The inability to think about what is happening around one, or to make a moral judgment about it, is a dangerous habit indeed.

The practice of institutionalized state torture requires precisely this "quite authentic inability to think" about the moral implications of one's actions. The torturer must learn how not to think about the prisoner's humanity, about effects of the torturer's own actions on the prisoner's mind and body, about how little the torturer knows about who this person is or why he or she "deserves" this torment. At the same time, the public also learns how not to think about what is being done in our name, for our "protection," while at the same moment "we munch a chocolate bar, smile at a lover, read a book, listen to a concerto, exercise in the morning." In this way, says the Chilean novelist Ariel Dorfman, "torture also corrupts the whole social fabric."[73]

What does it mean to say that torture "corrupts the whole social fabric" of a nation, to make that claim, for example, about the United States? Certainly only a tiny proportion of Americans have been engaged in torture since the attacks of September 11, 2001. However, no adult American can now legitimately claim that there is no evidence of institutional support for torture within the U.S. government. Such a claim has been patently untrue, at least since stories of CIA methods began to surface in the U.S. press as long ago as March 2003.[74] Anyone who has wanted to know that torture was the policy of the Bush administration has had available a wide variety of newspaper and magazine articles. By 2004, the first books had begun to appear, such as Mark Danner's *Torture and Truth*.[75] The Internet has long provided access to English-language foreign reporting, which has often been more frank than the American press.

The refusal to acknowledge or to think about the evidence of torture that is right in front of us is a vice, one I have earlier called "culpable ignorance." It is the opposite of right reason, in that it constrains the ability to choose right actions when faced with an ethical challenge. It is not only the torturers' capacity for practical wisdom that institutionalized torture destroys. The rhetoric of denial, the theater of fear with its manipulations of threat levels and "striptease of power," the apologias for torture by present and former government officials, on the grounds that "it works": All these serve to diminish ordinary citizens' capacity to think clearly about moral questions.

Stanley Milgram describes with obvious contempt the attempts of one of his subjects to bring such prudential judgment to bear on what he is being asked to do. The gentleman in question is an elderly professor of Old Testament theology of whom Milgram reports that an "excessive fastidiousness characterizes all his actions." Milgram appears annoyed rather than pleased that, unlike his other subjects, the professor does not accord his white-coated experimenter the expected obedience. "In his discussion with the experimenter, the subject seems in no way intimidated by the experimenter's status but rather treats him as a dull technician." The professor refuses the experimenter's instructions "that the learner's protests are to be disregarded, and [that] the experiment must continue."[76] Milgram quotes the following bit of dialogue, after the professor refuses to administer any more shocks:

> EXPERIMENTER: It's absolutely essential to the experiment that we continue.
> SUBJECT: I understand that statement, but I don't understand why the experiment is placed above this person's life.
> EXPERIMENTER: There is no permanent tissue damage.
> SUBJECT: Well, that's your opinion. If he doesn't want to continue, I'm taking orders from him.[77]
> When [during a later discussion] the experimenter assures him of the safety of the shock generator, the subject, with some exasperation, brings up of the question of the emotional rather than physiological effects of the learner.
> SUBJECT (*spontaneously*): Surely you've considered the ethics of this thing. (extremely agitated) Here he doesn't want to go on, and you think the experiment is more important? Do you know what his physical state is? Say this man had a weak heart (quivering voice).
> EXPERIMENTER: We know the machine, sir.
> SUBJECT: But you don't know the man you're experimenting on.... That's very risky (gulping and tremulous). What about the fear that man had? It's impossible for you to determine what effect that has on him ... the fear that he himself is generating.... [78]

Here the prudence of Milgram's subject leads him to challenge the experimenter's characterization of the situation. He refuses to accept patently unreasonable assurances about the safety of the procedure; the experimenter may know his machine, but he doesn't know "the man [he's] experimenting on." With considerable perception, the professor identifies one of the key mechanisms of torture when he raises the possibility that harm may done not only directly through (to use Osvaldo Romo's words) the application of current, but also by the "learner's" own fear. His judgment of the situation is practical—it confronts the reality that he has encountered—but it transcends the merely instrumental. The professor has framed his objection to the experiment and the harm it might cause as a concern about "the ethics of this thing." This is prudence. This is Aquinas's "wisdom about human affairs."[79]

Milgram, however, dismisses his subject's "spontaneous mention of ethics" as unimportant, an issue "raised in a didactic manner and deriving from his professional position as a teacher of religion." One might have thought this subject's use of practical ethical reasoning was a useful datum in an experiment whose stated "true purpose" was to identify "the most effective way of strengthening resistance to inhumane authority."[80]

The various attempts of the Justice Department's Office of Legal Counsel to twist the law so that it appears to support torture and to exonerate both the torturers and their superiors is another example of the perversion of practical wisdom. Interpretation of law is an obvious locus for the use of the intellect in the service of judging what is right. It is a perversion of practical wisdom to use legal skills to so misinterpret laws and treaties against torture that they can be understood to permit the chaining of a human being to the ceiling by the wrists, so the prisoner remains standing for days without respite, sleepless, clothed only in an "adult diaper."[81]

Faith, Hope, and Love—A Brief Excursus

When Christian theologians speak of the three "graces," they are referring to a New Testament passage in which Paul discusses various spiritual gifts. The context is important: He has just finished his great remonstrance to the church at Corinth for the way they come together to celebrate what they call the Lord's supper, a ritual meal eaten at the end of the day in a church member's home. But all is not well in Corinth. Instead of sharing what each has to offer, the participants have managed to reproduce the class relations of the time. The rich people are off in a corner eating what they have brought with them, while the poorer folk, who often would have worked all day with little to sustain them, go hungry. Paul is furious. "Whoever, therefore, eats the bread or drinks the cup of the Lord in an unworthy manner," he writes to the Corinthians, "will be answerable for the body and blood of the Lord. Examine yourselves, and only then eat of the bread and drink of the cup. For all who eat and drink without discerning the body eat and drink judgment against themselves."[82]

For centuries, this passage was interpreted (by Catholic theologians especially) to pronounce judgment on anyone who receives communion while failing to believe that the bread and wine have literally become the body and blood of Jesus Christ. But many contemporary theologians prefer a different interpretation. The "body" that the people at Corinth have failed to recognize is their own community. By allowing some to eat well while others go hungry, rather than creating a shared feast, they have failed to discern their nature as a community.

Paul then launches into a description of the variety of spiritual gifts, or charisms, they might hope to receive, including the ability to teach, to prophesy,[83] or to speak in tongues. Each is valuable in its own way, but none is absolutely necessary to the good life of a member of a Christian community. The passage culminates in a description of the gifts that do endure: "And now faith, hope, and love abide, these three; and the greatest of these is love."[84] Again, the context is important. These are three qualities, Paul argues, that are necessary to sustain the life, not only of an individual but of a community. Paul is concerned that the people to whom he writes recognize that their lives are embedded in a larger community and that they develop the habits that make that community thrive. In this he is like Aristotle, who wrote that a human being is by nature a social animal and that because of this, society itself "is something that precedes the individual. Anyone who either cannot lead the common life or is so self-sufficient as not to need to, and therefore does not partake of society, is either a beast or a god."[85]

Aristotle believed that living in society requires certain virtues and that a good society will help people form those virtues. Similarly, Paul writes of faith, hope, and love as virtues that are necessary to the members of a community. In his case, it is a very particular kind of community—a Christian one preparing itself for the imminent return of Christ. I think, however, that these virtues are important ones for social animals in general and for a good society in particular, which, as Aristotle says, "precedes" and forms the individual.

Torture perverts faith, hope, and love in very particular ways. Torturers, their commanders, and a society where torture happens learn to keep faith with a debased simulacrum of a nation. Patriotism, fidelity to one's native place, is thus perverted into a faithfulness to the power of the state. Hope for the future is twisted into desperation; we no longer hope for a good life; we settle for a life that we believe can only be bought with other people's anguish. And love? Rather than expanding love's radius, torture encourages us to draw the circle tight, so that finally it encloses only ourselves and those most like us.

Notes

1. Daniel Stone, "Why 60 Percent of Young People Support Torture," *Daily Beast*, April 12, 2011. http://www.thedailybeast.com/articles/2011/04/12/red-cross-study-finds-60-percent-of-young-people-support-torture.html.
2. Alasdair MacIntyre, *After Virtue*, 2d ed. (Notre Dame. IN: Notre Dame University Press, 1984), 190.
3. For examples of the latter, see Sarah-Marie Belcastro, "The Home of Mathematical Knitting (Sarah–Marie's Mathematical Knitting Pages)." http://www.toroidalsnark.net/mathknit.html.

4. The word "goods" appears in quotation marks here, to indicate that just as torture is a false practice, the "goods" it produces are also false. But because this use of punctuation is distracting, it is dropped as the argument develops.

5. MacIntyre, *After Virtue*, 188.

6. Elaine Scarry, *The Body in Pain: The Making and Unmaking of the World* (New York: Oxford University Press, 1985), 56.

7. John Collier, "Thus I Refute Beelzy," in *Fancies and Goodnights*, by John Collier (New York: New York Review of Books, 2003), 196–200.

8. Ibid.

9. John Conroy, *Unspeakable Acts, Ordinary People: The Dynamics of Torture* (Berkeley: University of California Press, 2000), 9.

10. "One of Them Made Cuts in My Penis. I Was in Agony," *The Guardian*, August 2, 2005.

11. Ibid.

12. Dan Froomkin, "Torturing for Propaganda Purposes," *WashingtonPost.com*, April 22, 2009. http://voices.washingtonpost.com/white-house-watch/torture/torturing-for-propaganda-purpo.html.

13. Douglas Jehl, "Qaeda–Iraq Link U.S. Cited Is Tied to Coercion Claim," *New York Times*, December 9, 2005.

14. Lawrence Wilkerson, "The Truth About Richard Bruce Cheney," *The Washington Note*, May 13, 2009. http://www.thewashingtonnote.com/archives/2009/05/the_truth_about/.

15. U.S. Senate Committee on Armed Services, *Inquiry into the Treatment of Detainees in U.S. Custody*, 110 Cong., 2nd sess., 2008, 41.

16. Scarry, *The Body in Pain*, 36.

17. Ibid., 51.

18. Herbert C. Kelman, "The Social Context of Torture," in *The Politics of Pain: Torturers and Their Masters*, ed. Ronald D. Crelinsten and Alex Peter Schmid (Boulder, CO: Westview, 1995), 32.

19. Ian Fisher, "Iraqi Tells of U.S. Abuse, from Ridicule to Rape Threat," *New York Times*, May 14, 2004. Revelations in May 2009 about the Bush administration's use of torture to establish a nonexistent link between al Qaeda and Saddam Hussein shed new light on this story. It now appears that those interrogating prisoners in Abu Ghraib *after* the successful invasion of Iraq were still seeking to establish that link as a retroactive justification for war.

20. George Orwell, *1984* (New York: Harcourt, Brace, 1983), 266.

21. Michel Foucault, *Discipline and Punish: The Birth of the Prison* (New York: Vintage, 1995).

22. Talal Asad, *Formations of the Secular: Christianity, Islam, Modernity* (Stanford, CA: Stanford University Press, 2003), 105.

23. William T. Cavanaugh, *Torture and Eucharist: Theology, Politics, and the Body of Christ* (Malden, MA: Blackwell, 1998).

24. William T. Cavanaugh, "Making Enemies: The Imagination of Torture in Chile and the United States," *Theology Today* 63, no. 3 (2006), 312.

25. Jane Mayer, *Dark Side: The Inside Story of How the War on Terror Turned into a War on American Ideals* (New York: Doubleday, 2008), 9–10; emphasis in the original.

26. My partner and I became bit players in this airport comedy when in August 2002 we turned up on the FBI no-fly list at San Francisco International Airport. Three armed police officers stood guard over us for half an hour, while we waited to see whether our names would also appear on a mysterious roll called "the master list." After half an hour we were escorted to the loading area and allowed to board a plane for Boston. We have never learned why we were on the list, but we suspect it had something to do with our work with the newspaper *War Times/Tiempo de Guerras*, a publication opposing the "war on terror."

   Whatever the reason, we learned that the value of these lists must be largely cosmetic. Neither of us has had a problem flying since—except the only other time my partner flew on the same airline. If these lists are a sieve to catch terrorists, some of its holes are quite large.

27. Patrick Cockburn, "Torture? It Probably Killed More Americans Than 9/11," *London Independent*, April 26, 2009.

28. Alexander Maxwell, *How to Break a Terrorist: The U.S. Interrogators Who Used Brains, Not Brutality, to Take Down the Deadliest Man in Iraq* (New York: Free Press, 2008).

29. Asad, *Formations of the Secular*, 104.

30. Robin Wright, "Chinese Detainees Are Men without a Country," *Washington Post*, August 24, 2005.

31. BBC, "Guantanamo Uighurs Sent to Palau," *BBC World News*, October 31, 2009. http://news.bbc.co.uk/2/hi/8336343.stm.

32. Human Rights Watch, "US/Yemen: Break Impasse on Yemeni Returns from Guantanamo," March 29, 2009. http://www.hrw.org/en/news/2009/03/28/usyemen-break-impasse-yemeni-returns-guantanamo.

33. Human Rights Watch, *No Direction Home: Returns from Guantanamo to Yemen* (New York: Human Rights Watch, 2009). Note that in May of 2013 the majority of Guantánamo's remaining 166 prisoners were on extended hunger strike, in protest at their indefinite detention. On May 23, 2013 President Obama, in a major address on defense policy, reiterated his intention to close the prison at Guantánamo.

34. Cavanaugh, "Making Enemies," 307.

35. Ibid., 313–14.

36. Stanley Milgram, *Obedience to Authority: An Experimental View* (New York: Harper & Row, 1974), 10; emphasis in original.

37. Cavanaugh, "Making Enemies," 314.

38. Kelman, "The Social Context of Torture," 28.

39. Ibid., 31.

40. Janice T. Gibson, "Training People to Inflict Pain: State Terror and Social Learning," *Journal of Humanistic Psychology* 31, no. (1991), 80.

41. Alfred W. McCoy, *Closer Than Brothers: Manhood at the Philippine Military Academy* (New Haven, CT: Yale University Press, 1999), 199.

42. Nancy Guzmán Jasmen, *Romo, Confesiones De Un Torturador*, 1st ed. (Santiago, Chile: Editorial Planeta Chilena, 2000), 194.

43. Martha K. Huggins, Mika Haritos-Fatouros, and Philip G. Zimbardo, *Violence Workers: Police Torturers and Murderers Reconstruct Brazilian Atrocities* (Berkeley: University of California Press, 2002), 155.

44. Rebecca Gordon, *Letters from Nicaragua* (San Francisco: Spinster/Aunt Lute, 1986), 74.

45. Federico Allodi, "Somoza's National Guard: A Study of Human Rights Abuses, Psychological Health and Moral Development," in *The Politics of Pain: Torturers and Their Masters*, ed. Ronald D.Crelinsten and AlexPeter Schmid (Boulder, CO: Westview, 1995), 115.

46. Mika Haritos-Fatouros, *The Psychological Origins of Institutional Torture*, ed. W. Peter Robinson. Routledge Research International Series in Social Psychology (New York: Routledge, 2003), 176–77; ibid.

47. Lawrence Weschler, *A Miracle, a Universe: Settling Accounts with Torturers* (New York: Penguin, 1990), 40.

48. Ronald D. Crelinsten, "In Their Own Words," in *The Politics of Pain: Torturers and Their Masters*, ed. Ronald D. Crelinsten and Alex Peter Schmid (Boulder, CO: Westview, 1995), 47.

49. Kelman, "The Social Context of Torture," 31.

50. David Leigh, "UK Forces Taught Torture Methods," *The Guardian*, May 7, 2004. http://www.guardian.co.uk/Iraq/Story/0,2763,1212197,00.html.

51. "SERE Training," http://www.training.sfahq.com/survival_training.htm (accessed October 10, 2006).

52. Steven G. Bradbury, *Memorandum for John A. Rizzo, Senior Deputy General Counsel, Central Intelligence Agency, May 30, 2005. Re: Application of United States Obligations under Article 16 of the Convention against Torture to Certain Techniques That May Be Used in the Interrogation of High Value Al Qaeda Detainees*, May 30, 2005, http://www2.gwu.edu/~nsarchiv/torture_archive/docs/Bradbury%20memo.pdf, 12.

53. Gibson, "Training People to Inflict Pain," 82.

54. Huggins, Haritos-Fatouros, and Zimbardo, *Violence Workers*, 159; emphasis in the original.

55. Hannah Arendt, "Thinking and Moral Considerations: A Lecture," *Social Research* 38, no. 3 (1971).

56. Thomas Aquinas, *Summa Theologica*, trans. Fathers of the English Dominican Province (Notre Dame, IN: Ave Maria, 1981; reprint, 1981), II–II, Q.47 a.8.
57. See Chapter 2 for a discussion of the decision to call "prudence" "practical wisdom" rather than "practical reason," which is a more familiar rendering for Thomistic scholars.
58. MacIntyre, *After Virtue*, 187.
59. Christopher Stephen Lutz, *Tradition in the Ethics of Alasdair Macintyre: Relativism, Thomism, and Philosophy* (Lanham, MD: Lexington Books, 2004), 103.
60. Sandra Blakeslee, "Cells That Read Minds," *New York Times*, January 10, 2006.
61. Ariel Dorfman, "The Tyranny of Terror: Is Torture Inevitable in Our Century and Beyond?" in *Torture: A Collection*, ed. Sanford Levinson (Oxford: Oxford University Press, 2004), 9.
62. Charles Krauthammer, "Torture? No. Except . . . ," *Washington Post*, May 1, 2009.
63. Tony Hamden, "Barack Obama Visits CIA to Calm Uproar over Release of Secret Memos " *London Telegraph*, April 21, 2009.
64. Huggins, Haritos-Fatouros, and Zimbardo, *Violence Workers*, 205.
65. Aristotle, *Nicomachean Ethics*, trans. David Ross (New York: Oxford University Press, 1998), Book V, 1131a6–34a12.
66. Alasdair MacIntyre, *Dependent Rational Animals: Why Human Beings Need the Virtues*, The Paul Carus Lectures (Chicago: Open Court, 1999), 121–22.
67. Cavanaugh, "Making Enemies," 314.
68. Jonathan Alter, "Time to Think About Torture," *Newsweek*, November 5, 2001.
69. Richard Engel, "Former Drone Operator Says He's Haunted by His Part in More Than 1,600 Deaths," *NBC News*, June 6, 2013. http://openchannel.nbcnews.com/_news/2013/06/06/18787450-former-drone-operator-says-hes-haunted-by-his-part-in-more-than-1600-deaths.
70. Aquinas, *Summa*, I–II, Q58, a. 2. Thomas compares prudence to "art" (or technical intelligence), which is "right reason about things to be made."
71. Arendt, "Thinking and Moral Considerations."
72. Hannah Arendt, "Personal Responsibility under Dictatorship," in *Responsibility and Judgment*, ed. JeromeKohn (New York: Schocken Books, 2003), 24; emphasis in original.
73. Dorfman, "The Tyranny of Terror: Is Torture Inevitable in Our Century and Beyond?," 9.
74. Don Van Natta Jr., Raymond Bonner, and Amy Wandman, "Threats and Responses: Interrogations; Questioning Terror Suspects in a Dark and Surreal World," *New York Times*, March 9, 2003.
75. Mark Danner, *Torture and Truth: America, Abu Ghraib, and the War on Terror* (New York: New York Review Books, 2004).
76. Milgram, *Obedience to Authority*, 48.
77. Ibid.
78. Ibid.; ellipses in original.
79. Aquinas, *Summa*, I–II, Q.47, a.2.
80. Milgram, *Obedience to Authority*, 49.
81. Steven G. Bradbury, *Memorandum for John A. Rizzo, Senior Deputy General Counsel, Central Intelligence Agency, May 10, 2005. Re: Application of §§ 2340–2340a to Certain Techniques That May Be Used in the Interrogation of a High Value Al Qaeda Detainee*, May 10, 2005; Steven G. Bradbury, *Memorandum for John A. Rizzo, Senior Deputy General Counsel, Central Intelligence Agency, May 10, 2005. Re: Application of §§ 2340–2340a to the Combined Use of Certain Techniques in the Interrogation of High Value Al Qaeda Detainees*, May 10, 2005; Steven G. Bradbury, *Memorandum for John A. Rizzo, Senior Deputy General Counsel, Central Intelligence Agency, May 30, 2005. Re: Application of United States Obligations under Article 16 of the Convention against Torture to Certain Techniques That May Be Used in the Interrogation of High Value Al Qaeda Detainees*, May 30, 2005.
82. 1 Corinthians 11: 27–29.
83. Note that "to prophesy" in this context does not mean to predict the future but to speak some kind of holy truth, usually in opposition to the ruling powers of the day.
84. 1 Corinthians 13:13.
85. Aristotle, T. A. Sinclair, and Trevor J. Saunders, *The Politics*, rev. ed. (London: Penguin Books, 1992), 1253A.

Conclusion: What Is to Be Done?

"There was a before 9/11, and there was an after 9/11. After 9/11
the gloves came off."
—Cofer Black, *then Director of the CIA Counterterrorist Center,*
speaking to the House and Senate Intelligence Committees in 2002.[1]

Although he has since published a well-received history of Franklin Delano
Roosevelt's first hundred days in office and two books on Barack Obama's
presidency,[2] *Newsweek* columnist Jonathan Alter is probably still best known
as the first person to suggest in popular media that the attacks of September 11
meant someone ought to be tortured. "In this autumn of anger," Alter wrote on
November 5, 2001, "even a liberal can find his thoughts turning to . . . torture."
Apart from its being the opening contribution to an unprecedented public
conversation, Alter's column is remarkable for its frankness about why he was
thinking about torture: It appeared to be the best possible means to "jump-
start the stalled investigation of the greatest crime in American history." Alter
justified his thinking about torture not with the modern objective of obtaining
"actionable intelligence" about possible future dangers but with the ancient
view of torture as the surest means of identifying those guilty of crimes already
committed. Those who were uncomfortable with his thinking, he argued, were
"hopelessly 'Sept. 10'—living in a country that no longer exists."[3]

How different, really, is the United States of today from the United States
of September 10, 2001? In particular, how is it different in relation to the subject of this book, institutionalized state torture? Certainly, some things have
changed. For the first time a U.S. government has directly sanctioned the use
of torture on persons declared enemies of the state. And for the first time in
many years, a public debate on torture has re-opened ethical questions long
thought settled. Torture has in a sense been rehabilitated—cleaned up and
reintroduced into respectable society. The "rhetoric of denial" surrounding it
has been transformed into a rhetoric of sober approval, conceived by torture's
advocates as a necessary, honest, and even courageous discourse.[4]

This new conversation represents a genuine discontinuity with the "hopelessly 'Sept. 10'" assumption that torture is wrong. Prior to September 11, U.S. involvement in torture was generally indirect and covert. It was indirect, in that its main focus was on providing training and technical assistance to torture regimes outside this country. It was covert, in that such training, and the research supporting it, were never publicly acknowledged by government officials. The glaring exception, of course, is the practice of torture in U.S. jails and prisons, which is discussed in a previous chapter. Torture in prisons, however, continues to be cloaked less in a rhetoric of denial than in an almost complete lack of rhetoric. Apart from rare exceptions, it is rarely discussed in the mainstream U.S. press.[5]

This book has described a break with the pre-9/11 indirect and covert practice, by detailing an organized practice of torture in detention centers run by both the U.S. Department of Defense and the CIA. Chapters 1 and 5 have demonstrated the shift in U.S. government policy from secretive support for torture regimes in other countries' internal wars to a quasi-overt use of torture in its own "war on terror." Since President Obama first declared his intention of closing the prison at Guantánamo, this openness has only grown. Former members of the Bush administration, especially Vice President Dick Cheney, have argued publicly in favor of torture as a necessary measure to protect Americans. In May 2009, Cheney told an audience at the conservative American Enterprise Institute that "to completely rule out enhanced interrogation methods in the future is unwise in the extreme. It is recklessness cloaked in righteousness, and would make the American people less safe."[6] It would be a mistake, however, to think that such justifications of torture began only once Bush officials had left office. As long ago as 2006, Cheney described the decision to use waterboarding on Khalid Sheik Mohammed as a "no-brainer."[7]

Much work remains to be done in documenting the ongoing national conversation about torture. Chapter 3 of this book describes the new post-9/11 discourse in academic literature and in two nationally read newspapers. But a review of newspaper editorials only begins to touch on the nonacademic discussion of torture. Popular discourse has taken additional forms, ones that probably reach many more people than newspaper editorials. These include innovations in dramatic representations, such as routine threats on television shows like *Hawaii 5–0* or *NCIS Los Angeles* to ship suspects off to "GITMO" and the use of torture in *Zero Dark Thirty*, a film about the death of Osama bin Laden.

The mere depiction of torture in movies and on television is nothing new. The hugely popular 1976 film *Marathon Man*, for example, featured a now-famous torture scene. What has changed is the role of the hero. Dustin Hoffman's Babe Levi is the torture victim in *Marathon Man*. In the television show *24*, Kiefer

Sutherland's Jack Bauer is the torturer. Here is a fertile field for more research. We need serious studies by communication experts of the changes in on-screen depictions of torture before and after September 11, 2001, to improve our understanding of the dialectical relationship between entertainment media and public attitudes toward torture. It would also be interesting to see whether the routine depictions of police abuse and threats of prison rape used to extract information and confessions have changed in number or severity from the days of the 1990s hit *NYPD Blue* to today's police procedurals.

More direct public conversation about the ethics of torture has also taken place on talk radio programs, beginning at least as early as the revelations of abuse at Abu Ghraib. In-depth studies of these would also be valuable, as would content analyses of letters to editors of local and national newspapers and examinations of Internet discourse on the subject. Pre- and post-9/11 comparative studies of the latter present other difficulties: The exponential growth of on-line discussion makes the Internet a very different, much more populous and more segmented place than it was in 2001. Careful comparison of polling data across the years following 9/11 would also offer some insight into changes in attitudes toward torture in this country.

If the start of the "war on terror" marked a departure in U.S. torture policy, it also represented something less than a complete break with the past. The infrastructure of torture was not created from scratch in the days after the September 11 attacks. As we have seen, the CIA has a over half a century of experience in torture research and in training officials of other countries in torture methods. Long before 9/11 the agency already had an "extraordinary rendition" program, which involved the shipping of captives to other countries for torture. However, as Daniel Coleman an FBI interrogation expert, told journalist Jane Mayer, this program "really went out of control" after 9/11. Besides an increase in the number of renditions, the CIA had begun to use the resources of other countries to conduct its own abusive interrogations: "Now instead of just sending people to third countries, we're holding them ourselves. We're taking people, and keeping them in our own custody in third countries." Nor, as we have seen, were these renditions and interrogations rare events. They became standard operating procedure. In the new period, Coleman said, torture had "become bureaucratized."[8]

Similarly, the use of torture by the U.S. uniformed armed forces has a conflicted history. On one hand, the U.S. military has long respected the Geneva Conventions' protections for prisoners of war, at least in part because the Conventions also cover U.S. soldiers should they be captured. On the other hand, military intelligence services have a history of cooperation with CIA interrogation programs. One example is the CIA's project of torture and assassination in Vietnam, known as the "Phoenix Program," which is described in the introduction to this book. Army intelligence personnel participated in this program. Techniques used in Phoenix also became part of Army Intelligence's Project X, begun in the mid-1960s. Project X, says historian Alfred McCoy, "was designed, according to a confidential Pentagon memo, 'to provide counterinsurgency techniques learned in Vietnam to Latin American countries.' " Training provided to Latin American torture regimes by the U.S. military included "techniques" such as "use of sodiopentathol [sic] compound in interrogation, abduction of adversary family members to influence the adversary, prioritization of adversary personalities for abduction, exile, physical beatings and execution. . . . For the next quarter of a century," adds McCoy, "the Army would transmit these extreme tactics, both by direct training and mailings of manuals, to the armies of at least ten Latin American nations."[9]

The Challenge: What Is to Be Done?

> For we are inquiring not in order to know what virtue is, but in order to become good, since otherwise our inquiry would have been of no use.
> —Aristotle, *Nicomachean Ethics*[10]

I have often thought that the entire content of this book could be expressed in five words: *Torture is wrong. Stop it.* Most of the foregoing chapters have been devoted to the three-word declarative portion of this formula. I now take up the two-word imperative. What can be done to bring an end to the practice of torture in and by the United States? Some answers to this question will necessarily entail policy recommendations, such as proposals to reorganize the multiple "intelligence" services of the federal government or reforms to incarceration practices at all levels of the criminal justice system. To make such policy recommendations falls outside the particular expertise of an ethicist, at least of this one. Insofar as I have opinions on these issues, they can carry no more or less weight than those of any other concerned citizen of a democratic state.

Other recommendations, however, do derive at least in part from an ethicist's knowledge and training. These include the need for a full accounting of, and accountability for, the quasi-overt practice of torture in the "war on terror"; some further thoughts on the vices leading to and reinforced by the practice of torture; and some thoughts about where we might look to find or to establish practices that make it easier to resist the temptations of torture.

In his inaugural address of 1797, President John Adams said, "The existence of such a government as ours for any length of time is a full proof of a general dissemination of knowledge and virtue throughout the whole body of the people." He went on to speak of national pride, saying that if it "is ever justifiable or excusable it is when it springs, not from power or riches, grandeur or glory, but from conviction of national innocence, information, and benevolence."[11]

These words of the second president of the United States might serve as a warning to any descendants of his audience who are considering the meaning of U.S. citizenship in the twenty-first century. Certainly the general understanding of who constitutes "the whole body of the people" has expanded beyond the set of white men of property contemplated in Adams's time. In the intervening centuries, descendants of African slaves, descendants of the native peoples of North America, a vast variety of immigrants, women in general— all these have claimed membership in that body, some more successfully than others. Such membership is still contested today by immigrants living and working as noncitizens in this country.

As the nature—and numbers—of "the whole body of the people" have expanded since Adams's day, so has the relationship of that people to a vastly more complex government, a relationship that has grown increasingly distant and indirect. Adams believed that the continued existence of "such a government" as the one he was elected to lead proved something positive about the "dissemination of knowledge and virtue" among the people. It could be argued today that the continued existence of the huge bureaucratic apparatus that is the U.S. government owes less to the knowledge and virtue of the 315.9 million inhabitants of this country than to the inevitable inertia of anything so large.

Nevertheless, it is not entirely unreasonable to ask what the existence "for any length of time" of a largely democratic government that has institutionalized the practice of torture demonstrates about the knowledge and virtue of the present body of the people. This is a very large question. It should not be answered glibly, and it cannot be answered well without the devoted empirical study and wisdom of a new generation of Tocquevilles.[12] In this conclusion I shall only sketch some areas that might usefully be explored by social theorists, students of culture, and ethicists who seek to understand the meaning of institutionalized state torture for the character of the people in whose name it is practiced.

Short-Range Actions

Look at the current situation, where we are force-feeding detainees who are being held on a hunger strike. . . . Is this who we are? Is that something our Founders foresaw? Is that the America we want to leave our children? Our sense of justice is stronger than that.[13]

—President Barack Obama, May 2013

Put a real end to the Bush administration-era policies. The day after his inauguration, President Obama ordered the prison at Guantánamo shut within a year. The same executive order also required the CIA to shut down its network of secret prisons developed over the seven years following 9/11 and in future to use only those interrogation methods found in the *Army Field Manual on Interrogation.* This is certainly a good beginning, but it does not guarantee that, as Gerald Ford once said in another context, "Our long national nightmare is over."[14] A practice developed over decades and supported by an expansive infrastructure does not end with one executive order.

In May 2013 the prison at Guantánamo was still open. President Obama again expressed his desire to close it, in a speech to the National Defense University, which is quoted above. He blamed congressional recalcitrance for his inability to close the prison during his first four years in office. Certainly, congressional actions have made it harder to try Guantánamo's prisoners in civilian courts or to set free the more than sixty still being held there who have been cleared for release. He also acknowledged the difficulties involved in deciding "just how to deal with those GTMO detainees who we know have participated in dangerous plots or attacks." The problem is that these people cannot be prosecuted, either because the evidence is "compromised," or, as the President delicately put it, it "is inadmissible in a court of law." In other words, the evidence was obtained through torture.[15]

Nor is the CIA prepared to end all its torture programs. According to Leon Panetta, the CIA's first director under President Obama, the agency will continue to use "extraordinary rendition," the transfer of prisoners to other countries where torture can be expected to follow. In his confirmation hearings, Panetta also told members of Congress that "if the approved techniques were 'not sufficient' to get a detainee to divulge details he was suspected of knowing about an imminent attack, he would ask for 'additional authority' to use other methods."[16]

As we have seen, for example in the arguments of Jean Arrigo, the actual capacity to implement any tortures approved under such "additional authority" requires an extant torture infrastructure. Being prepared to torture by necessity implies maintaining the necessary resources—human and material—in good working order.[17] Leon Panetta left the CIA in 2011. The director at this writing, John Brennan, is a long-time agency employee, one who has in the past defended CIA "enhanced interrogation" methods. In 2007 he told CBS that these techniques produced "a lot of information and help." By the next year, however, he had changed his position, telling an audience at the Center for Strategic and International Studies, "Tactics such as waterboarding were not in keeping with our values as Americans, and these practices have been rightly terminated and should not, and will not, happen again." In addition to concerns about American values, Brennan advanced another, more instrumentalist objection to torture; it creates a "recruitment bonanza for terrorists."[18]

The President ordered the CIA to close its secret prisons, but the very fact that their locations are secret renders it difficult for a president and impossible for ordinary citizens to verify that this has been done. The best hope in this regard is that the journalists who have followed this story, from the *Washington Post's* Dana Priest to Eric Schmitt, Charlie Savage, and Mark Mazetti of the *New York Times* to the *New Yorker's* Jane Mayer and Seymour Hersh, will continue their excellent and necessary work.

Medium-Range Actions

There must be a full, public accounting of, and full, public accountability for, the torture practiced in the "war on terror." President Obama has argued that "nothing will be gained by spending our time and energy laying blame for the past," but this is not true.[19] What will be gained is the possibility of developing a public consensus that the United States should not practice torture any longer. Here I am thinking, for example, of the sort of consensus that has developed in this country that the World War II imprisonment of Japanese-American citizens was wrong.

Such a consensus about torture does not exist today. This is made evident by the contradictory views examined in Chapter 3. Public opinion is similarly divided. Polling suggests that this division has remained remarkably stable in the five years since the revelations about Abu Ghraib. In eight surveys between April 2004 and February 2009 the Pew Center for People and the Press asked respondents, "Do you think the use of torture against suspected terrorists to gain important information can often be justified, sometimes be justified, rarely be justified or never be justified?" Note that this question does not specify what sort of information is involved—only that it is "important"—or any degree of certainty about the potential target's identity as a "terrorist." In other words, these are not even the special constraints that characterize the ticking-bomb scenario. Nevertheless, the percentage of respondents answering that torture can "often" or "sometimes" be justified ranges between 43 and 48 percent in all the polls. If those who would permit torture "rarely" are added to the total, the percentage increases to between 63 and 69 percent.

In a 2012 *Foreign Policy* article called "Torture Creep," Amy Zegart took an updated look at polling on torture. Zegart commissioned a poll of one thousand Americans, which ran in August 2012. In addition to the startling fact that one-fourth of the respondents approve the use of a nuclear bomb against "terrorists," she finds "more Americans accepting Bush-era policies than ever before." For example, "in an October 2007 Rasmussen poll, 27 percent

of Americans surveyed said the United States should torture prisoners captured in the fight against terrorism, while 53 percent said it should not." In
Zegart's poll, "41 percent said they would be willing to use torture—a gain of
14 points—while 34 percent would not, a decline of 19 points."[20]

Zegart included some of the same questions that appeared in a 2005 USA
Today/CNN/Gallup poll to gauge changes in respondents' approval of specific techniques. Her results:

> Respondents in 2012 are more pro-waterboarding, pro-threatening pris-
> oners with dogs, pro-religious humiliation, and pro-forcing-prisoners-
> to-remain-naked-and-chained-in-uncomfortable-positions-in-cold-
> rooms. In 2005, 18 percent said they believed the naked chaining
> approach was OK, while 79 percent thought it was wrong. In 2012, 30
> percent of Americans thought this technique was right, an increase of 12
> points, while just 51 percent thought it was wrong, a drop of 28 points.
> In 2005, only 16 percent approved of waterboarding suspected terror-
> ists, while an overwhelming majority (82 percent) thought it was wrong
> to strap people on boards and force their heads underwater to simulate
> drowning. Now, 25 percent of Americans believe in waterboarding ter-
> rorists, and only 55 percent think it's wrong. The only specific interroga-
> tion technique that is less popular now than in 2005, strangely enough, is
> prolonged sleep deprivation.[21]

It is certainly worth asking whether these numbers would change if U.S.
citizens had a more complete understanding of what has been done in their
names.[22]

Even should the United States decide to do so, it would be impossible to dismantle our practice of institutionalized torture without understanding the full
extent of what has been done, the chronology of events, and the roles played
by officials and agents of the state at all levels. It might be argued that human
rights organizations, journalists, and academics are already constructing such
an accounting, as the articles, reports, and books detailing torture under the
Bush administration pile up. This is important work, but by itself it is incomplete for at least two reasons.

First, the literature that has developed to date is necessarily partial, as each
author follows one or two threads of the story. So, for example, Philippe Sands
has documented the role of the Department of Defense, its then-Secretary
Donald Rumsfeld, and his coterie of neoconservative subordinates in the development of torture at Guantánamo;[23] In the same context, Joseph Margulies
has looked at the role of the president's office;[24] Jane Mayer has focused on

the role of Vice President Dick Cheney and his legal staff in the use of torture both at military and CIA sites and the role of the SERE program;[25] Seymour Hersh has followed the chain of command to identify responsibility for Abu Ghraib;[26] and Alfred McCoy has laid the foundation with his history of the CIA's torture research and practice.[27] However, as yet no single complete chronology has been assembled, let alone a full account of the nature and extent of the U.S. torture program. This is hardly surprising; it is a big project, and one as much for historians as for journalists. As with any history, that of the Bush administration will necessarily be assembled from a variety of overlapping and competing narratives. Nor, alas, does the story end with the end of the Bush administration.

There is another reason, however, why these necessary, essential accounts are not sufficient: they do not bear any government imprimatur. They are not "the official story." They do not represent an attempt on the part of the whole nation to come to grips with this recent past. This is not to say that an official account can or should be an uncontested account. But an official account of what has happened can lay the groundwork for a national consensus against the future use of torture. We might compare such a step to the (not uncontested) 2008 decision of the Australian government to make a formal apology to Australian Aborigines for their treatment at the hands of European settlers, and especially for the government policy of removing children from Aboriginal homes, a policy that lasted through the1970s.[28] It is unlikely that the Australian citizenry were unanimous in making this apology, but the government action marks an important stage in Australia's understanding of its own history.[29]

At this writing, such an accounting does not appear likely. In December 2012 the Senate Intelligence Committee approved the CIA's own six thousand-page report on its treatment of prisoners during the "war on terror," but the report remains classified.[30] A few years earlier, former U.S. ambassador to the United Nations Thomas Pickering and former FBI director William Sessions argued for the creation of a presidential commission "to investigate the post-Sept. 11 policies and actions regarding the detention, treatment and transfer of security detainees."[31] When it became clear that the Obama administration had no appetite for such an investigation, the two chose to collaborate instead with the Constitution Project, which in 2013 produced a five hundred-page report on detainee treatment during the "war on terror."[32] Even if Pickering and Sessions had succeeded in their call for a presidential commission they still envisioned a clearly circumscribed role for such a body: "The mandate of this commission would not be to conduct a criminal investigation," they say, because "that is the job of our criminal justice system."[33]

And it is a job that our criminal justice system ought to do. Since 9/11, the long-standing U.S. practice of covert support for torture by other states was transformed into a quasi-overt practice conducted by this state. Those responsible should be held accountable, so that such an escalation cannot easily happen again. As Senator Carl Levin, then-Chair of the House Armed Services Committee has said, "The seeds of Abu Ghraib's rotten fruit were sown by civilians at the highest levels of our government."[34] Now-retired Maj. General Antonio Taguba, whose military career was cut short by his report on the abuses at Abu Ghraib, said the same in 2008, speaking of the Bush administration. "After years of disclosures by government investigations, media accounts, and reports from human rights organizations," he wrote, "there is no longer any doubt as to whether the current administration has committed war crimes. The only question that remains to be answered is whether those who ordered the use of torture will be held to account." Years later, with a new administration in its second term, this question still "remains to be answered."[35]

What is true for Abu Ghraib is true for the rest of the U.S. torture program under the Bush administration. Ultimate responsibility lies with the leaders of that administration. One difficulty in bringing these men to account is that no one in government, not even Senator Levin, will name them directly. Just as the grand jury investigating the break-in at Democratic Party Headquarters in 1972 referred to President Nixon only as an "unindicted co-conspirator," George W. Bush, Dick Cheney, and Donald Rumsfeld remained unnamed "civilians at the highest levels of our government."

The idea that a former president and vice president might face charges for human rights crimes is almost unthinkable. I suspect that this is true for the same reasons that until very recently the idea that the United States might be practicing torture has fallen outside the bounds of licit discourse, that is, because it has appeared to be a contradiction in terms. Just as being "a state that does not torture" has been understood as one of the defining characteristics of the United States of America, "persons who do not commit war crimes" has been a self-evident part of the definition of those who hold the highest positions in U.S. government. Certainly other nations' leaders have been accused of war crimes and legitimately so, at least in the imagination of the U.S. public. But these are Serbs like Slobodan Milošević or Africans like Charles Taylor of Liberia or Omar Hassan Ahmad al-Bashir of Sudan, all of whom have been indicted in international courts.

Sometimes torturers are held to account in their own countries. In 2012, Argentina's former dictator Jorge Videla received a fifty-year sentence for his involvement in the theft of babies taken from prisoners disappeared in that country's Dirty War. Videla died in prison the following year. Earlier, Argentine General (and dictator from 1982 to 1983) Reynaldo Bignone, along with six other members of the military or police, were handed sentences of up to twenty-five years for their involvement in torture and disappearances. In 2013, Guatemala's former president Efraín Rios Montt was tried for and convicted of genocide in his nation's "counterinsurgency" war of the 1980s, in which thousands of indigenous people were murdered. A Guatemalan appellate court overturned that conviction in April 2013, but the case remains alive. The likelihood is quite small that members of the former Bush administration will face criminal charges any time soon, at least in this country. But that does not mean that they cannot be held accountable by history.

Why is it not sufficient simply to have a full public accounting of torture in the post-9/11 period, a project that is difficult enough in and of itself? Why must officials also be held accountable? One reason is that an accounting is primarily a descriptive exercise; as such it is an important step in forming a public consensus in opposition to torture. But description without interpretation is insufficient. An interpretation of the meaning of state torture, such as the one presented in this book, is a work of normative, ethical judgment. I would suggest that without such judgment, and preferably an official, state-sanctioned judgment, justice cannot be done.

Justice for whom? To begin, there are the victims of torture, some of whom are already seeking legal redress in U.S. courts. Unfortunately, the new administration appears to have adopted the tactics of the previous one, when faced with cases such as that brought by Binyam Mohammed against a subsidiary of the Boeing corporation. Mohammed contends that this company was responsible for his rendition flight to Morocco, where he suffered eighteen months of torture. Although the details of his torture, provided here in Chapter 1, are easily available to anyone who seeks them, the Obama administration has refused to allow them to be presented in court, on the grounds that such details are "state secrets."[36]

Then there are the few individuals who have been convicted of abusing prisoners, such as the seven soldiers prosecuted for abuses at Abu Ghraib. It is clear that they have borne the shame and punishment, not only for their own crimes but also for the crimes of their superiors. Speaking of the House Armed Services Committee's eighteen-month investigation into treatment of detainees in the "war on terror," Senator Carl Levin observed in 2009:

When former Vice President Cheney said last week that what happened at Abu Ghraib was the work of "a few sadistic prison guards" acting on their own, he bore false witness. And when he said last week there was no link between the techniques used at Abu Ghraib and those approved for use in the CIA's secret prisons, he again strayed from the truth. . . .

Our bipartisan Committee report found that on December 2, 2002, techniques that we saw in photos at Abu Ghraib—including nudity, stress positions, and dogs—were formally approved by Secretary of Defense Rumsfeld for use by Department of Defense personnel against detainees at Guantanamo. Our report showed, in about 20 pages of detail, how the Secretary of Defense's 2002 authorization of the aggressive techniques at Guantanamo led to their use in Afghanistan and in Iraq, including at Abu Ghraib.[37]

Is justice done when a few low-level Army Reservists bear all responsibility for policies directed by "civilians at the highest levels of our government"?

Finally, there is the question of how failing to assign accountability might affect the ordinary citizens of this country. If justice is indeed a virtue, then, like all virtues, it is a settled disposition to act in certain ways in certain kinds of situations. It is, as Aristotle, Aquinas, and MacIntyre all have said, a habit. We become just by doing just acts. Justice in this case requires asking ourselves what responsibility the citizens of an at least nominally democratic state may justly be said to bear for the practices of that state. This is a question that cannot be answered by trials or truth commissions, necessary as they may be. It is a question about the relationship between human beings' quest for the good and the modern nation state. It is a question about how the practice of torture should be addressed in the future.

In the Long Run: Looking Forward

Thus, in one word, states of character arise out of like activities. . . . It makes no small difference, then, whether we form habits of one kind or of another from our very youth; it makes a very great difference, or rather *all* the difference.

—Aristotle, *Nicomachean Ethics*[38]

I have argued that torture is a false practice. That is, it is a practice in which the quest for the good life has been diverted and in which the cardinal virtues of justice, courage, temperance, and prudence, or "wisdom about human affairs," which I have called "practical wisdom," are deformed.[39] I have said something about justice already. Here I offer some thoughts about the moral virtues of courage and temperance and the intellectual virtue of prudence.

Courage: Aristotle argued that "by doing the acts that we do in the presence of danger, and by being habituated to feel fear or confidence, we become brave or cowardly."[40] Since September 11, 2001, the people of this country have been systematically "habituated to feel fear" of terrorism. The rhetoric of the Bush administration, accompanied by the theater of rising "threat levels," terrorist watch lists with thousands of names,[41] and repetition by a Greek chorus of officials of the words "September 11" have combined to remind Americans that we should always be afraid. We have been taught to look for danger where it does not exist—for example, in an Iraqi nuclear arsenal—and where it may exist we have been taught to magnify it in our imaginations.

Furthermore, the goal of keeping Americans "safe" has been posited as the legitimate basis for any government action, including, of course, torture. U.S. citizens have been instructed to take as our whole *telos* our own personal survival. The quest for the good life, we have been told, begins and ends in the preservation of our own lives. Journalist Gary Kamiya puts this very clearly. "Because terrorism in our national imagination is simultaneously villain and nemesis, human and inhuman, the 'war' against terrorism slips into becoming a war not just against fanatical jihadis but against our own death, against the very idea of death." As we accept this "repression of reality," he continues, it "and the infantile fantasy of perfect safety—in other words, cowardice—become the driving forces of our lives."[42]

Institutionalized torture is not the only U.S. government practice deployed in the "war on terror." In June of 2013, a former CIA contractor named Edward Snowden released thousands of top secret documents to reporters at the U.K. *Guardian* and the *Washington Post.* The papers detailed two National Security Agency data surveillance programs of breathtaking scope, begun under the Bush administration and continued under President Obama. The first involves the collection of "metadata" (everything about a phone call except its actual content—date, time, sending and receiving phone numbers) for every phone call made through the largest U.S. phone service company, Verizon. The second program, called PRISM, collects not only the metadata, but also the content of online interactions between persons in the United States and anyone in a foreign country.

The mere existence of these two programs was a state secret of the highest, "top," order. Had Snowden not perceived this secret as what he termed an "existential threat to democracy," we might never have heard of them at all. The programs' defenders, including the president and his staff, and the few members of Congress who were briefed, emphasize a different "existential" threat, the one represented by "terrorism." The *Wall Street Journal* concurred.[43] Not surprisingly, Republican Speaker of the House John Boehner denounced Snowden as a traitor who "puts Americans at risk" by disclosing to "our adversaries what our capabilities are."[44] Revelations about the scope of these programs, like those about U.S. torture programs, serve to remind people in this country of the need to be afraid. They encourage us to respond to that fear by sanctioning any government action that might keep us a little safer, a little while longer.

Philip Zimbardo has addressed the issue of fear in the conclusion of *The Lucifer Effect*. Here he calls for a new understanding of heroism, one that incorporates the facing of social and economic, as well as physical, risks. Working with his colleague Zeno Franco, Zimbardo has elaborated a new taxonomy of heroism, which he defines as having "four key features":

> (a) it must be engaged in voluntarily; (b) it must involve a risk or potential sacrifice, such as the threat of death, an immediate threat to physical integrity, a long-term threat to health, or the potential for serious degradation of one's quality of life; (c) it must be conducted in service to one or more other people or the community as a whole; and (d) it must be without secondary, extrinsic gain anticipated at the time of the act.[45]

This is a solid definition of heroism, but it shares a certain defect with most definitions of torture: it treats heroism as an "act" or "deed." In Zimbardo's construction, people do not act bravely or with cowardice as a result of any dispositional tendencies. There are, he declares, "no special inner attributes of either pathology or goodness residing within the human psyche or the human genome." His point here is not only that heroes and torturers are not born but made but also that they are made suddenly, "in a decisive decisional moment," in which situational forces "combine to increase the probability of one's acting to harm others or acting to help others."

Zimbardo calls these forces "situational action vectors" and includes among them "group pressures and group identity, the diffusion of responsibility for the action; a temporal focus on the immediate moment without concern for consequences stemming from the act in the future, presence of social models, and commitment to an ideology." Heroism is not, in Zimbardo's understanding, the expression of courage formed by practices; it is rather the result of "strong situational forces" that "most often impulsively drive the person to action." In fact, "any of us could as easily become heroes as perpetrators of evil depending on how we are influenced by situational forces."[46]

Zimbardo makes a distinction between "heroes of the moment" and "lifetime heroes." He takes as one example of a "hero of the moment" Rosa Parks on the day she refused to give up her seat to a white passenger on a Montgomery, Alabama, bus.[47] But his choice of Rosa Parks actually makes my point: Heroism is not a sudden decision, but the expression of virtue formed in practice. Rosa Parks' decision to keep her seat was not "impulsively" driven by situational forces of the moment. It was the outcome of a life of practice, including participation in organizing training at the Highlander Folk School in Tennessee. As that institution's history puts it, "while Rosa Parks was indeed remarkable, her story is also about collective action, willed risk, intentional plans and mass movement." The courage Rosa Parks displayed on December 1, 1955 was a born of a long habit of acting bravely in the face of danger:

> At the time of her arrest, Rosa Parks was a respected community leader already working to counter humiliating racist laws and traditions. She became secretary of the Montgomery NAACP chapter as early as 1943 and tried to register to vote three times before doing so for the first time in 1945. As a member of the NAACP, she worked on voter registration and youth programs, and in fact on that particular December 1st, she needed to get home to prepare for a youth workshop she was conducting that weekend.[48]

Zimbardo's solution to the problem of cowardly or evil acts is two-fold. First, we must discover "how to limit, constrain, and prevent the situational and systemic forces that propel some of us toward social pathology." Second, "every society" should "foster a 'heroic imagination' in its citizenry" and "be preparing laurel leaves for all those who will discover their reservoir of hidden strengths and virtues enabling them to come forth to act against injustice and cruelty and to stand up for their principled values."[49] But how is that "hidden reservoir" of virtues to be filled in the first place? How are we to recognize injustice if we have no experience of behaving in just ways? How are we to know the difference between cruelty and necessary pain if we have not developed the intellectual apparatus, the practical wisdom, that allows us to make such judgments?

I suspect that more is required than fostering a heroic imagination, which is no bad thing in itself, but is not sufficient to teach us the courage to confront and dismantle the practice of torture. Recall Alasdair MacIntyre's illustration, the case of the German citizen he calls "J." You may remember that J is a hypothetical train operator in Nazi Germany who rejects any responsibility or blame for his failure to ask what (or whom) his train is carrying. For J to have questioned the nature and destination of his cargo would have required a kind of courage that is not "discovered" in a moment of extremity but rather developed through practice and practices. For MacIntyre, virtues such as courage arise and have their meaning in a social context in which "social relationships and types of activity" can foster "systematic dialogue" with other people, and "critical scrutiny" by them of one's behavior and practices. "It is only in and through such milieus [of dialogue and mutual critique]," says MacIntyre, "that moral agents become able to understand themselves as accountable to others in respect of the human virtues."[50] It is within a social context that fosters a habit of bravery that we can learn to be brave.

Temperance: Thomas Aquinas says that "temperance is about pleasures of touch," in which he includes our appetites for food and drink and for sexual pleasure. These direct, physical pleasures Thomas considers "the most difficult to moderate," but there are other pleasures that also require moderation, so that "any virtue that is effective of moderation in some matter or other, and restrains the appetite in its impulse towards something, may be reckoned a part of temperance."[51] Temperance is the virtue that allows our desires to be brought under the control of reason.

Just as Americans have been taught that our lives must always be preserved at any cost, the conduct of the "war on terror" has taught that the "American way of life" must be similarly preserved. This way of life is generally understood as a variety of individual rights and liberties, combined with a high standard of living, defined as the consumption of endless material abundance. It was the latter to which George H. W. Bush referred when, while attending the 1992 Earth Summit at Rio de Janeiro, he explained why the United States would not sign a global warming treaty that contained any specific emissions goals. "The American way of life," he said, "is not negotiable."

In the aftermath of the September 11 attacks, U.S. citizens learned that the act of heroism our president hoped that we would perform in this moment of extremity was—to go shopping. The reopening of the New York Stock Exchange was celebrated as a national holiday, with a New York firefighter ringing the opening bell. In San Francisco, where I live, a poster appeared in many store windows—a drawing of an upended American flag, from which sprouted two handles at the top. The flag had become a shopping bag. "America: Open for Business" read the poster's printed slogan. I would argue that the "war on terror" has not helped the people of this country to moderate our grasping at the material things that bring us pleasure. The "American way of life" may not be negotiable, but neither is it sustainable, for several reasons. First, it contributes to the destruction of ecosystems and to potentially disastrous climate change. Second, it cannot be maintained without the disproportionate flow of natural resources, especially, but not only, of fossil fuels, from other countries to this one. The desire to maintain that flow has stretched the military capacity of even the world's only superpower to the breaking point. No empire in history has survived forever at the apex of world power.

In discussing the virtue of temperance, St. Thomas names other passions that may properly be moderated by it, or by its subsidiary virtues. He speaks of the "inward movement" toward a desired object, and of the "daring" that results from the hope of attaining that object. This daring, he suggests, ought to be moderated by the virtue of humility. Humility's role is "to temper and restrain the mind, lest it tend to high things immoderately." Humility is the virtue that allows us to reason well enough to avoid arrogating to ourselves a greatness that we do not possess. "It restrains the appetite from aiming at great things against right reason."[52] It is precisely the virtue needed to recognize and resist the logic of torture: the belief that we *cannot* do wrong because by definition we are people who *do* not do wrong; that we torture to bring about a greater good than the evil we inflict; that we have the ability to know with a certainty that the prisoner in front of us is a terrorist with life-saving information, and not just some hapless foot soldier scooped up on an Afghan battlefield; that we are those special few called to make a sacrifice of our own consciences at the altar of public safety.

Another "inward movement," says Thomas, "is that of anger, which tends towards revenge, and this is restrained by 'meekness' or 'mildness.'" I have just argued that one effect of the conduct of the "war on terror" and the practice of torture in that context has been the engendering or sustaining of a tendency toward cowardice. At the same time that we have been told to be afraid, we have also been encouraged to nurture our desire for revenge for the horrors of September 11, 2001. The Bush administration played on this desire when it sought to convince U.S. citizens that Saddam Hussein was responsible for the attacks. By September 2003, six months after the invasion, a *Washington Post* poll reported that 69 percent of respondents believed that "it is likely the Iraqi leader was personally involved in the attacks carried out by al-Qaeda." Nor was this belief limited to administration supporters. "A majority of Democrats, Republicans and independents believe it's likely Saddam was involved." A Time/ CNN poll taken at about the same time showed that 63 percent believed that the United States had been right to go to war.[53]

It is, I would submit, a failure of that part of temperance that Thomas calls meekness or mildness to be willing to destroy another country in an act of revenge. It is also a failure of mildness to use torture, as the Bush administration did, to attempt to justify such revenge by tormenting prisoners until they admitted a false connection between Saddam Hussein and the attacks of September 11.[54]

Prudence: I have argued throughout this book that institutionalized state torture represents a failure of prudence, which is the use of practical reason to understand what ought to be done and how to do it. I have argued that the failure of prudence encompasses, for example, the efforts of Bush administration lawyers to distort the legal definitions of torture beyond recognition. I would add here that failures of prudence include the general use of the rhetoric of denial to distort and erase the reality of the practice of torture.

The failure of prudence also extends to that failure to recognize what one's own government is doing, which I have called culpable ignorance. MacIntyre agrees that questions about who ought to know, and what they ought to know, are central to moral life in a modern state. "Conflicts about

whose responsibility it is to know about this or that are ... among those that
... especially in the circumstances of distinctively modern societies, provide content for the requirements of morality." In other words, he argues,
there is in modern societies, precisely because their structures act to obscure truth, a moral imperative to lift the veil. "Ask about your own social
and cultural order what it needs you and others not to know," he says, "has
become an indispensable moral maxim."[55]

Prudence, however, extends beyond the ability to acquire particular bits of
data. It also involves a capacity for critical thinking that makes it possible to as-
semble information into meaningful patterns. It includes the ability to analyze
an argument, both to determine whether the factual assertions it contains are
well supported and whether its claims are supported by evidence and reasonable dependence of one proposition upon another. Finally, prudence requires
the capacity to understand that knowledge very often has moral dimensions,
both in the implicit and explicit goods that it expresses and in the implications
for necessary action that it may present.

It is prudence that enables a person to understand, for example, what it
means when a former vice president of the United State says in as public a way
as possible that "to completely rule out enhanced interrogation methods in the
future is unwise in the extreme. It is recklessness cloaked in righteousness,
and would make the American people less safe." It enables the hearer to understand that "enhanced interrogation methods" means the practice of torture,
with everything that practice implies; that a reference to "recklessness clothed
in righteousness" is an attempt forestall any ethical judgment against the practice of torture, by suggesting that anyone who might make such a judgment is
an arrogant fool; and that the whole argument is grounded in an appeal to a
presumably shared belief that anything is permissible that might prevent the
smallest diminishing of public safety.[56]

I have argued in these pages that institutionalized state torture is a false
practice that destroys individual minds and bodies; that it thereby also dis-
rupts and disables social bodies, which are often themselves the sites of true
practices; that it is likely to deform the characters and intellects of those who
practice it; and that it may very well contribute to the same deformations in the
larger society in which it exists.

I do not pretend to know how to engender and sustain virtue in a complex modern society like the United State. But building a movement to end
the practice of institutionalized state torture might be a good place to begin.
Members of such a movement might transform the very work of dismantling a
false practice into a true practice, in the process of which we might be formed
in virtues such as justice, courage, temperance, and prudence.

Some Final, Personal Words

Some time during the early 1990s in San Francisco, California, I attended the speech of a Salvadoran trade unionist. Her name was Gloria. I had travelled to El Salvador myself in 1989 as the interpreter for a solidarity delegation. At that time, the U.S.-backed Salvadoran government had a strategy of kidnapping, torturing, and often murdering the middle-level leadership of trade unions, which they understood as a threat to their power. Indeed, during the two weeks while we were in El Salvador, one of our union liaison members was arrested. We were able to visit him a few days later in prison, where he described how he had been tortured.

Gloria's purpose that evening in San Francisco was to inform her audience about the dangers in El Salvador to union members like herself. By way of illustration, she related the story of her own capture and torture by the notorious Salvadoran Treasury Police. She told us that it was only the pressure of phone calls and letters from *la solidaridad internacional* (international solidarity) that had finally forced the police to set her free. As Gloria spoke, I began to shiver. I remembered that I had heard—and spoken—her name before. I realized that I myself had made some of those calls.

This happened because my friend Sharon Martinas organized an informal phone tree among her Spanish-speaking friends. When news of police kidnappings reached her from El Salvador, she would provide the necessary information to telephone the appropriate police force or military service (El Salvador had several) and demand the victim's release. Sharon would keep us updated about what was known of the victim's whereabouts and supply us with the relevant telephone numbers. That night, I remembered my phone calls to the Treasury Police, remembered insisting that we knew that they had Gloria, that she had been seen in the prison at Ilopango, which they controlled. Sharon's numbers were very good, and I remembered talking directly with the head of the prison there, insisting despite his denials that they were holding Gloria, that she had been seen entering the prison, and that she must be set free immediately.

As Gloria told her story, I was seized with a sort of retrospective horror. *Suppose Sharon's little group had failed to make those calls?* What if we had been too busy in the days of Gloria's capture to add our voice to those of others demanding her reappearance? What if no one in this country had sought to understand and counteract the practical implications of our own government's policies? But there was Gloria, alive, and continuing her work.

We had better get on with ours.

Notes

1. Cofer Black, "Joint Investigation into September 11th: Fifth Public Hearing," September 20, 2002.

2. Jonathan Alter, *The Defining Moment: FDR's Hundred Days and the Triumph of Hope* (New York: Simon & Schuster, 2006).

3. Jonathan Alter, "Time to Think About Torture," *Newsweek*, November 5, 2001. The problem, as Alter saw it, was that "right now, four key hijacking suspects aren't talking at all." Three of the four never did "talk," because they had nothing to say. The fourth, the mentally unstable Zacarias Moussaoui, was convicted in 2006 of conspiring to kill U.S. citizens in the September 11 attacks, although, as the *Washington Post* reported, "three jurors took it upon themselves to write that Moussaoui had 'limited knowledge of the 9/11 attack plans.'" Jaweed Azmath and Alub Ali Khan were eventually convicted of credit card fraud and deported to India. The fourth, Nabil Almarrabh, was held incommunicado in New York State prisons for eight months as a material witness. He was sentenced to less than time served for immigration violation. For more information, see James Beckman, *Comparative Legal Approaches to Homeland Security and Anti-Terrorism* (Aldershot; Burlington, VT: Ashgate, 2007), 33; Benjamin Weiser, "Threats and Responses: Sentencing; Ex-Suspect Expects Deportation," *New York Times*, September 19, 2002; Robert F. Worth, "Man Detained after 9/11 Says Rights Were Ignored," *New York Times*, May 11, 2002; Jerry Markon and Timothy Dwyer, "Jurors Reject Death Penalty for Moussaoui," *Washington Post*, May 4, 2006.

4. The phrase "rhetoric of denial," first mentioned in Chapter 1, is Talal Asad's. See Talal Asad, *Formations of the Secular: Christianity, Islam, Modernity* (Stanford, CA: Stanford University Press, 2003), 105.

5. One such exception is Atul Gawande's writing on solitary confinement. Atul Gawande, "Hellhole," *New Yorker*, March 30, 2009.

6. Dick Cheney, "Text of Dick Cheney's National Security Speech at AEI," May 21, 2009. http://www.foxnews.com/politics/2009/05/21/raw-data-text-dick-cheneys-national-security-speech-aei/.

7. Dave Eggen, "Cheney's Remarks Fuel Torture Debate: Critics Say He Backed Waterboarding," *Washington Post*, October 27, 2006.

8. Daniel Coleman, quoted in Jane Mayer, *Dark Side: The Inside Story of How the War on Terror Turned into a War on American Ideals* (New York: Doubleday, 2008), 117.

9. Alfred W. McCoy, *A Question of Torture: C.I.A. Interrogation, from the Cold War to the War on Terror*, 1st ed. The American Empire Project. (New York: Metropolitan Books/Henry Holt, 2006), 71.

10. Aristotle, *Nicomachean Ethics*, trans. David Ross (New York: Oxford University Press, 1998), 1103b26.

11. John Adams, "Inaugural Address" (Philadelphia: 1797).

12. This work was certainly begun by the authors of *Habits of the Heart*, who sought to identify some general qualities common to many Americans in the second half of the twentieth century. See Robert N. Bellah, Richard Madsen, William M. Sullivan, Ann Swidler, and Steven M. Tipton, *Habits of the Heart: Individualism and Commitment in American Life* (New York: Harper & Row, 1985).

13. Barack Obama, "Obama's Speech on Drone Policy," *New York Times*, May 24, 2013. http://www.nytimes.com/2013/05/24/us/politics/transcript-of-obamas-speech-on-drone-policy.html?pagewanted = all&_r = 0.

14. Remarks of Gerald Ford on the occasion of his swearing-in as President of the United States after the resignation of Richard Nixon, August 9, 1974.

15. Obama, "Obama's Speech on Drone Policy."

16. Charlie Savage, "Obama's War on Terror May Resemble Bush's in Some Areas," *New York Times*, February 18, 2009.

17. Jean Maria Arrigo, "A Consequentialist Argument against Torture Interrogation of Terrorists," paper presented at Joint Services Conference on Professional Ethics. (Springfield,

Virginia, January 30–31, 2003). Vittorio Bufacchi and Jean Maria Arrigo, "Torture, Terrorism and the State: A Refutation of the Ticking–Bomb Argument," *Journal of Applied Philosophy* 23, no. 3 (2006).

18. "Who Runs Gov: John O. Brennan," *Washington Post.* http://www.washingtonpost.com/politics/john-o-brennan/gIQA9SFs9O_topic.html.

19. Mark Mazetti and Scott Shane, "Interrogation Memos Detail Harsh Tactics by the C.I.A.," *New York Times*, April 16, 2009. It is possible that President Obama believed that shielding former Bush administration officials from prosecution would allow him future leverage with those institutions, such as the CIA, which he seeks to rein in. Such a bargain need not be stated explicitly to have binding force. If this were the case, even in *realpolitik* terms, it would be a strategic error, because it allows the institutions to define the boundaries of possible action for the president, rather than the other way around.

20. Amy Zegart, "Torture Creep: Why Are More Americans Accepting Bush-Era Policies Than Ever Before?" *Foreign Policy*, September 25, 2012. http://www.foreignpolicy.com/articles/2012/09/25/torture_creep.

21. Ibid.

22. Pew Center for People & the Press, *Pew Research Center for the People & the Press, February 2009 Political and Economic Survey* (Washington, DC: 2009). Table 7.1 provides my tabulation of answers to the question on torture:

Table 7.1 **Americans' views on torture, 2004–2009**

Q. 48F1	Do you think the use of torture against suspected terrorists in order to gain important information can often be justified, sometimes be justified, rarely be justified, or never be justified?							
	Feb. 2009 (%)	Feb. 2008 (%)	Nov. 2007 (a%)	Jan. 2007 (%)	Oct. 2006 (%)	Oct. 2005 (%)	March 2005 (%)	July 2004 (%)
Often	16	17	18	12	18	15	15	15
Sometimes	28	31	30	31	28	31	30	28
Rarely	20	20	21	25	19	17	24	21
Never	31	30	27	29	32	32	27	32
Don't know	5	2	4	3	3	5	4	4
	100	100	100	100	100	100	100	100
Often, sometimes, or rarely	64	68	69	68	65	63	69	64
Often or sometimes	44	48	48	43	46	46	45	43

23. Philippe Sands, *Torture Team: Rumsfeld's Memo and the Betrayal of American Values*, 1st ed. (New York: Palgrave MacMillan, 2008).

24. Joseph Margulies, *Guantánamo and the Abuse of Presidential Power* (New York: Simon & Schuster, 2006).

25. Jane Mayer, "The Experiment: The Military Trains People to Withstand Interrogation. Are Those Methods Being Misused at Guantánamo?" *New Yorker*, July 11, 2005; Jane Mayer, *Dark Side: The Inside Story of How the War on Terror Turned into a War on American Ideals*.

26. Seymour M. Hersh, *Chain of Command: The Road from 9/11 to Abu Ghraib* (New York: HarperCollins, 2004).

27. McCoy, *A Question of Torture*.

28. Tim Johnston, "Australia Says 'Sorry' to Aborigines for Mistreatment " *New York Times*, February 13, 2008.

29. It is also worth noting that the Australian government's action in 2008 was not in instance of spontaneous generation; it was the result of a popular movement, which eight years earlier, on May 29, 2000, had brought 200,000 people into the streets of Sydney in "the largest civil rights demonstration in Australian history." For details, see "Australians March in Support of Aborigines," *New York Times*, May 29, 2009.

30. Scott Shane, "Senate Panel Approves Findings Critical of Detainee Interrogations," *New York Times*, December 13, 2012.

31. Thomas R. Pickering and William S. Sessions, "Moving Forward by Looking Back: Why a Presidential Commission on Torture Is Critical to America's Security," *Washington Post*, March 23, 2009.

32. The Constitution Project, *The Report of the Constitution Project's Task Force on Detainee Treatment* (Washington, DC: Constitution Project, 2013).

33. Pickering and Sessions, "Moving Forward by Looking Back."

34. Senator Carl Levin, "Remarks of Senator Carl Levin at the Foreign Policy Association 2009 Annual Dinner," May 27, 2009. http://www.levin.senate.gov/newsroom/press/release/?id=4ca3eb9b-2e44-42f1-b4eb-c4c24829784f.

35. Antonio M. Taguba, "Preface," in *Broken Laws, Broken Lives: Medical Evidence of Torture by US Personnel and Its Impact*, by Physicians for Human Rights (Washington, DC: Physicians for Human Rights, 2008), viii. For the effects on Maj. Gen. Taguba's career of his work on Abu Ghraib, see Seymour M. Hersh, "The General's Report: How Antonio Taguba, Who Investigated the Abu Ghraib Scandal, Became One of Its Casualties," *New Yorker*, June 25, 2007.

36. Raymond Bonner, "Guantánamo Detainee's Campaign Reaches to Obama, " *New York Times*, February 11, 2009.

37. Levin, "Remarks of Senator Carl Levin at the Foreign Policy Association 2009 Annual Dinner."

38. Aristotle, *Nicomachean Ethics*, Book II, 1103b25; emphasis in original.

39. Thomas Aquinas, *Summa Theologica*, trans. Fathers of the English Dominican Province (Notre Dame, IN: Ave Mari, 1981; reprint, 1981), II–II, q.47 a.2.

40. Aristotle, *Nicomachean Ethics*, 1103b.

41. Including, at one point, my own and that of my partner. See David Kravets, "Feds Agree to Pay ACLU over No-Fly List," *Associated Press*, January 24, 2006.

42. Gary Kamiya, "In the Shadow of Cheney," *Salon*, May 28, 2009. http://www.salon.com/opinion/kamiya/2009/05/28/culture_of_fear/index.html. Kamiya is the editor of the online magazine *Salon*.

43. A *Journal* editorial downplayed the importance of Snowden's revelations. "He has mainly exposed a few voyeuristic details about the NSA's antiterror technical capacity regarding programs," said the editors somewhat disingenuously, "that were already widely known to exist." They faulted Snowden for being more concerned about the dangers posed by programs designed to "prevent terrorism" than about terrorism itself. See "Snowden's 'Conscience,'" *Wall Street Journal*, June 11, 2013.

44. Aaron Blake, "Boehner: Snowden Is 'a Traitor,'" *Washington Post*, June 11, 2013. http://www.washingtonpost.com/blogs/post-politics/wp/2013/06/11/boehner-snowden-is-a-traitor/.

45. Philip Zimbardo, *The Lucifer Effect: Understanding How Good People Turn Evil* (New York: Random House, 2007), 466ff.

46. ibid., 486.

47. Ibid.

48. Highlander Research and Education Center, "A Tribute to Rosa Parks." http://www.peaceworkmagazine.org/pwork/0511/051124.htm (accessed 11/25/13).

49. Zimbardo, *Lucifer Effect*, 486.

50. Alasdair MacIntyre, "Social Structures and Their Threat to Moral Agency," in *Ethics and Politics: Selected Essays*, ed. AlasdairMacIntyre (New York: Cambridge University Press, 2006), 195–96.
51. Aquinas, *Summa*, II–II, q.143 a.1.
52. Ibid., II–II, Q.143 a.1; II–II, Q. 61, a.2.
53. Associated Press, " Poll: 70% Believe Saddam, 9–11 Link," *USA Today*, September 6, 2003.
54. This is documented in Chapter 4. See U.S. Senate Committee on Armed Services, *Inquiry into the Treatment of Detainees in U.S. Custody*, 110 Cong., 2nd sess., 2008). 41.
55. MacIntyre, "Social Structures and Their Threat to Moral Agency," 194.
56. Cheney, "Text of Dick Cheney's National Security Speech at AEI."

INDEX